FALL OF CTHULHU

THE GATHERING

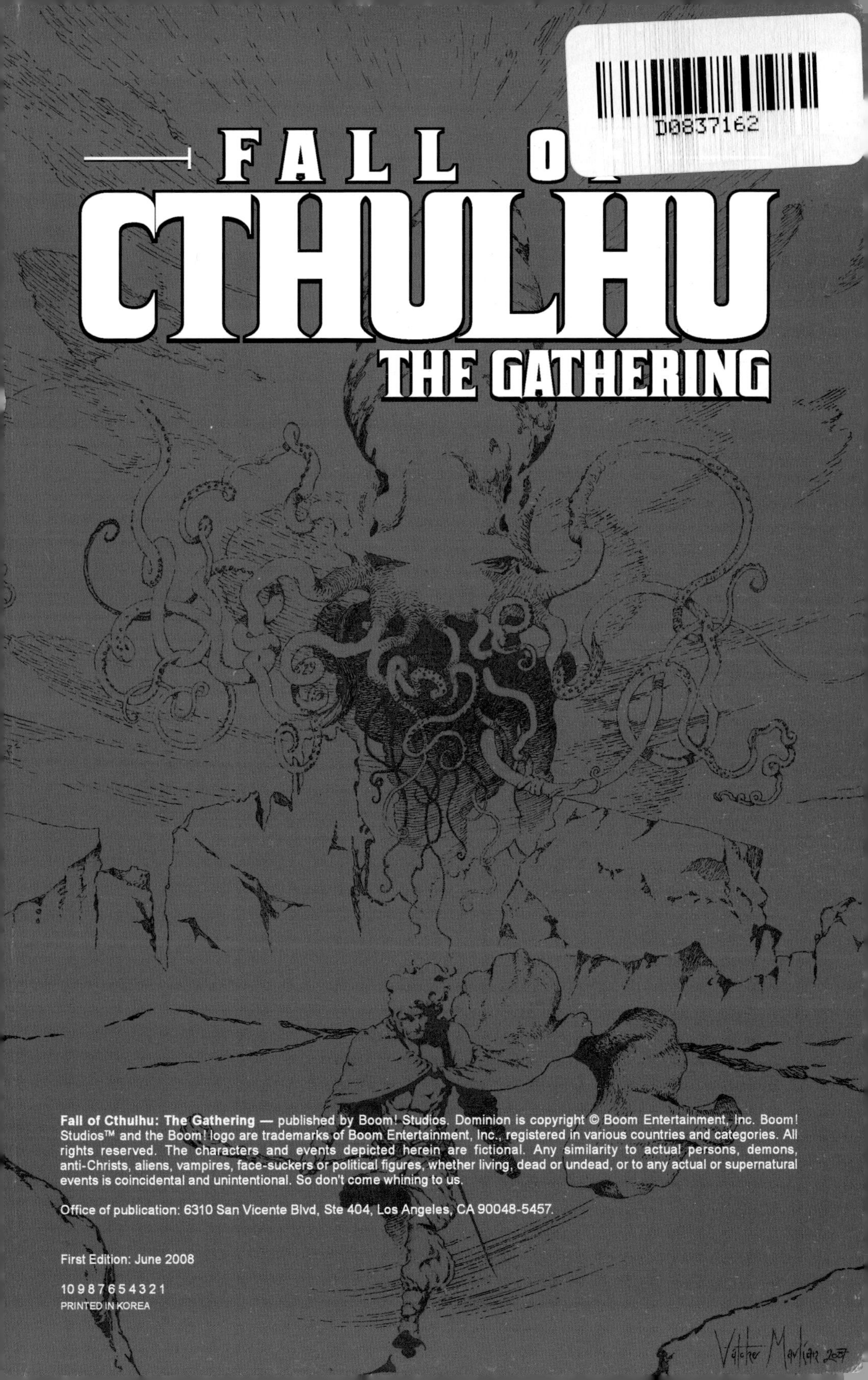

Fall of Cthulhu: The Gathering — published by Boom! Studios. Dominion is copyright © Boom Entertainment, Inc. Boom! Studios™ and the Boom! logo are trademarks of Boom Entertainment, Inc., registered in various countries and categories. All rights reserved. The characters and events depicted herein are fictional. Any similarity to actual persons, demons, anti-Christs, aliens, vampires, face-suckers or political figures, whether living, dead or undead, or to any actual or supernatural events is coincidental and unintentional. So don't come whining to us.

Office of publication: 6310 San Vicente Blvd, Ste 404, Los Angeles, CA 90048-5457.

First Edition: June 2008

10 9 8 7 6 5 4 3 2 1
PRINTED IN KOREA

FALL OF CTHULHU
THE GATHERING

PART I

MICHAEL ALAN NELSON
story

GREG SCOTT
art

JOEL SEGUIN
colors

ED DUKESHIRE
managing editor & letterer

PART II

MICHAEL ALAN NELSON
story

MARCO RUDY
art

MARC RUEDA
colors

MARSHALL DILLON
managing editor & letterer

JOYCE EL HAYEK
assistant editor

PART III

MICHAEL ALAN NELSON
story

TIM HAMILTON
& MICHEL FIFFE
art

MARC RUEDA
colors

MARSHALL DILLON
managing editor & letterer

JOYCE EL HAYEK
assistant editor

PART IV & V

MICHAEL ALAN NELSON
story

PABLO E. QUILIGOTTI
art & colors

TERRI DELGADO AND
MARSHALL DILLON
letters

MARSHALL DILLON
managing editor

ANDREW COSBY
ROSS RICHIE
founders

MARK WAID
editor-in-chief

WENDY WALLACE
general manager

ADAM FORTIER
vice president,
new business

CHIP MOSHER
marketing &
sales director

ED DUKESHIRE
designer

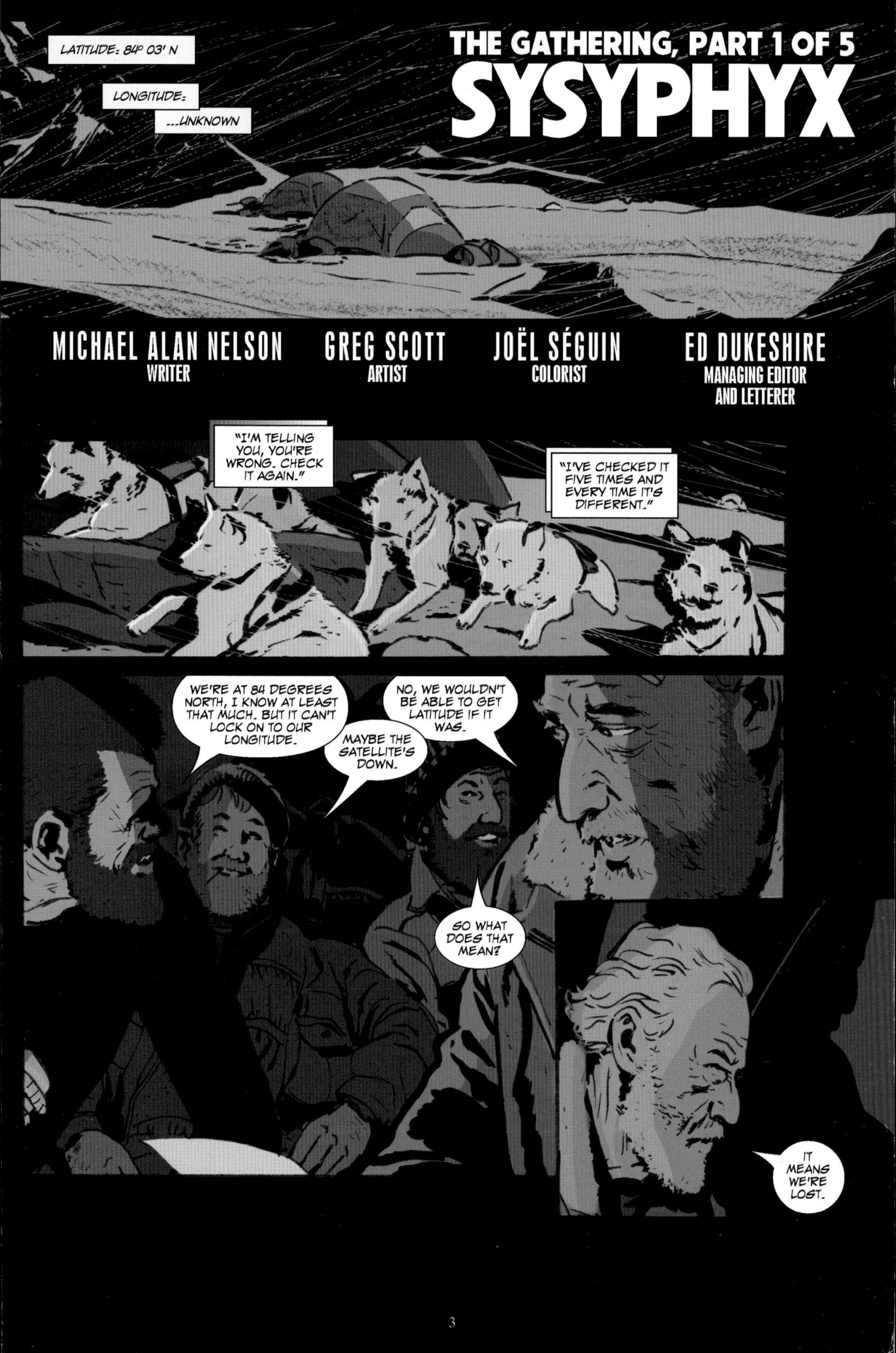
LATITUDE: 84° 03' N
LONGITUDE:
...UNKNOWN
THE GATHERING, PART 1 OF 5
SYSYPHYX
MICHAEL ALAN NELSON
WRITER
GREG SCOTT
ARTIST
JOËL SÉGUIN
COLORIST
ED DUKESHIRE
MANAGING EDITOR AND LETTERER
"I'M TELLING YOU, YOU'RE WRONG. CHECK IT AGAIN."
"I'VE CHECKED IT FIVE TIMES AND EVERY TIME IT'S DIFFERENT."
WE'RE AT 84 DEGREES NORTH, I KNOW AT LEAST THAT MUCH. BUT IT CAN'T LOCK ON TO OUR LONGITUDE.
MAYBE THE SATELLITE'S DOWN.
NO, WE WOULDN'T BE ABLE TO GET LATITUDE IF IT WAS.
SO WHAT DOES THAT MEAN?
IT MEANS WE'RE LOST.

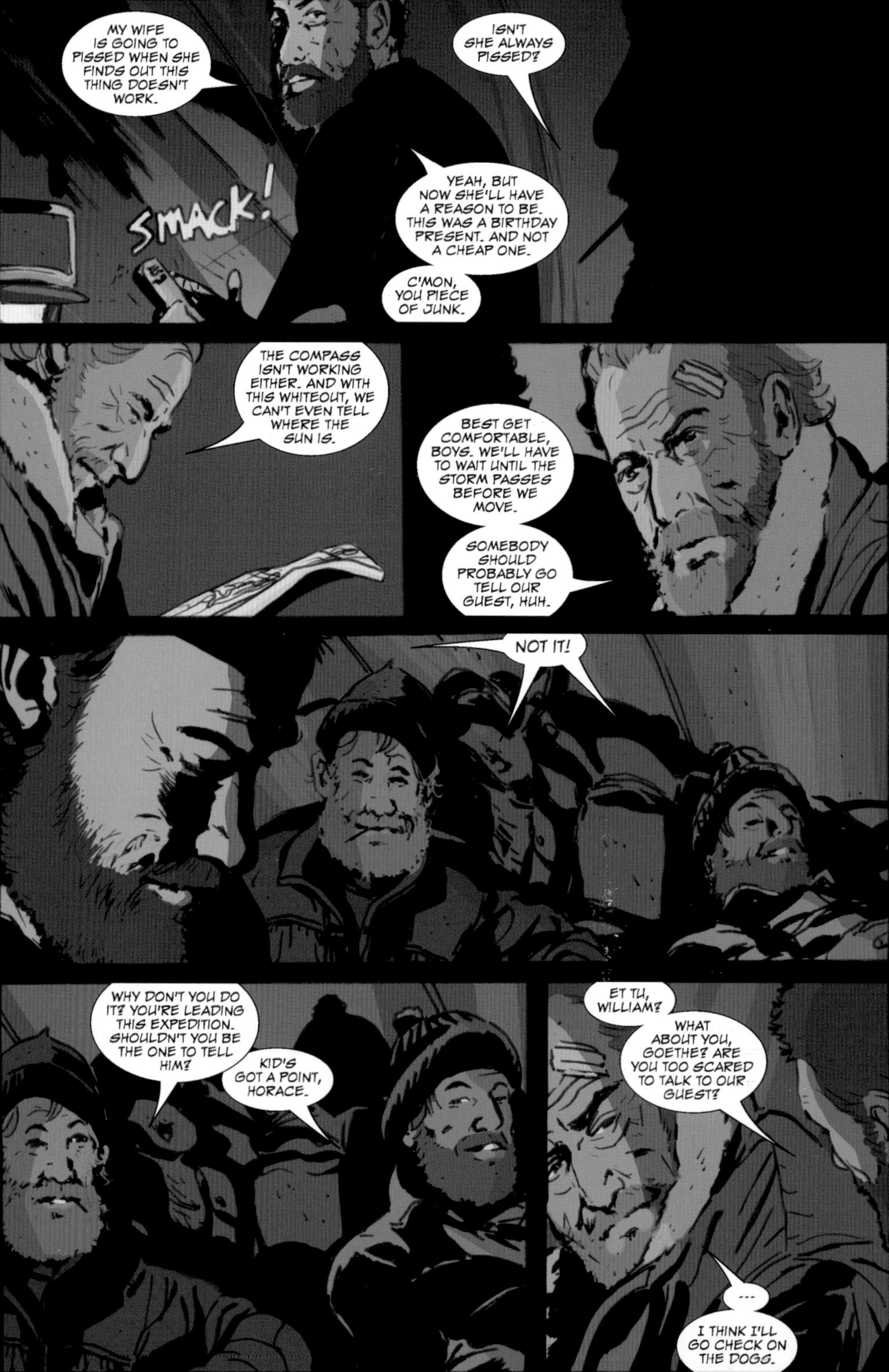
MY WIFE IS GOING TO PISSED WHEN SHE FINDS OUT THIS THING DOESN'T WORK.
ISN'T SHE ALWAYS PISSED?
SMACK!
YEAH, BUT NOW SHE'LL HAVE A REASON TO BE. THIS WAS A BIRTHDAY PRESENT. AND NOT A CHEAP ONE.
C'MON, YOU PIECE OF JUNK.
THE COMPASS ISN'T WORKING EITHER. AND WITH THIS WHITEOUT, WE CAN'T EVEN TELL WHERE THE SUN IS.
BEST GET COMFORTABLE, BOYS. WE'LL HAVE TO WAIT UNTIL THE STORM PASSES BEFORE WE MOVE.
SOMEBODY SHOULD PROBABLY GO TELL OUR GUEST, HUH.
NOT IT!
WHY DON'T YOU DO IT? YOU'RE LEADING THIS EXPEDITION. SHOULDN'T YOU BE THE ONE TO TELL HIM?
KID'S GOT A POINT, HORACE.
ET TU, WILLIAM?
WHAT ABOUT YOU, GOETHE? ARE YOU TOO SCARED TO TALK TO OUR GUEST?
...
I THINK I'LL GO CHECK ON THE DOGS.

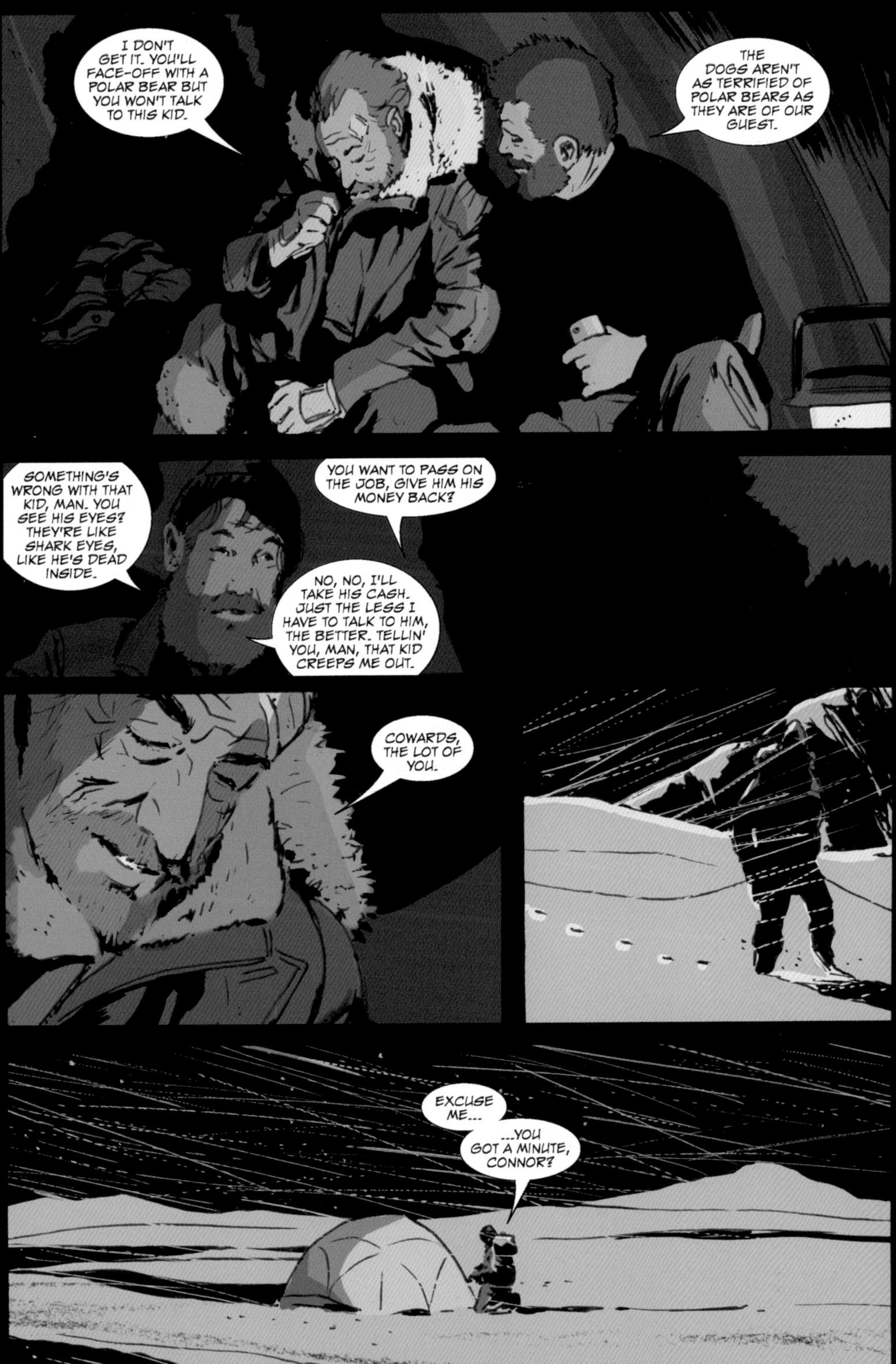
I DON'T GET IT. YOU'LL FACE-OFF WITH A POLAR BEAR BUT YOU WON'T TALK TO THIS KID.
THE DOGS AREN'T AS TERRIFIED OF POLAR BEARS AS THEY ARE OF OUR GUEST.
SOMETHING'S WRONG WITH THAT KID, MAN. YOU SEE HIS EYES? THEY'RE LIKE SHARK EYES, LIKE HE'S DEAD INSIDE.
YOU WANT TO PASS ON THE JOB, GIVE HIM HIS MONEY BACK?
NO, NO, I'LL TAKE HIS CASH. JUST THE LESS I HAVE TO TALK TO HIM, THE BETTER. TELLIN' YOU, MAN, THAT KID CREEPS ME OUT.
COWARDS, THE LOT OF YOU.
EXCUSE ME...
...YOU GOT A MINUTE, CONNOR?

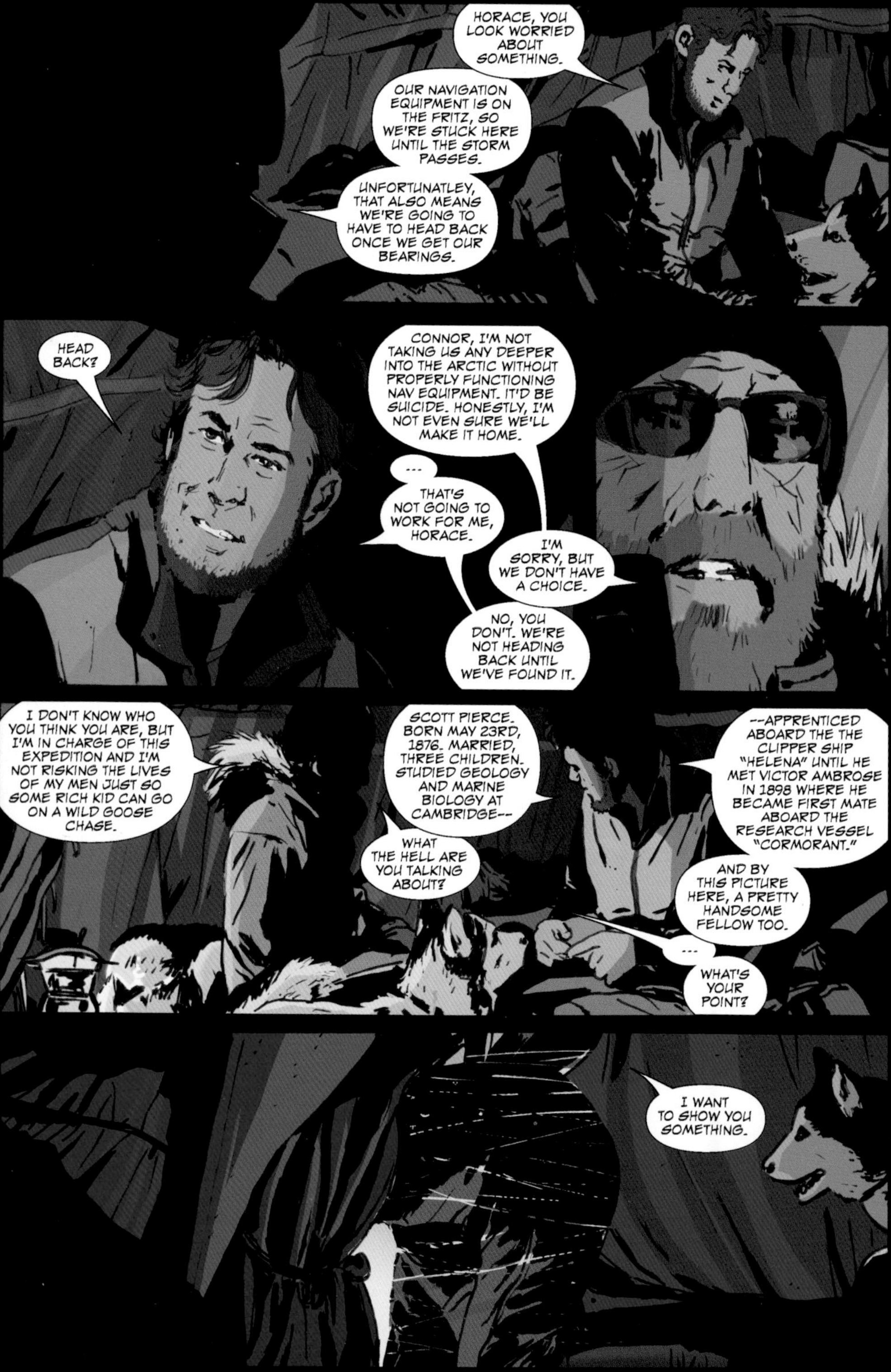
HORACE, YOU LOOK WORRIED ABOUT SOMETHING.
OUR NAVIGATION EQUIPMENT IS ON THE FRITZ, SO WE'RE STUCK HERE UNTIL THE STORM PASSES.
UNFORTUNATLEY, THAT ALSO MEANS WE'RE GOING TO HAVE TO HEAD BACK ONCE WE GET OUR BEARINGS.
HEAD BACK?
CONNOR, I'M NOT TAKING US ANY DEEPER INTO THE ARCTIC WITHOUT PROPERLY FUNCTIONING NAV EQUIPMENT. IT'D BE SUICIDE. HONESTLY, I'M NOT EVEN SURE WE'LL MAKE IT HOME.
...
THAT'S NOT GOING TO WORK FOR ME, HORACE.
I'M SORRY, BUT WE DON'T HAVE A CHOICE.
NO, YOU DON'T. WE'RE NOT HEADING BACK UNTIL WE'VE FOUND IT.
I DON'T KNOW WHO YOU THINK YOU ARE, BUT I'M IN CHARGE OF THIS EXPEDITION AND I'M NOT RISKING THE LIVES OF MY MEN JUST SO SOME RICH KID CAN GO ON A WILD GOOSE CHASE.
SCOTT PIERCE. BORN MAY 23RD, 1876. MARRIED, THREE CHILDREN. STUDIED GEOLOGY AND MARINE BIOLOGY AT CAMBRIDGE--
WHAT THE HELL ARE YOU TALKING ABOUT?
--APPRENTICED ABOARD THE THE CLIPPER SHIP "HELENA" UNTIL HE MET VICTOR AMBROSE IN 1898 WHERE HE BECAME FIRST MATE ABOARD THE RESEARCH VESSEL "CORMORANT."
AND BY THIS PICTURE HERE, A PRETTY HANDSOME FELLOW TOO.
...
WHAT'S YOUR POINT?
I WANT TO SHOW YOU SOMETHING.

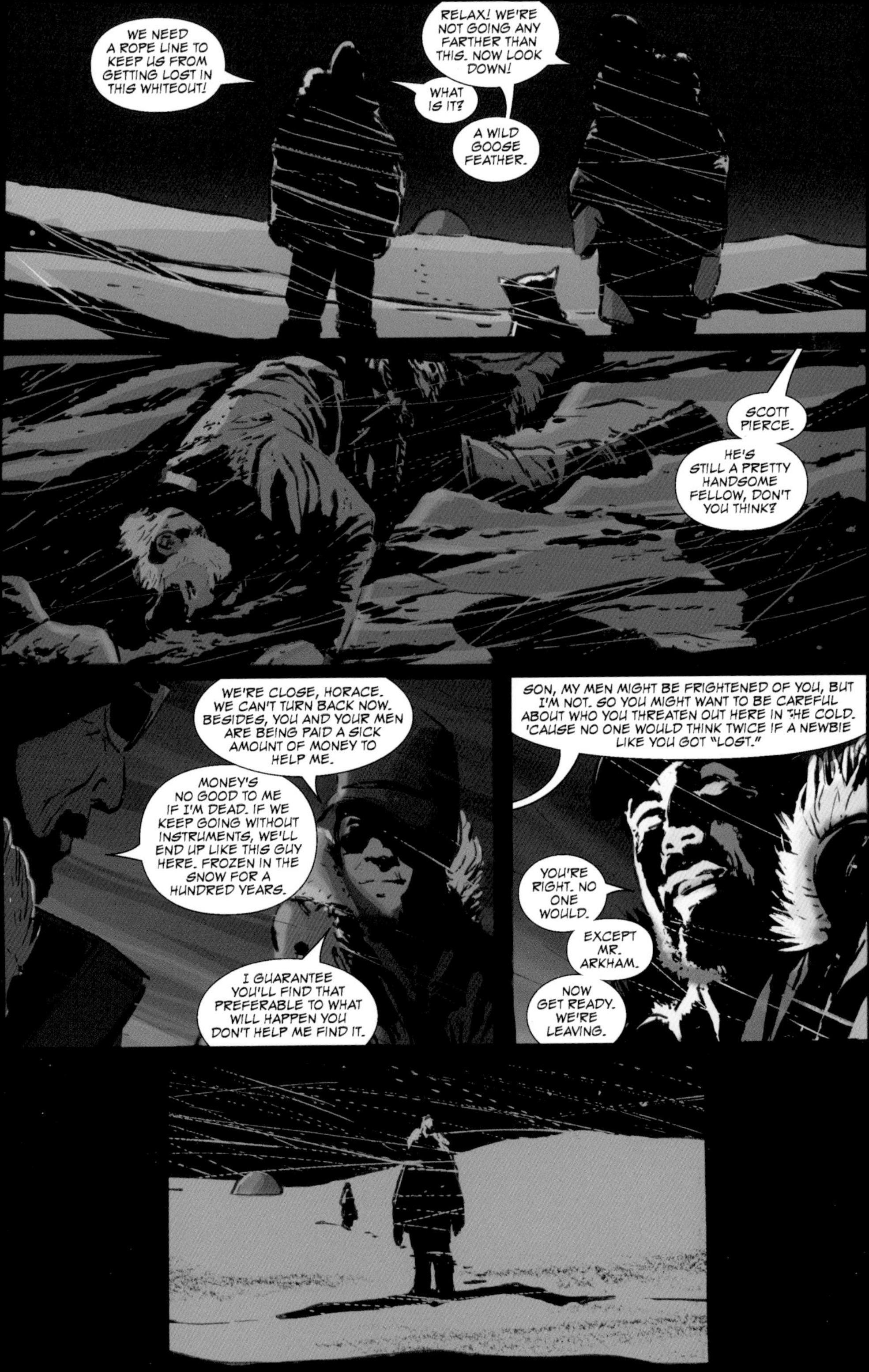
WE NEED A ROPE LINE TO KEEP US FROM GETTING LOST IN THIS WHITEOUT!
RELAX! WE'RE NOT GOING ANY FARTHER THAN THIS. NOW LOOK DOWN!
WHAT IS IT?
A WILD GOOSE FEATHER.
SCOTT PIERCE.
HE'S STILL A PRETTY HANDSOME FELLOW, DON'T YOU THINK?
WE'RE CLOSE, HORACE. WE CAN'T TURN BACK NOW. BESIDES, YOU AND YOUR MEN ARE BEING PAID A SICK AMOUNT OF MONEY TO HELP ME.
MONEY'S NO GOOD TO ME IF I'M DEAD. IF WE KEEP GOING WITHOUT INSTRUMENTS, WE'LL END UP LIKE THIS GUY HERE. FROZEN IN THE SNOW FOR A HUNDRED YEARS.
I GUARANTEE YOU'LL FIND THAT PREFERABLE TO WHAT WILL HAPPEN YOU DON'T HELP ME FIND IT.
SON, MY MEN MIGHT BE FRIGHTENED OF YOU, BUT I'M NOT. SO YOU MIGHT WANT TO BE CAREFUL ABOUT WHO YOU THREATEN OUT HERE IN THE COLD. 'CAUSE NO ONE WOULD THINK TWICE IF A NEWBIE LIKE YOU GOT "LOST."
YOU'RE RIGHT. NO ONE WOULD.
EXCEPT MR. ARKHAM.
NOW GET READY. WE'RE LEAVING.

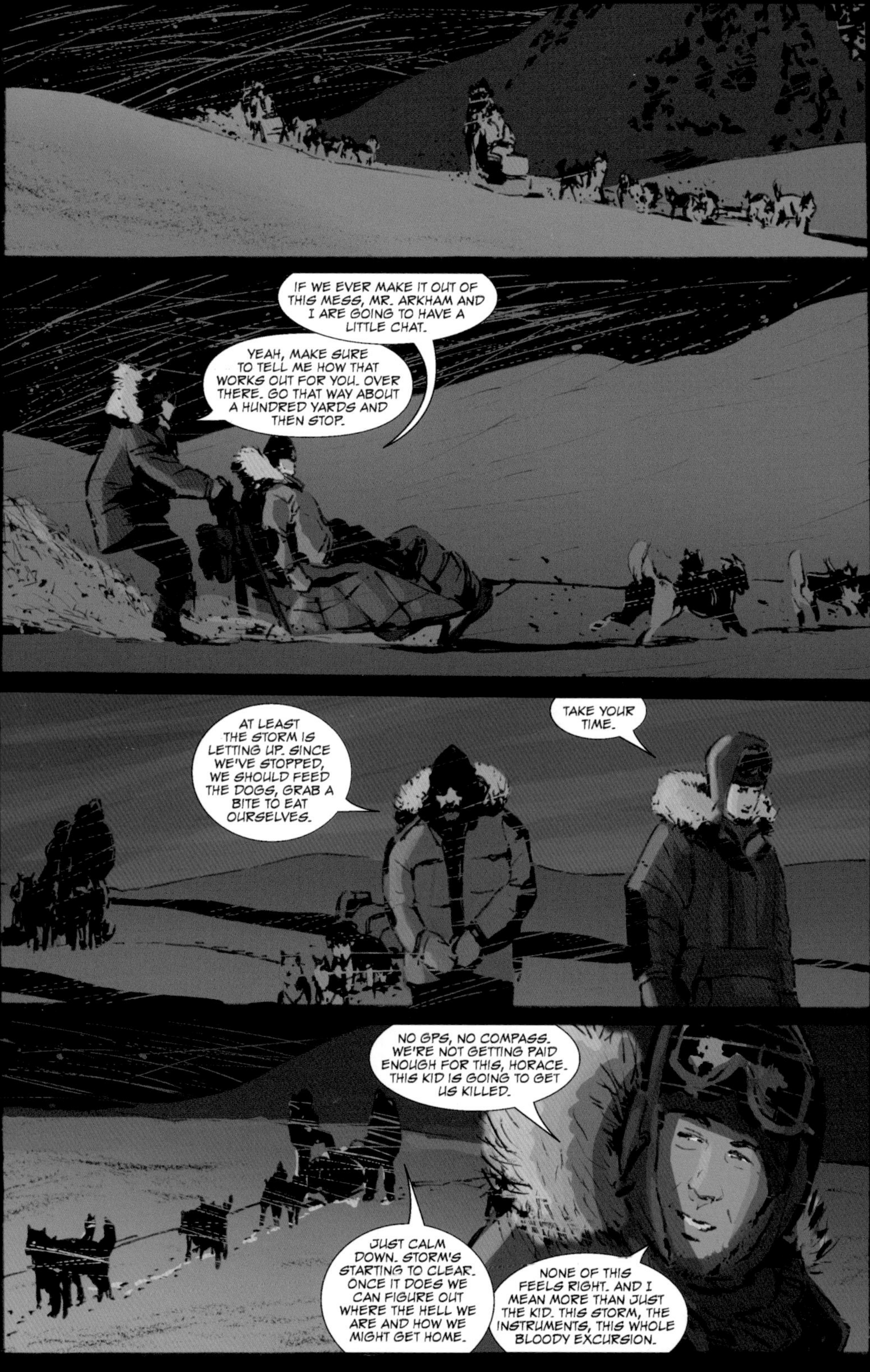
IF WE EVER MAKE IT OUT OF THIS MESS, MR. ARKHAM AND I ARE GOING TO HAVE A LITTLE CHAT.
YEAH, MAKE SURE TO TELL ME HOW THAT WORKS OUT FOR YOU. OVER THERE. GO THAT WAY ABOUT A HUNDRED YARDS AND THEN STOP.
AT LEAST THE STORM IS LETTING UP. SINCE WE'VE STOPPED, WE SHOULD FEED THE DOGS, GRAB A BITE TO EAT OURSELVES.
TAKE YOUR TIME.
NO GPS, NO COMPASS. WE'RE NOT GETTING PAID ENOUGH FOR THIS, HORACE. THIS KID IS GOING TO GET US KILLED.
JUST CALM DOWN. STORM'S STARTING TO CLEAR. ONCE IT DOES WE CAN FIGURE OUT WHERE THE HELL WE ARE AND HOW WE MIGHT GET HOME.
NONE OF THIS FEELS RIGHT. AND I MEAN MORE THAN JUST THE KID. THIS STORM, THE INSTRUMENTS, THIS WHOLE BLOODY EXCURSION.

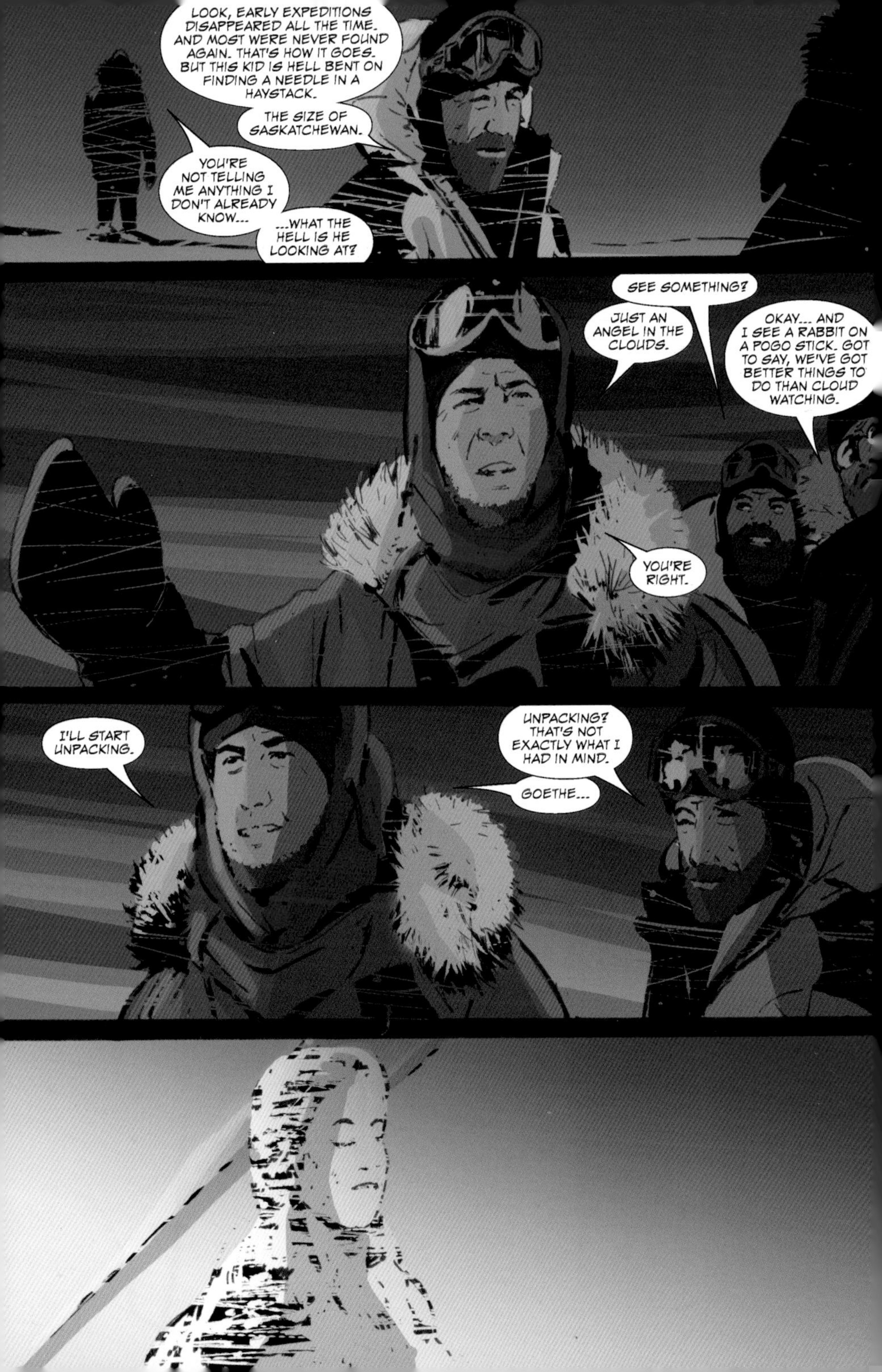
LOOK, EARLY EXPEDITIONS DISAPPEARED ALL THE TIME. AND MOST WERE NEVER FOUND AGAIN. THAT'S HOW IT GOES. BUT THIS KID IS HELL BENT ON FINDING A NEEDLE IN A HAYSTACK.
THE SIZE OF SASKATCHEWAN.
YOU'RE NOT TELLING ME ANYTHING I DON'T ALREADY KNOW...
...WHAT THE HELL IS HE LOOKING AT?
SEE SOMETHING?
JUST AN ANGEL IN THE CLOUDS.
OKAY... AND I SEE A RABBIT ON A POGO STICK. GOT TO SAY, WE'VE GOT BETTER THINGS TO DO THAN CLOUD WATCHING.
YOU'RE RIGHT.
I'LL START UNPACKING.
UNPACKING? THAT'S NOT EXACTLY WHAT I HAD IN MIND.
GOETHE...

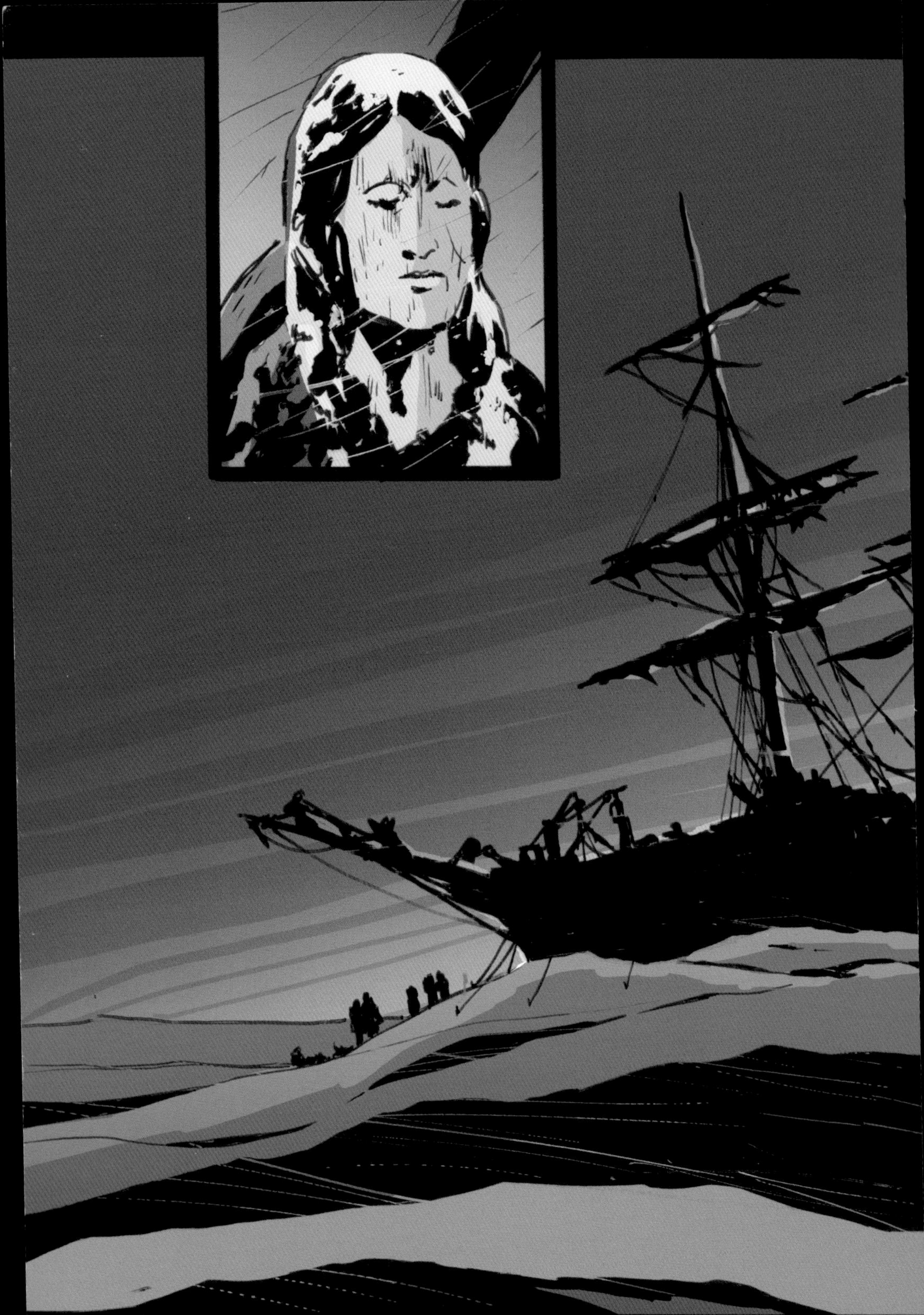

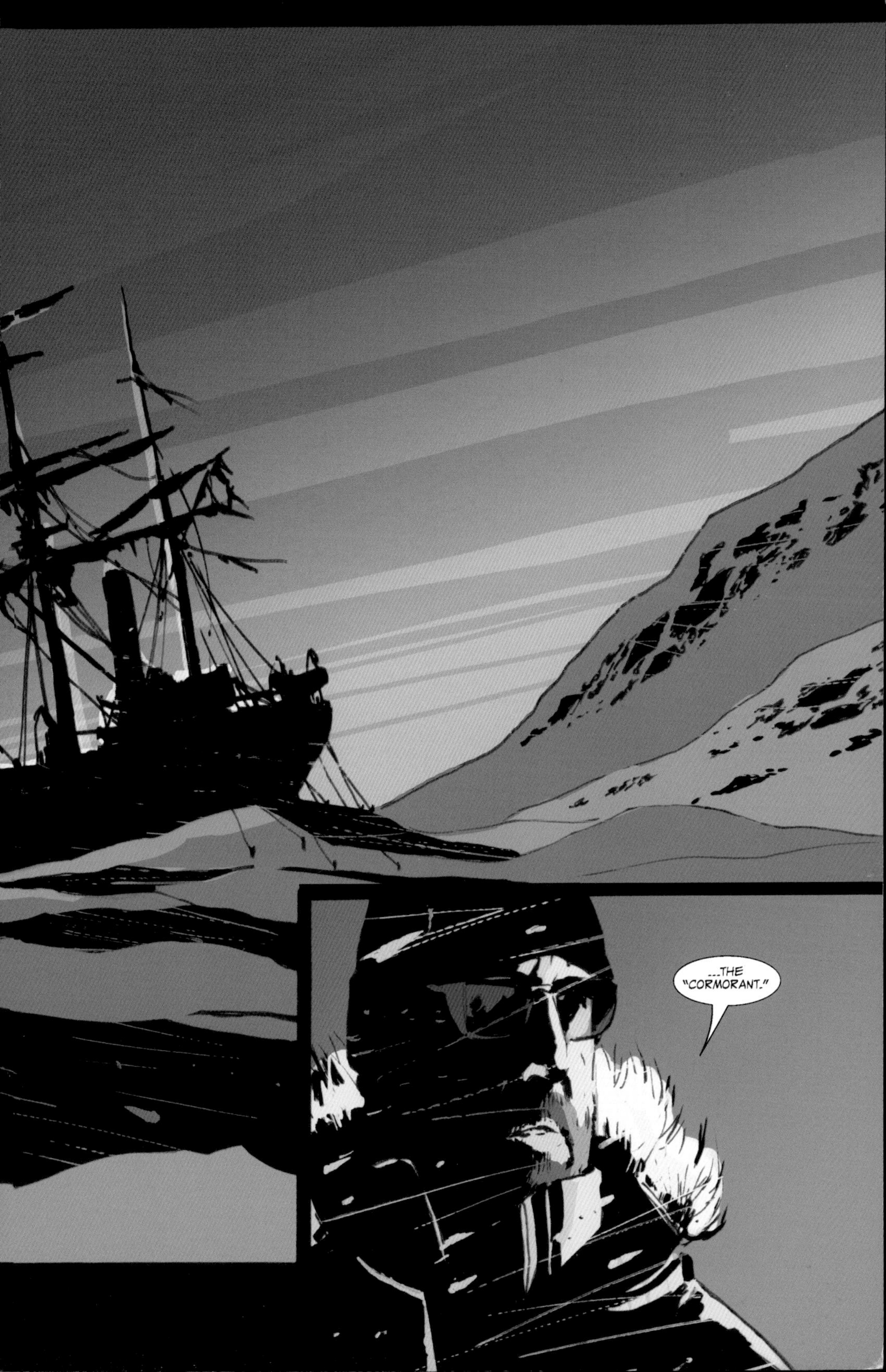
...THE "CORMORANT."

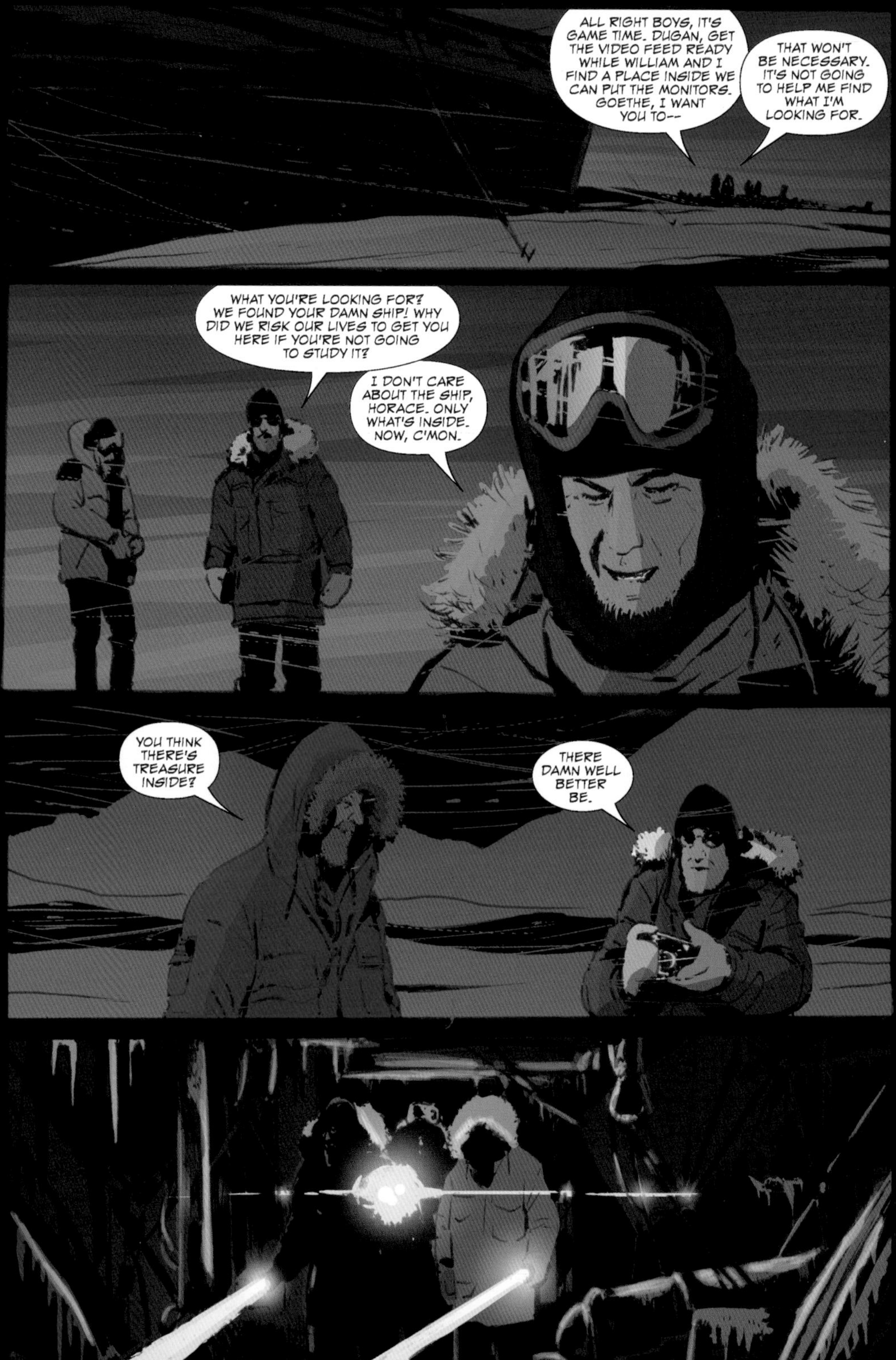
ALL RIGHT BOYS, IT'S GAME TIME. DUGAN, GET THE VIDEO FEED READY WHILE WILLIAM AND I FIND A PLACE INSIDE WE CAN PUT THE MONITORS. GOETHE, I WANT YOU TO--
THAT WON'T BE NECESSARY. IT'S NOT GOING TO HELP ME FIND WHAT I'M LOOKING FOR.
WHAT YOU'RE LOOKING FOR? WE FOUND YOUR DAMN SHIP! WHY DID WE RISK OUR LIVES TO GET YOU HERE IF YOU'RE NOT GOING TO STUDY IT?
I DON'T CARE ABOUT THE SHIP, HORACE. ONLY WHAT'S INSIDE. NOW, C'MON.
YOU THINK THERE'S TREASURE INSIDE?
THERE DAMN WELL BETTER BE.

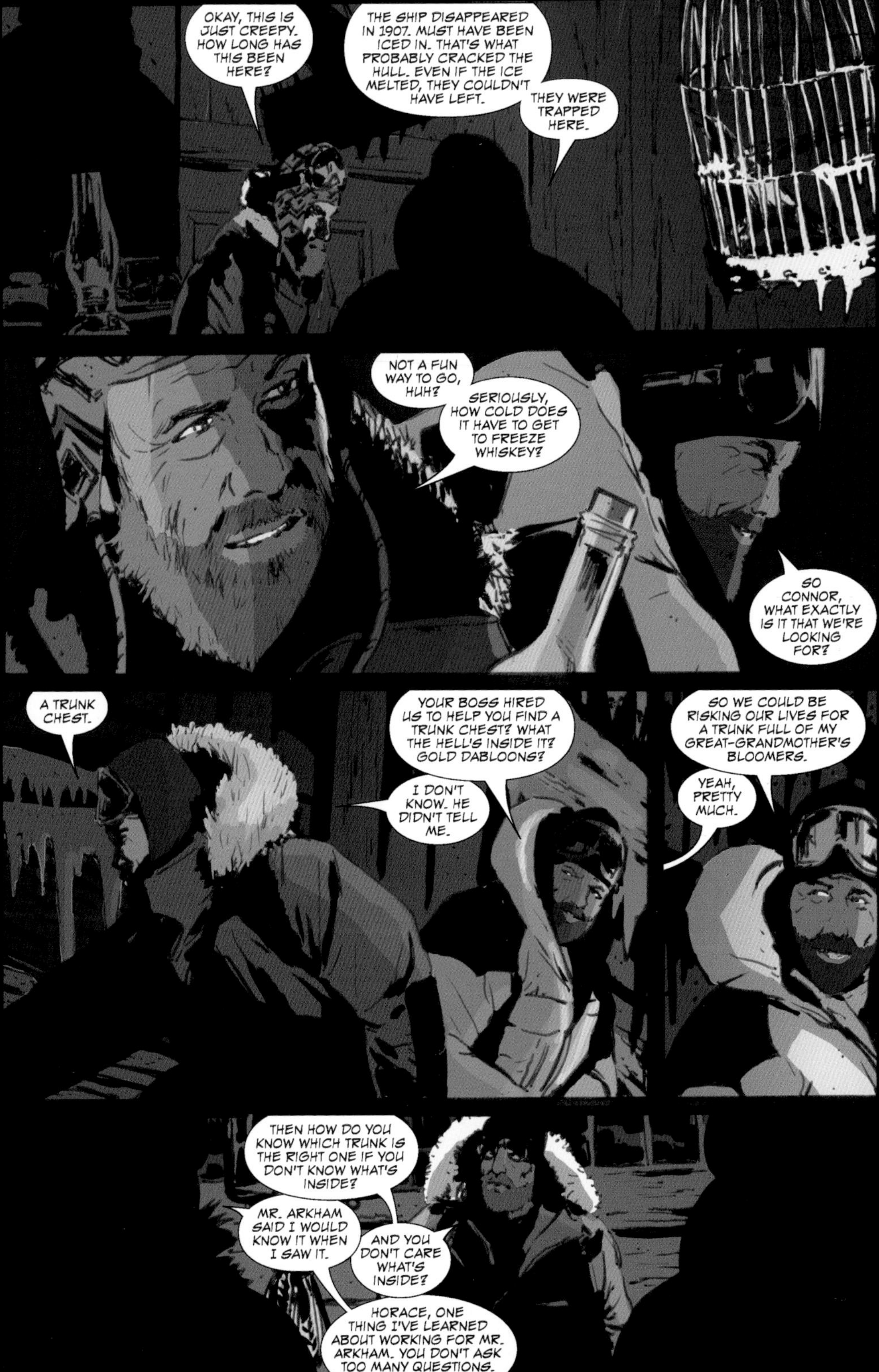
OKAY, THIS IS JUST CREEPY. HOW LONG HAS THIS BEEN HERE?
THE SHIP DISAPPEARED IN 1907. MUST HAVE BEEN ICED IN. THAT'S WHAT PROBABLY CRACKED THE HULL. EVEN IF THE ICE MELTED, THEY COULDN'T HAVE LEFT.
THEY WERE TRAPPED HERE.
NOT A FUN WAY TO GO, HUH?
SERIOUSLY, HOW COLD DOES IT HAVE TO GET TO FREEZE WHISKEY?
SO CONNOR, WHAT EXACTLY IS IT THAT WE'RE LOOKING FOR?
A TRUNK CHEST.
YOUR BOSS HIRED US TO HELP YOU FIND A TRUNK CHEST? WHAT THE HELL'S INSIDE IT? GOLD DABLOONS?
I DON'T KNOW. HE DIDN'T TELL ME.
SO WE COULD BE RISKING OUR LIVES FOR A TRUNK FULL OF MY GREAT-GRANDMOTHER'S BLOOMERS.
YEAH, PRETTY MUCH.
THEN HOW DO YOU KNOW WHICH TRUNK IS THE RIGHT ONE IF YOU DON'T KNOW WHAT'S INSIDE?
MR. ARKHAM SAID I WOULD KNOW IT WHEN I SAW IT.
AND YOU DON'T CARE WHAT'S INSIDE?
HORACE, ONE THING I'VE LEARNED ABOUT WORKING FOR MR. ARKHAM. YOU DON'T ASK TOO MANY QUESTIONS.

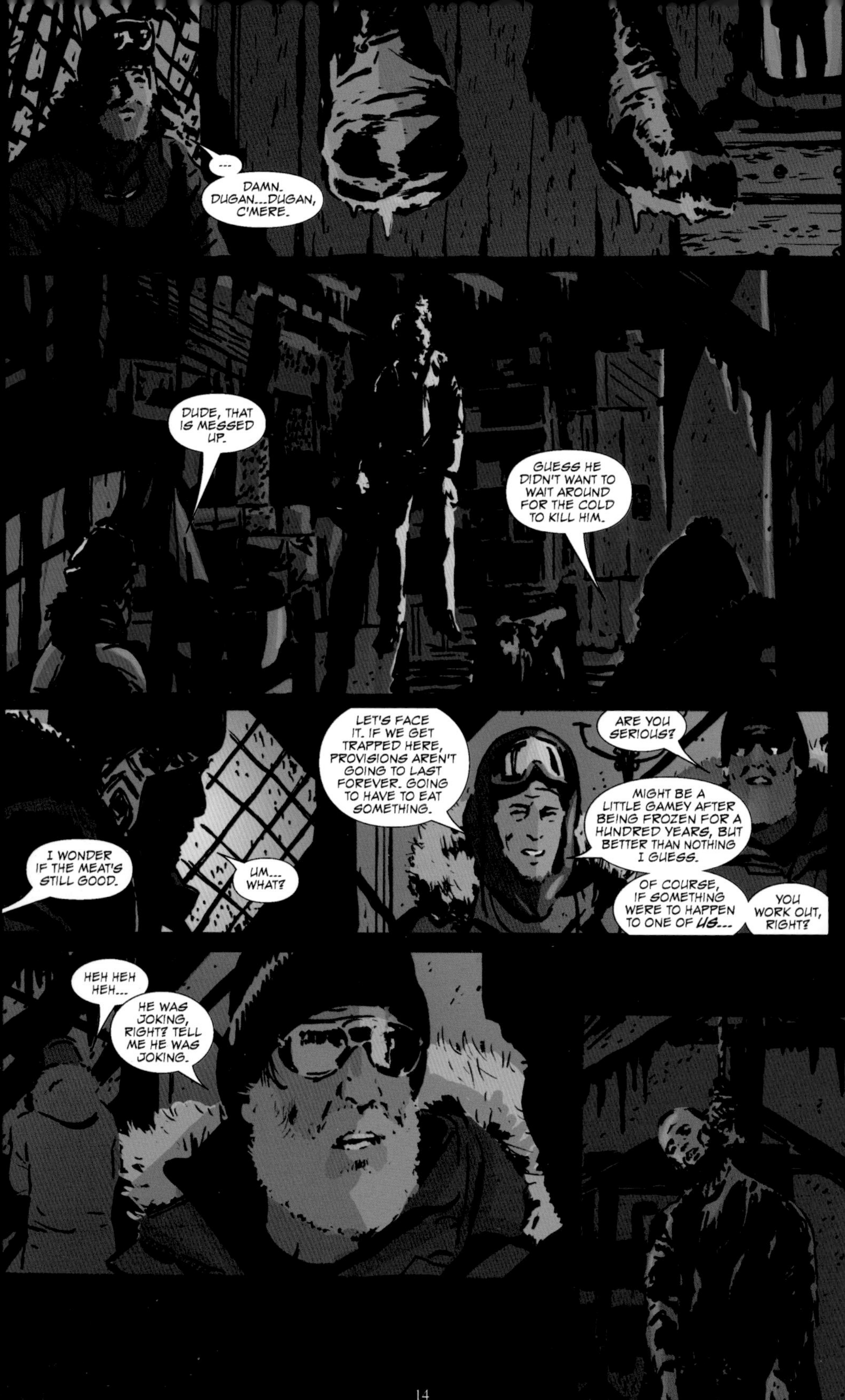

DAMN. DUGAN...DUGAN, C'MERE.
DUDE, THAT IS MESSED UP.
GUESS HE DIDN'T WANT TO WAIT AROUND FOR THE COLD TO KILL HIM.
I WONDER IF THE MEAT'S STILL GOOD.
UM... WHAT?
LET'S FACE IT. IF WE GET TRAPPED HERE, PROVISIONS AREN'T GOING TO LAST FOREVER. GOING TO HAVE TO EAT SOMETHING.
ARE YOU SERIOUS?
MIGHT BE A LITTLE GAMEY AFTER BEING FROZEN FOR A HUNDRED YEARS, BUT BETTER THAN NOTHING I GUESS.
OF COURSE, IF SOMETHING WERE TO HAPPEN TO ONE OF US...
YOU WORK OUT, RIGHT?
HEH HEH HEH...
HE WAS JOKING, RIGHT? TELL ME HE WAS JOKING.

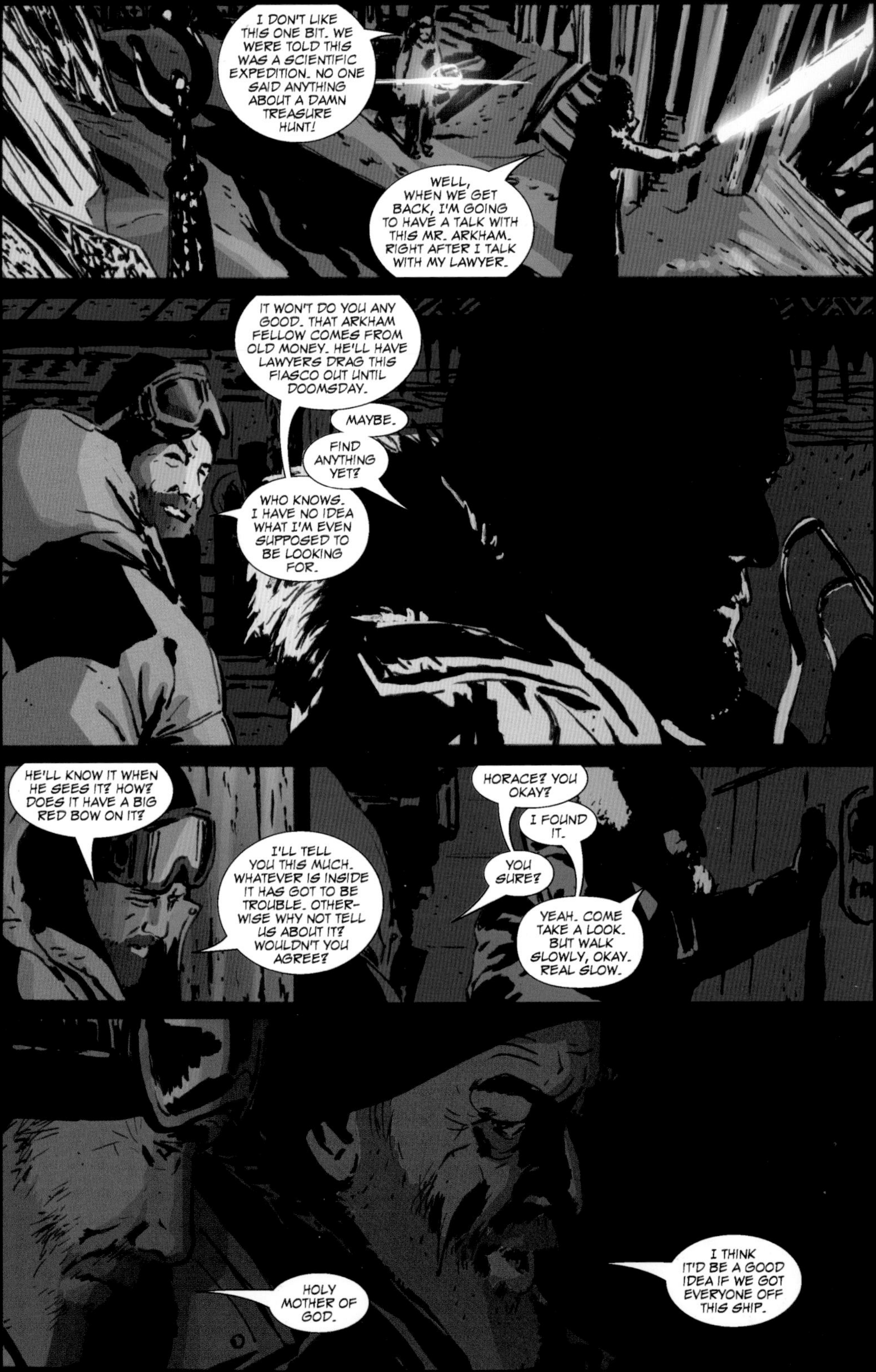
I DON'T LIKE THIS ONE BIT. WE WERE TOLD THIS WAS A SCIENTIFIC EXPEDITION. NO ONE SAID ANYTHING ABOUT A DAMN TREASURE HUNT!
WELL, WHEN WE GET BACK, I'M GOING TO HAVE A TALK WITH THIS MR. ARKHAM. RIGHT AFTER I TALK WITH MY LAWYER.
IT WON'T DO YOU ANY GOOD. THAT ARKHAM FELLOW COMES FROM OLD MONEY. HE'LL HAVE LAWYERS DRAG THIS FIASCO OUT UNTIL DOOMSDAY.
MAYBE.
FIND ANYTHING YET?
WHO KNOWS. I HAVE NO IDEA WHAT I'M EVEN SUPPOSED TO BE LOOKING FOR.
HE'LL KNOW IT WHEN HE SEES IT? HOW? DOES IT HAVE A BIG RED BOW ON IT?
I'LL TELL YOU THIS MUCH. WHATEVER IS INSIDE IT HAS GOT TO BE TROUBLE. OTHER-WISE WHY NOT TELL US ABOUT IT? WOULDN'T YOU AGREE?
HORACE? YOU OKAY?
I FOUND IT.
YOU SURE?
YEAH. COME TAKE A LOOK. BUT WALK SLOWLY, OKAY. REAL SLOW.
HOLY MOTHER OF GOD.
I THINK IT'D BE A GOOD IDEA IF WE GOT EVERYONE OFF THIS SHIP.

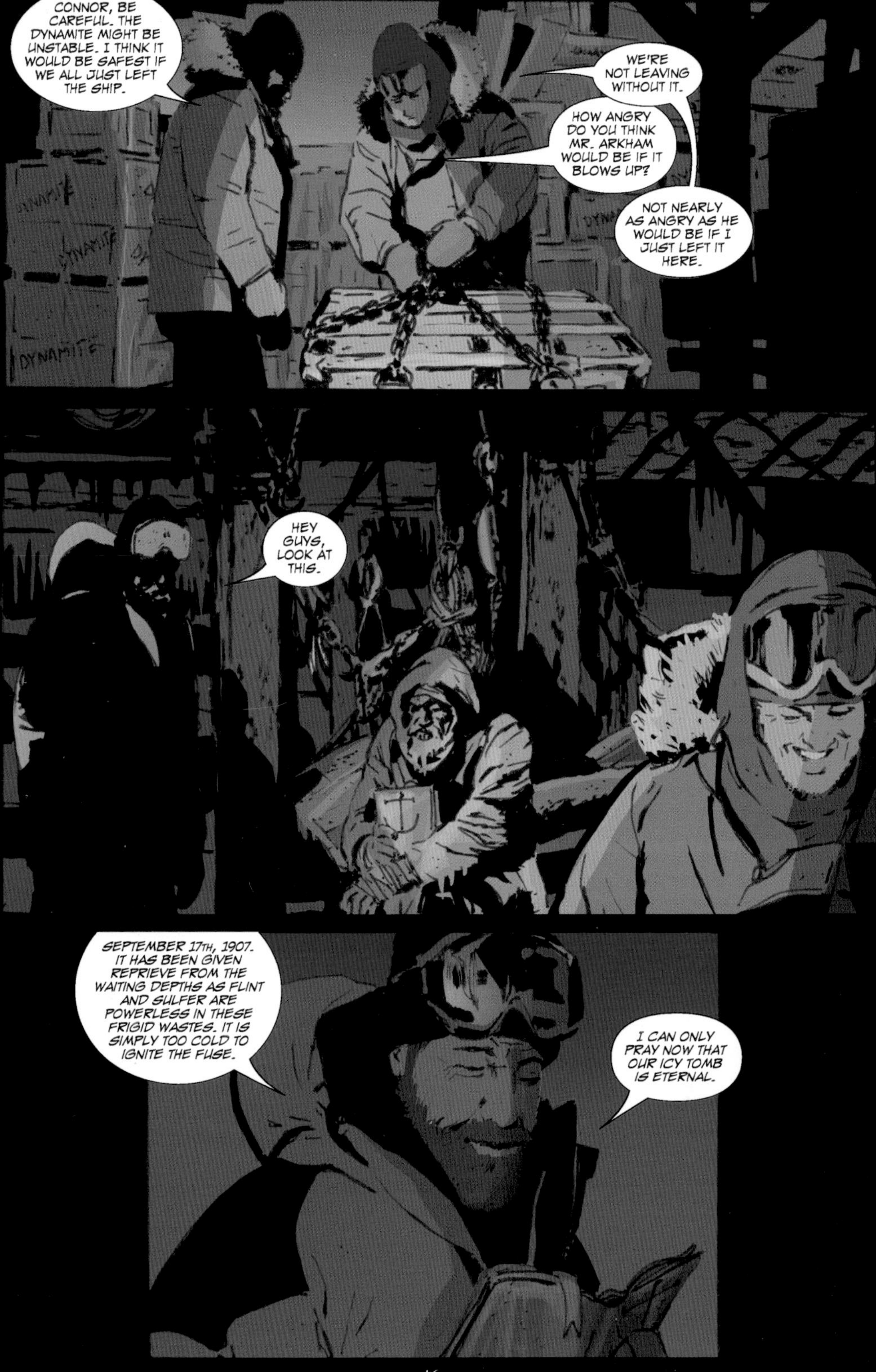
CONNOR, BE CAREFUL. THE DYNAMITE MIGHT BE UNSTABLE. I THINK IT WOULD BE SAFEST IF WE ALL JUST LEFT THE SHIP.
WE'RE NOT LEAVING WITHOUT IT.
HOW ANGRY DO YOU THINK MR. ARKHAM WOULD BE IF IT BLOWS UP?
NOT NEARLY AS ANGRY AS HE WOULD BE IF I JUST LEFT IT HERE.
DYNAMITE
DYNAMITE
DYNAMITE
HEY GUYS, LOOK AT THIS.
SEPTEMBER 17TH, 1907. IT HAS BEEN GIVEN REPRIEVE FROM THE WAITING DEPTHS AS FLINT AND SULFER ARE POWERLESS IN THESE FRIGID WASTES. IT IS SIMPLY TOO COLD TO IGNITE THE FUSE.
I CAN ONLY PRAY NOW THAT OUR ICY TOMB IS ETERNAL.

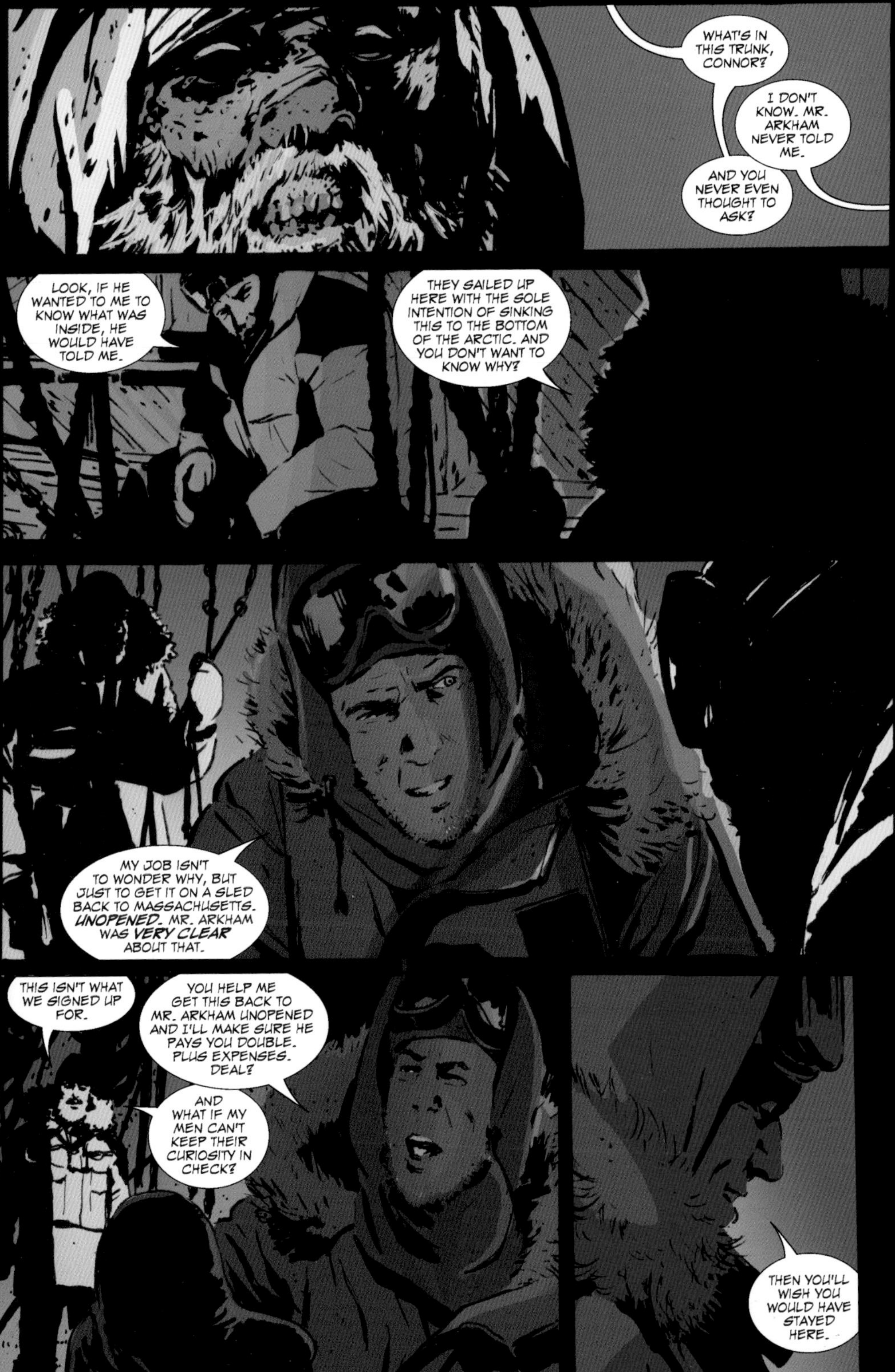
WHAT'S IN THIS TRUNK, CONNOR?
I DON'T KNOW. MR. ARKHAM NEVER TOLD ME.
AND YOU NEVER EVEN THOUGHT TO ASK?
LOOK, IF HE WANTED TO ME TO KNOW WHAT WAS INSIDE, HE WOULD HAVE TOLD ME.
THEY SAILED UP HERE WITH THE SOLE INTENTION OF SINKING THIS TO THE BOTTOM OF THE ARCTIC. AND YOU DON'T WANT TO KNOW WHY?
MY JOB ISN'T TO WONDER WHY, BUT JUST TO GET IT ON A SLED BACK TO MASSACHUSETTS. UNOPENED. MR. ARKHAM WAS VERY CLEAR ABOUT THAT.
THIS ISN'T WHAT WE SIGNED UP FOR.
YOU HELP ME GET THIS BACK TO MR. ARKHAM UNOPENED AND I'LL MAKE SURE HE PAYS YOU DOUBLE. PLUS EXPENSES. DEAL?
AND WHAT IF MY MEN CAN'T KEEP THEIR CURIOSITY IN CHECK?
THEN YOU'LL WISH YOU WOULD HAVE STAYED HERE.

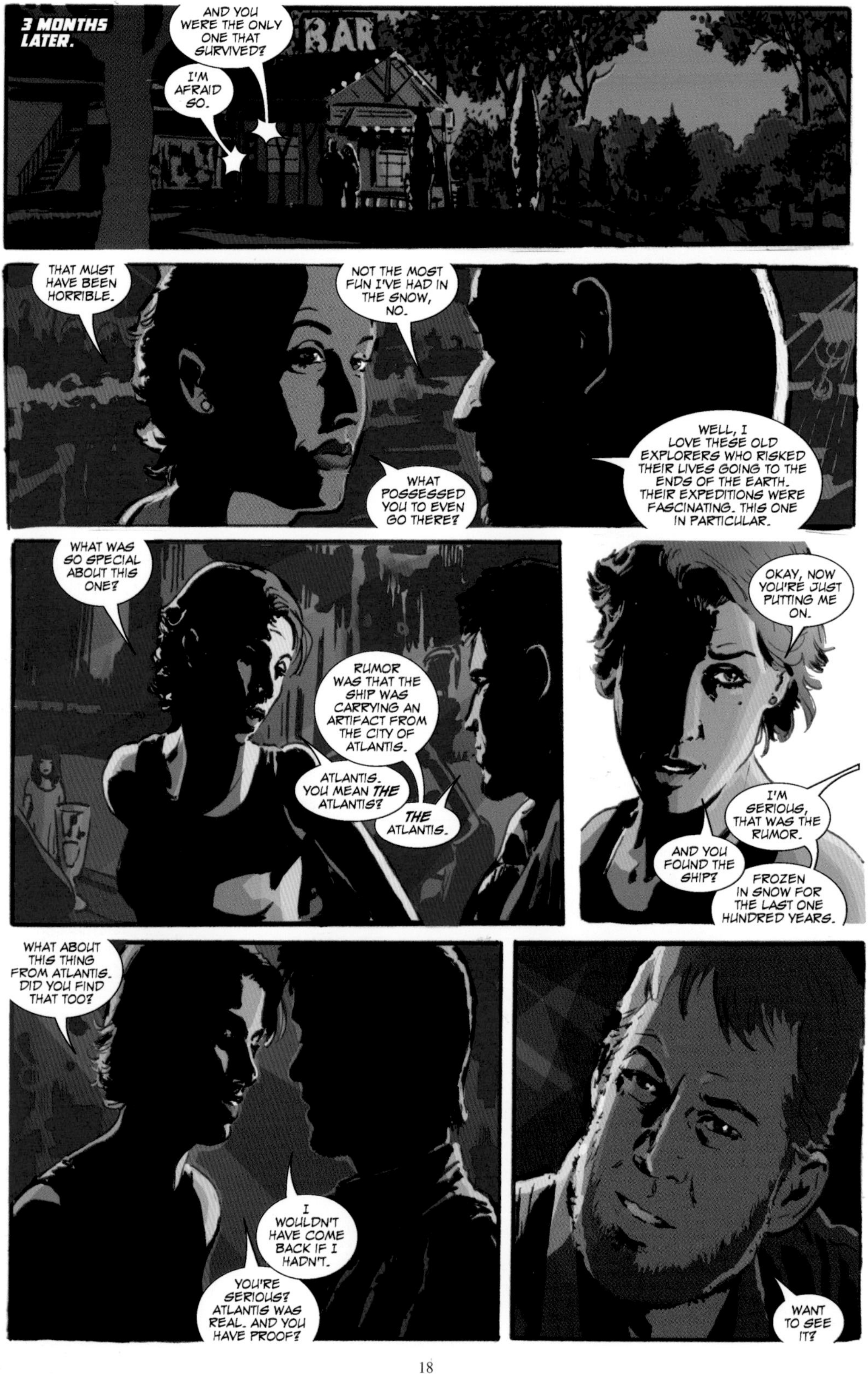
3 MONTHS LATER.
BAR
AND YOU WERE THE ONLY ONE THAT SURVIVED?
I'M AFRAID SO.
THAT MUST HAVE BEEN HORRIBLE.
NOT THE MOST FUN I'VE HAD IN THE SNOW, NO.
WHAT POSSESSED YOU TO EVEN GO THERE?
WELL, I LOVE THESE OLD EXPLORERS WHO RISKED THEIR LIVES GOING TO THE ENDS OF THE EARTH. THEIR EXPEDITIONS WERE FASCINATING. THIS ONE IN PARTICULAR.
WHAT WAS SO SPECIAL ABOUT THIS ONE?
RUMOR WAS THAT THE SHIP WAS CARRYING AN ARTIFACT FROM THE CITY OF ATLANTIS.
ATLANTIS. YOU MEAN *THE* ATLANTIS?
THE ATLANTIS.
OKAY, NOW YOU'RE JUST PUTTING ME ON.
I'M SERIOUS, THAT WAS THE RUMOR.
AND YOU FOUND THE SHIP?
FROZEN IN SNOW FOR THE LAST ONE HUNDRED YEARS.
WHAT ABOUT THIS THING FROM ATLANTIS. DID YOU FIND THAT TOO?
I WOULDN'T HAVE COME BACK IF I HADN'T.
YOU'RE SERIOUS? ATLANTIS WAS REAL. AND YOU HAVE PROOF?
WANT TO SEE IT?

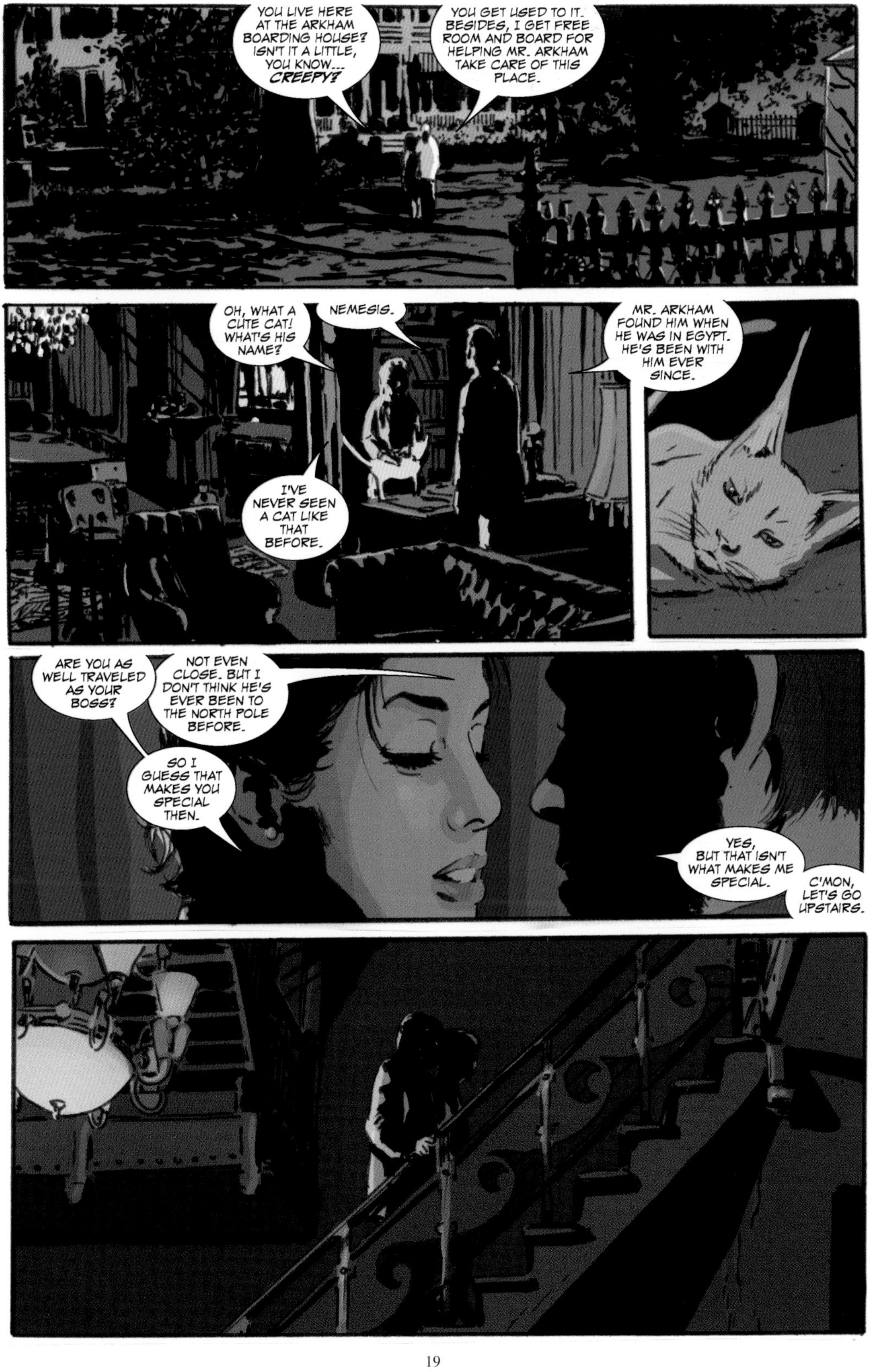
YOU LIVE HERE AT THE ARKHAM BOARDING HOUSE? ISN'T IT A LITTLE, YOU KNOW... CREEPY?
YOU GET USED TO IT. BESIDES, I GET FREE ROOM AND BOARD FOR HELPING MR. ARKHAM TAKE CARE OF THIS PLACE.
OH, WHAT A CUTE CAT! WHAT'S HIS NAME?
NEMESIS.
I'VE NEVER SEEN A CAT LIKE THAT BEFORE.
MR. ARKHAM FOUND HIM WHEN HE WAS IN EGYPT. HE'S BEEN WITH HIM EVER SINCE.
ARE YOU AS WELL TRAVELED AS YOUR BOSS?
NOT EVEN CLOSE. BUT I DON'T THINK HE'S EVER BEEN TO THE NORTH POLE BEFORE.
SO I GUESS THAT MAKES YOU SPECIAL THEN.
YES, BUT THAT ISN'T WHAT MAKES ME SPECIAL.
C'MON, LET'S GO UPSTAIRS.

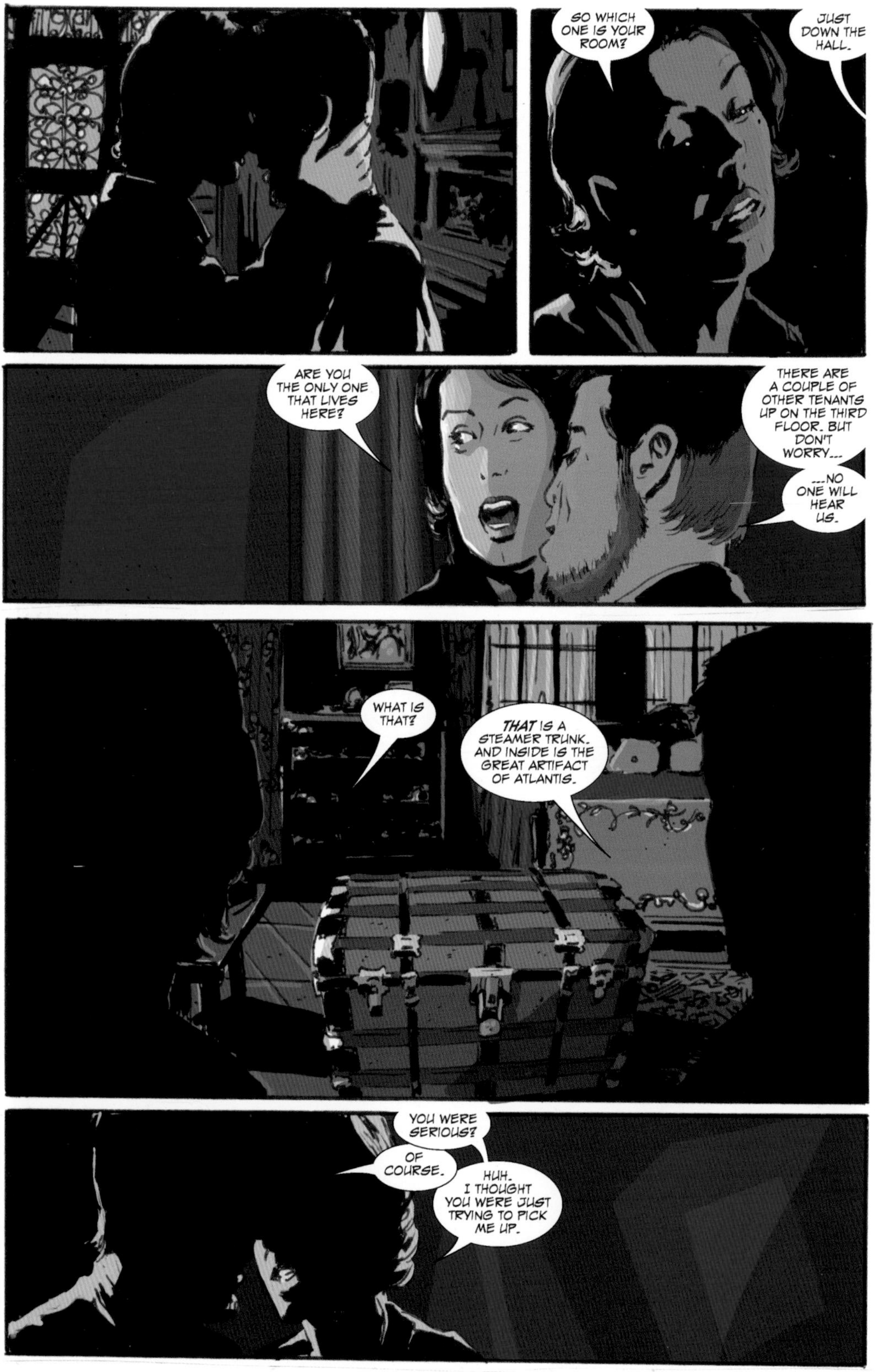
SO WHICH ONE IS YOUR ROOM?
JUST DOWN THE HALL.
ARE YOU THE ONLY ONE THAT LIVES HERE?
THERE ARE A COUPLE OF OTHER TENANTS UP ON THE THIRD FLOOR. BUT DON'T WORRY...
...NO ONE WILL HEAR US.
WHAT IS THAT?
THAT IS A STEAMER TRUNK. AND INSIDE IS THE GREAT ARTIFACT OF ATLANTIS.
YOU WERE SERIOUS?
OF COURSE.
HUH. I THOUGHT YOU WERE JUST TRYING TO PICK ME UP.

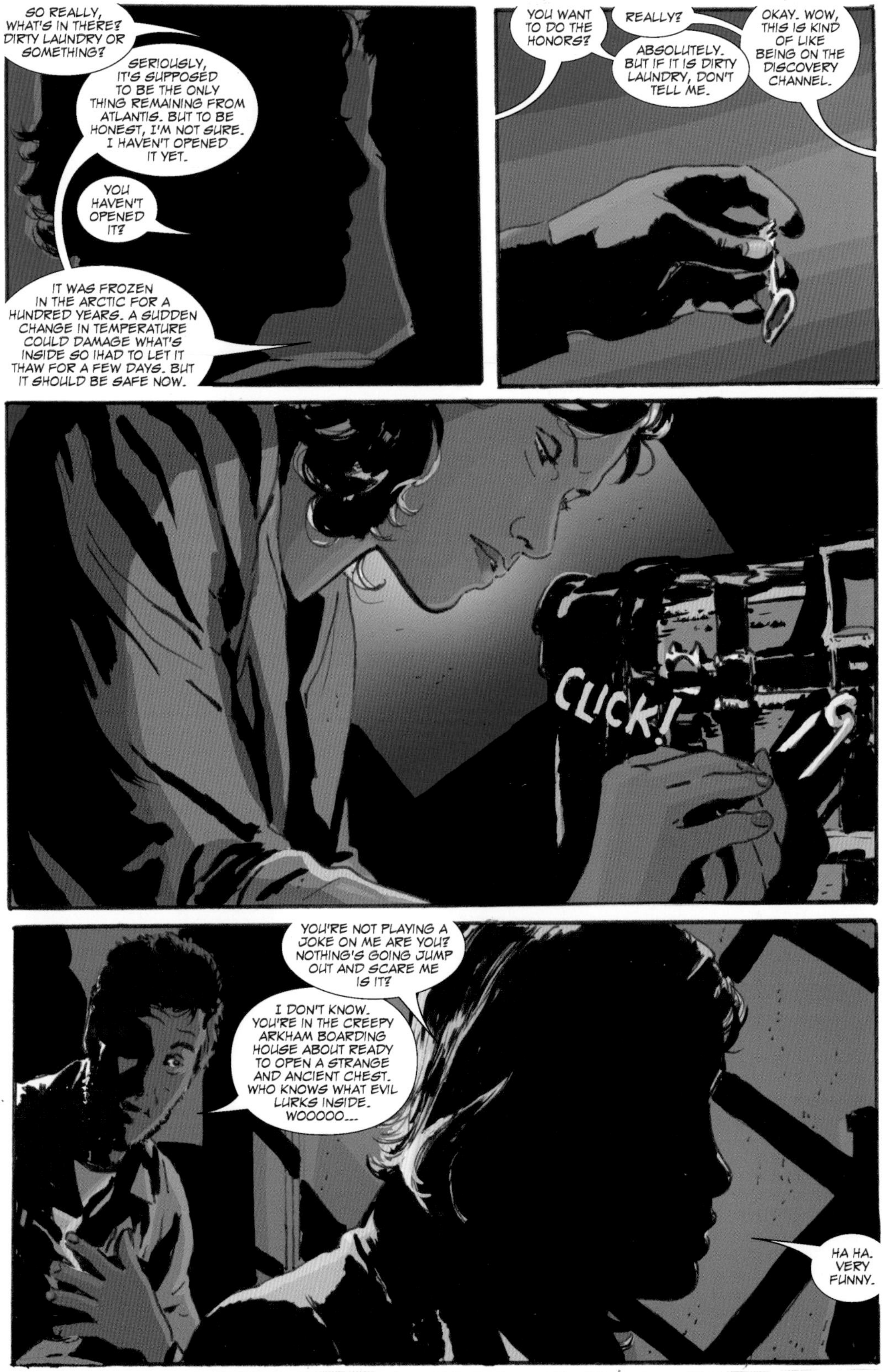
SO REALLY, WHAT'S IN THERE? DIRTY LAUNDRY OR SOMETHING?
SERIOUSLY, IT'S SUPPOSED TO BE THE ONLY THING REMAINING FROM ATLANTIS. BUT TO BE HONEST, I'M NOT SURE. I HAVEN'T OPENED IT YET.
YOU HAVEN'T OPENED IT?
IT WAS FROZEN IN THE ARCTIC FOR A HUNDRED YEARS. A SUDDEN CHANGE IN TEMPERATURE COULD DAMAGE WHAT'S INSIDE SO IHAD TO LET IT THAW FOR A FEW DAYS. BUT IT SHOULD BE SAFE NOW.
YOU WANT TO DO THE HONORS?
REALLY?
ABSOLUTELY. BUT IF IT IS DIRTY LAUNDRY, DON'T TELL ME.
OKAY. WOW, THIS IS KIND OF LIKE BEING ON THE DISCOVERY CHANNEL.
CLICK!
YOU'RE NOT PLAYING A JOKE ON ME ARE YOU? NOTHING'S GOING JUMP OUT AND SCARE ME IS IT?
I DON'T KNOW. YOU'RE IN THE CREEPY ARKHAM BOARDING HOUSE ABOUT READY TO OPEN A STRANGE AND ANCIENT CHEST. WHO KNOWS WHAT EVIL LURKS INSIDE. WOOOOO...
HA HA. VERY FUNNY.

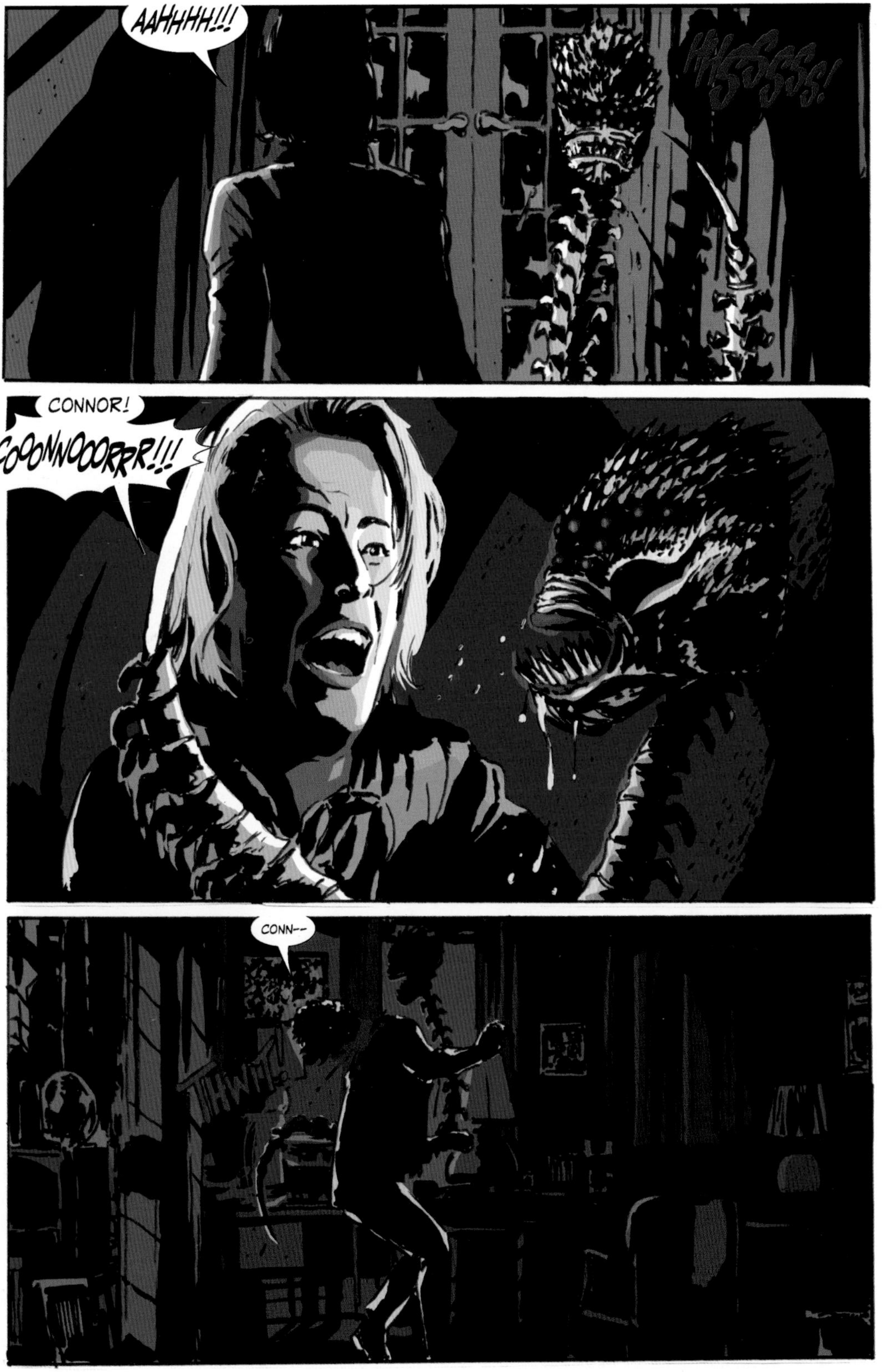
AAHHHH!!!
HISSSSS!
CONNOR!
COOONNOOORRRR!!!
CONN--
THWIP!

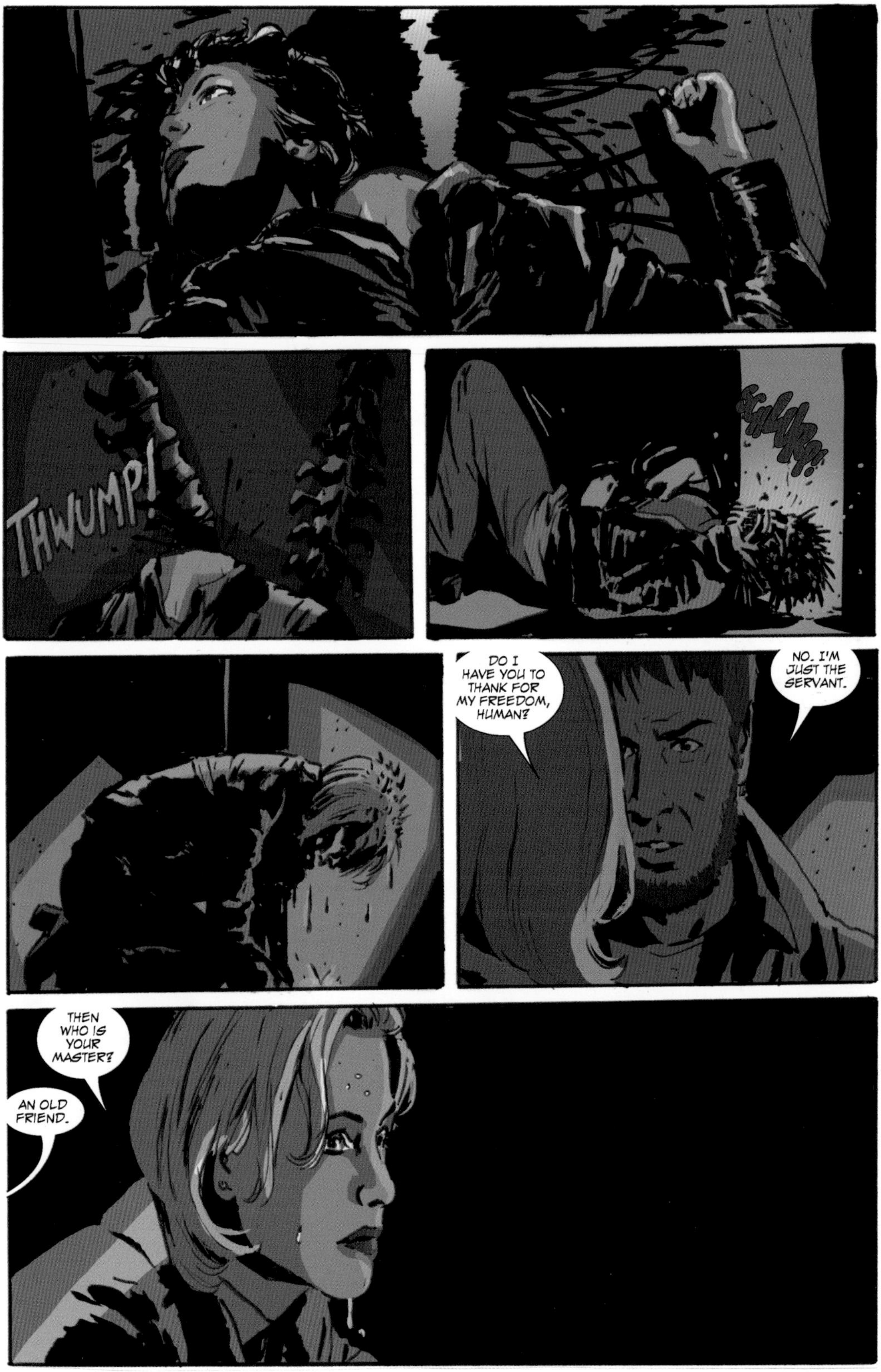
THWUMP!
DO I HAVE YOU TO THANK FOR MY FREEDOM, HUMAN?
NO. I'M JUST THE SERVANT.
THEN WHO IS YOUR MASTER?
AN OLD FRIEND.

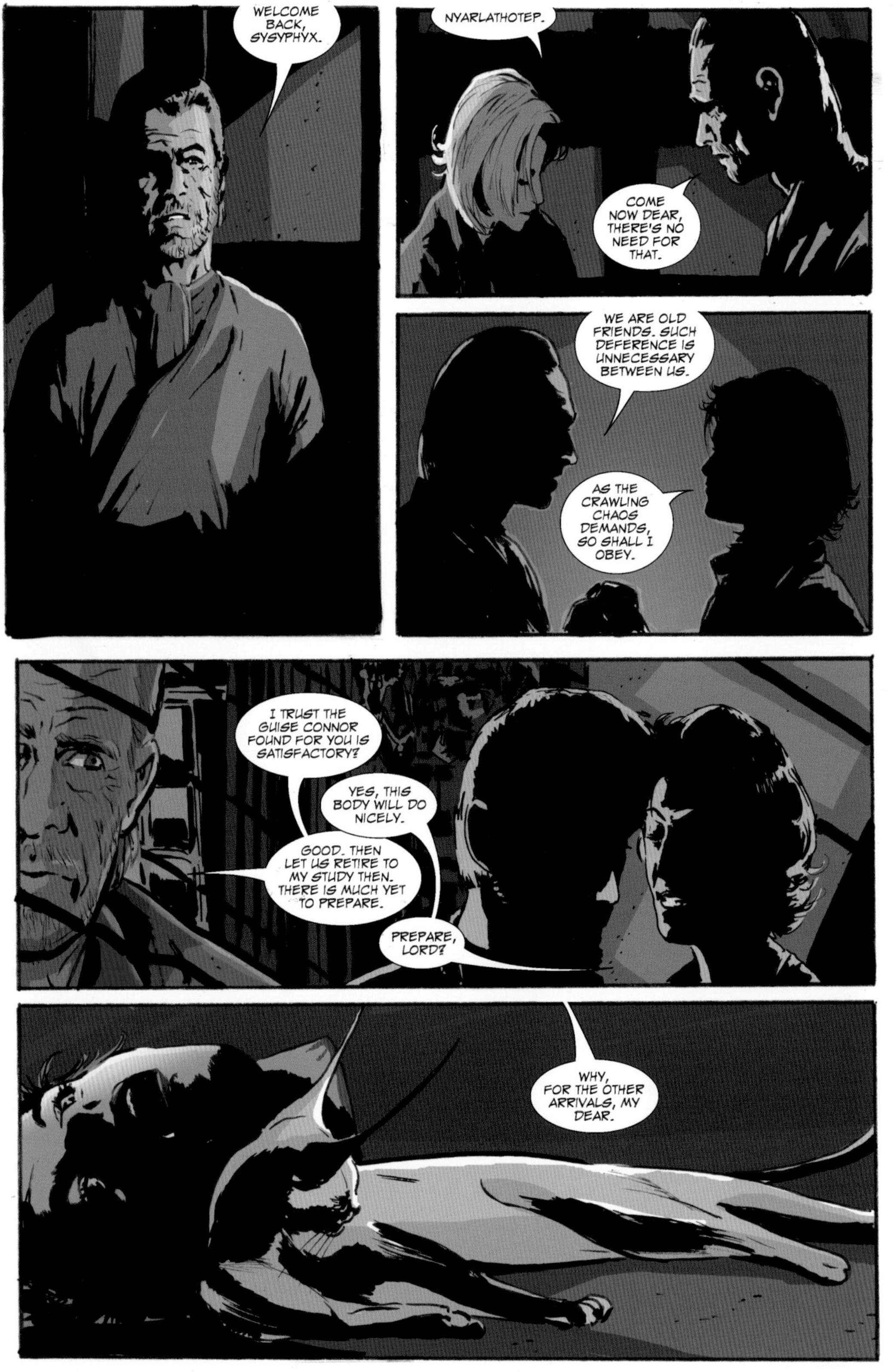
WELCOME BACK, SYSYPHYX.
NYARLATHOTEP.
COME NOW DEAR, THERE'S NO NEED FOR THAT.
WE ARE OLD FRIENDS. SUCH DEFERENCE IS UNNECESSARY BETWEEN US.
AS THE CRAWLING CHAOS DEMANDS, SO SHALL I OBEY.
I TRUST THE GUISE CONNOR FOUND FOR YOU IS SATISFACTORY?
YES, THIS BODY WILL DO NICELY.
GOOD. THEN LET US RETIRE TO MY STUDY THEN. THERE IS MUCH YET TO PREPARE.
PREPARE, LORD?
WHY, FOR THE OTHER ARRIVALS, MY DEAR.

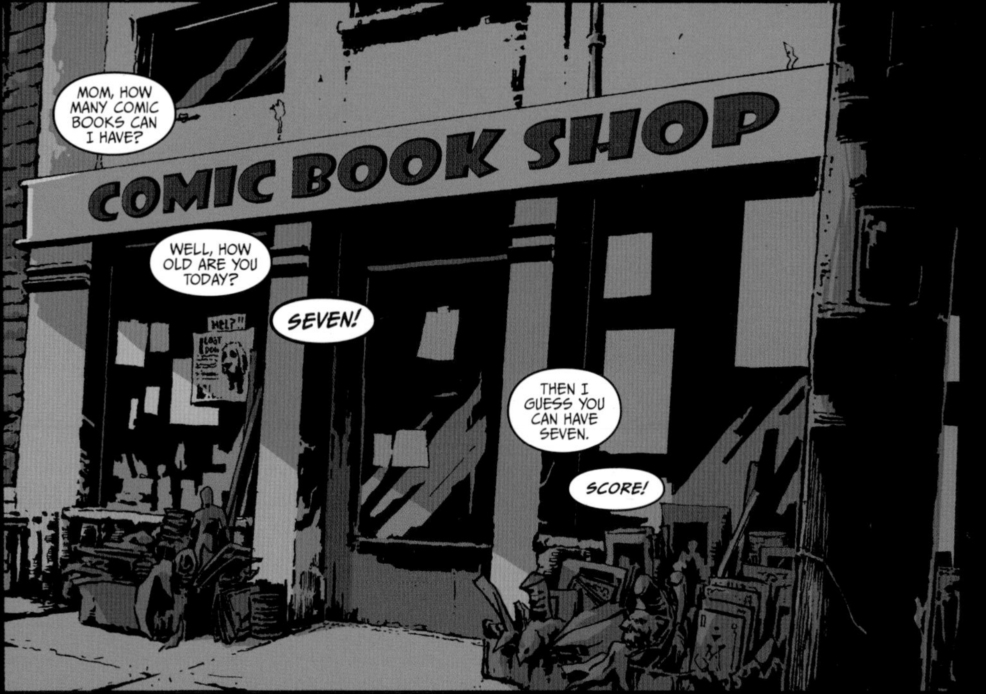
COMIC BOOK SHOP
MOM, HOW MANY COMIC BOOKS CAN I HAVE?
WELL, HOW OLD ARE YOU TODAY?
SEVEN!
THEN I GUESS YOU CAN HAVE SEVEN.
SCORE!

THE GATHERING

PART 2 of 5

"Happy Birthday"

MICHAEL ALAN NELSON
WRITER

MARCO RUDY
ARTIST

MARC RUEDA
COLORIST

MARSHALL DILLON
LETTERER

VATCHE MAVILIAN
COVER A ARTIST

PATRICK McEVOY
COVER B ARTIST

MARSHALL DILLON
MANAGING EDITOR

JOYCE EL HAYEK
ASSISTANT EDITOR

SHANNON McDONNELL
COPY EDITOR

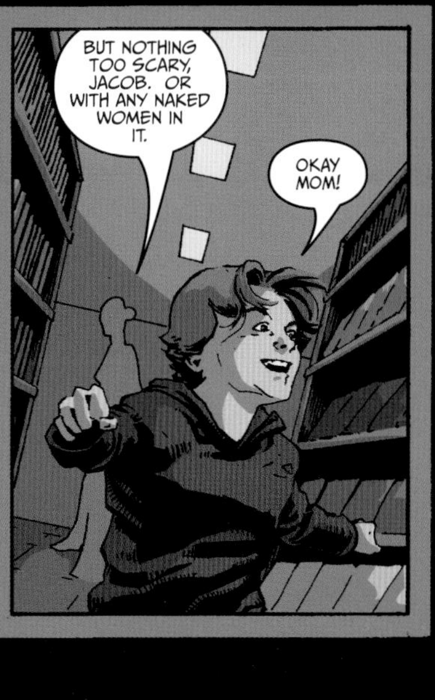
BUT NOTHING TOO SCARY, JACOB. OR WITH ANY NAKED WOMEN IN IT.
OKAY MOM!

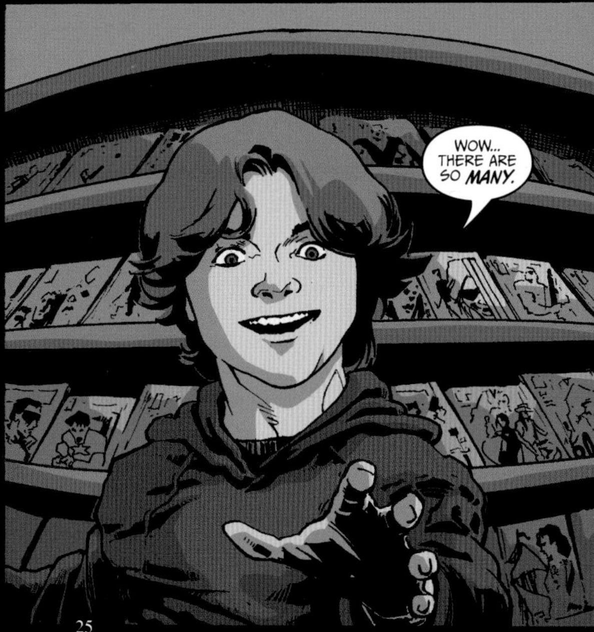
WOW... THERE ARE SO *MANY*.

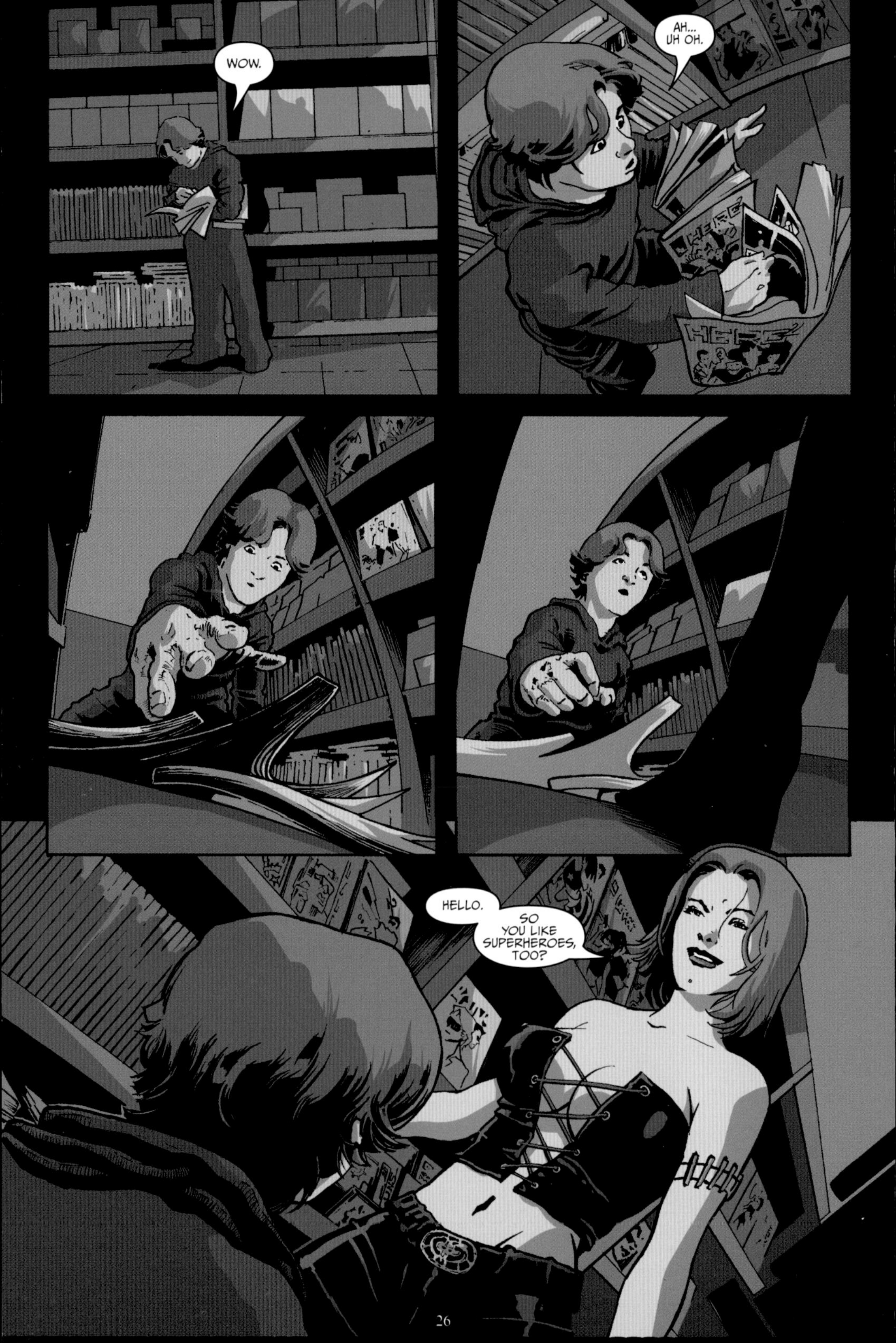
WOW.
AH... UH OH.
HELLO.
SO YOU LIKE SUPERHEROES, TOO?

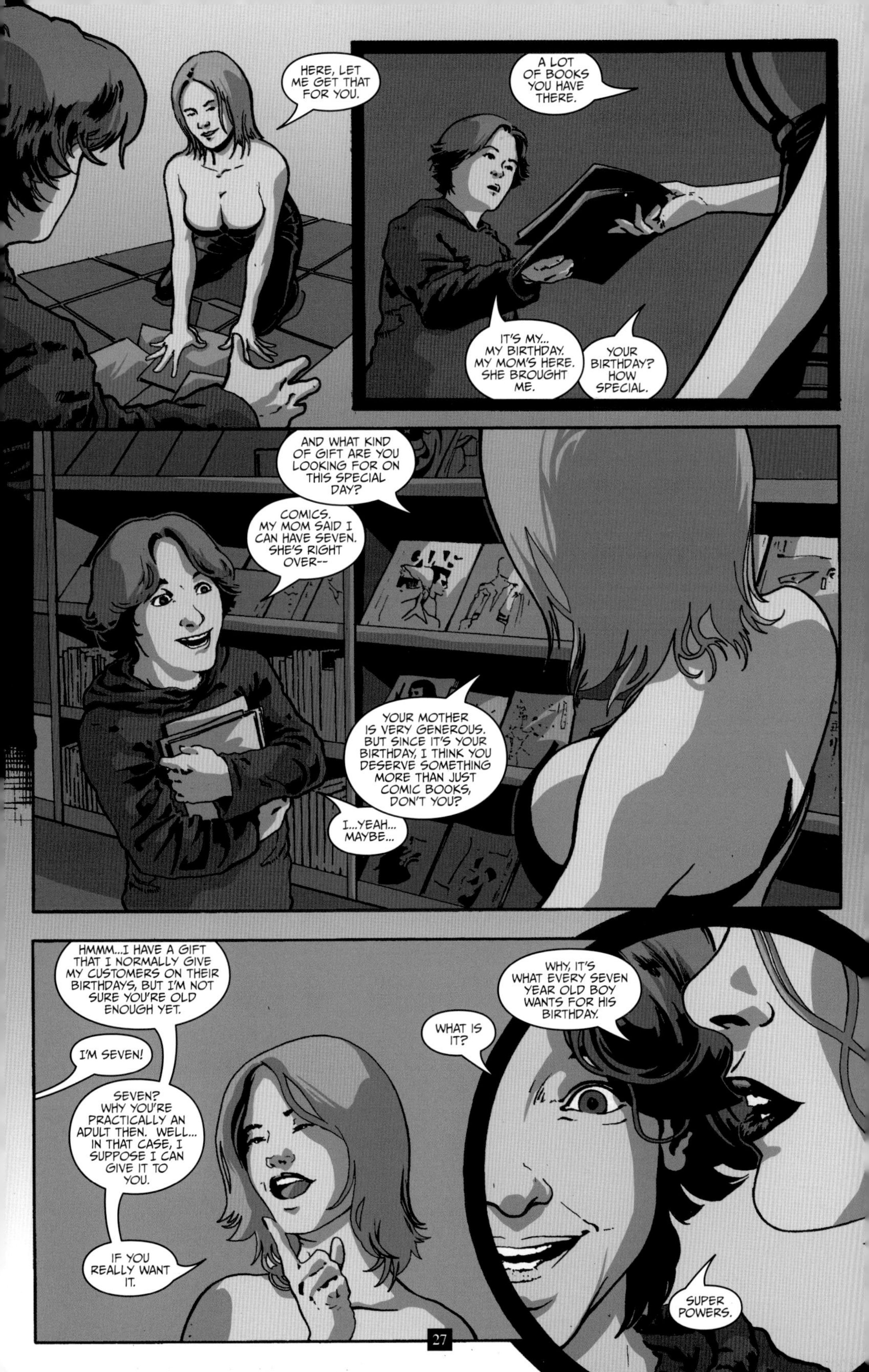
HERE, LET ME GET THAT FOR YOU.
A LOT OF BOOKS YOU HAVE THERE.
IT'S MY... MY BIRTHDAY. MY MOM'S HERE. SHE BROUGHT ME.
YOUR BIRTHDAY? HOW SPECIAL.
AND WHAT KIND OF GIFT ARE YOU LOOKING FOR ON THIS SPECIAL DAY?
COMICS. MY MOM SAID I CAN HAVE SEVEN. SHE'S RIGHT OVER--
YOUR MOTHER IS VERY GENEROUS. BUT SINCE IT'S YOUR BIRTHDAY, I THINK YOU DESERVE SOMETHING MORE THAN JUST COMIC BOOKS, DON'T YOU?
I...YEAH... MAYBE...
HMMM...I HAVE A GIFT THAT I NORMALLY GIVE MY CUSTOMERS ON THEIR BIRTHDAYS, BUT I'M NOT SURE YOU'RE OLD ENOUGH YET.
I'M SEVEN!
SEVEN? WHY YOU'RE PRACTICALLY AN ADULT THEN. WELL... IN THAT CASE, I SUPPOSE I CAN GIVE IT TO YOU.
IF YOU REALLY WANT IT.
WHAT IS IT?
WHY, IT'S WHAT EVERY SEVEN YEAR OLD BOY WANTS FOR HIS BIRTHDAY.
SUPER POWERS.

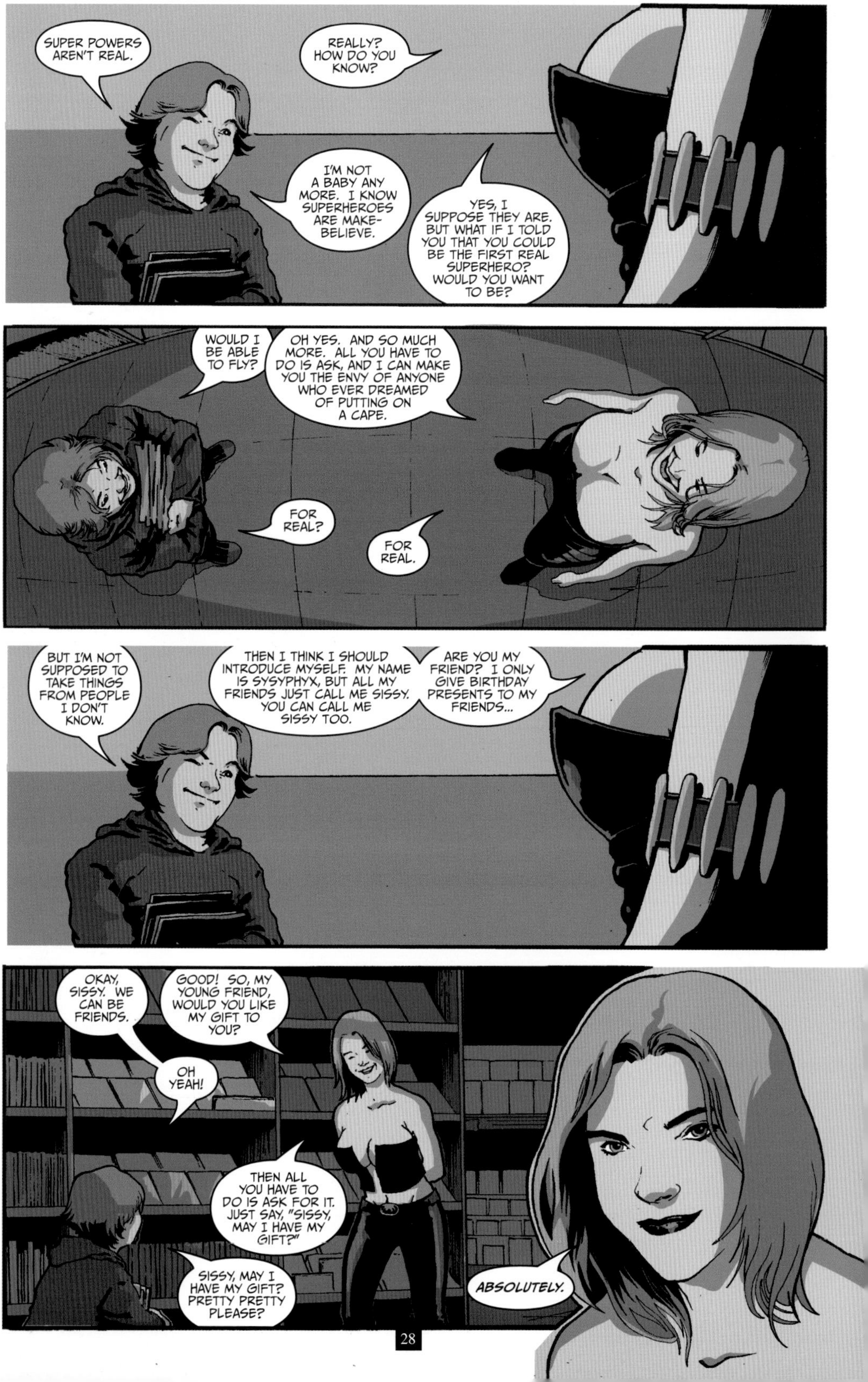
SUPER POWERS AREN'T REAL.
REALLY? HOW DO YOU KNOW?
I'M NOT A BABY ANY MORE. I KNOW SUPERHEROES ARE MAKE-BELIEVE.
YES, I SUPPOSE THEY ARE. BUT WHAT IF I TOLD YOU THAT YOU COULD BE THE FIRST REAL SUPERHERO? WOULD YOU WANT TO BE?
WOULD I BE ABLE TO FLY?
OH YES. AND SO MUCH MORE. ALL YOU HAVE TO DO IS ASK, AND I CAN MAKE YOU THE ENVY OF ANYONE WHO EVER DREAMED OF PUTTING ON A CAPE.
FOR REAL?
FOR REAL.
BUT I'M NOT SUPPOSED TO TAKE THINGS FROM PEOPLE I DON'T KNOW.
THEN I THINK I SHOULD INTRODUCE MYSELF. MY NAME IS SYSYPHYX, BUT ALL MY FRIENDS JUST CALL ME SISSY. YOU CAN CALL ME SISSY TOO.
ARE YOU MY FRIEND? I ONLY GIVE BIRTHDAY PRESENTS TO MY FRIENDS...
OKAY, SISSY. WE CAN BE FRIENDS.
GOOD! SO, MY YOUNG FRIEND, WOULD YOU LIKE MY GIFT TO YOU?
OH YEAH!
THEN ALL YOU HAVE TO DO IS ASK FOR IT. JUST SAY, "SISSY, MAY I HAVE MY GIFT?"
SISSY, MAY I HAVE MY GIFT? PRETTY PRETTY PLEASE?
ABSOLUTELY.

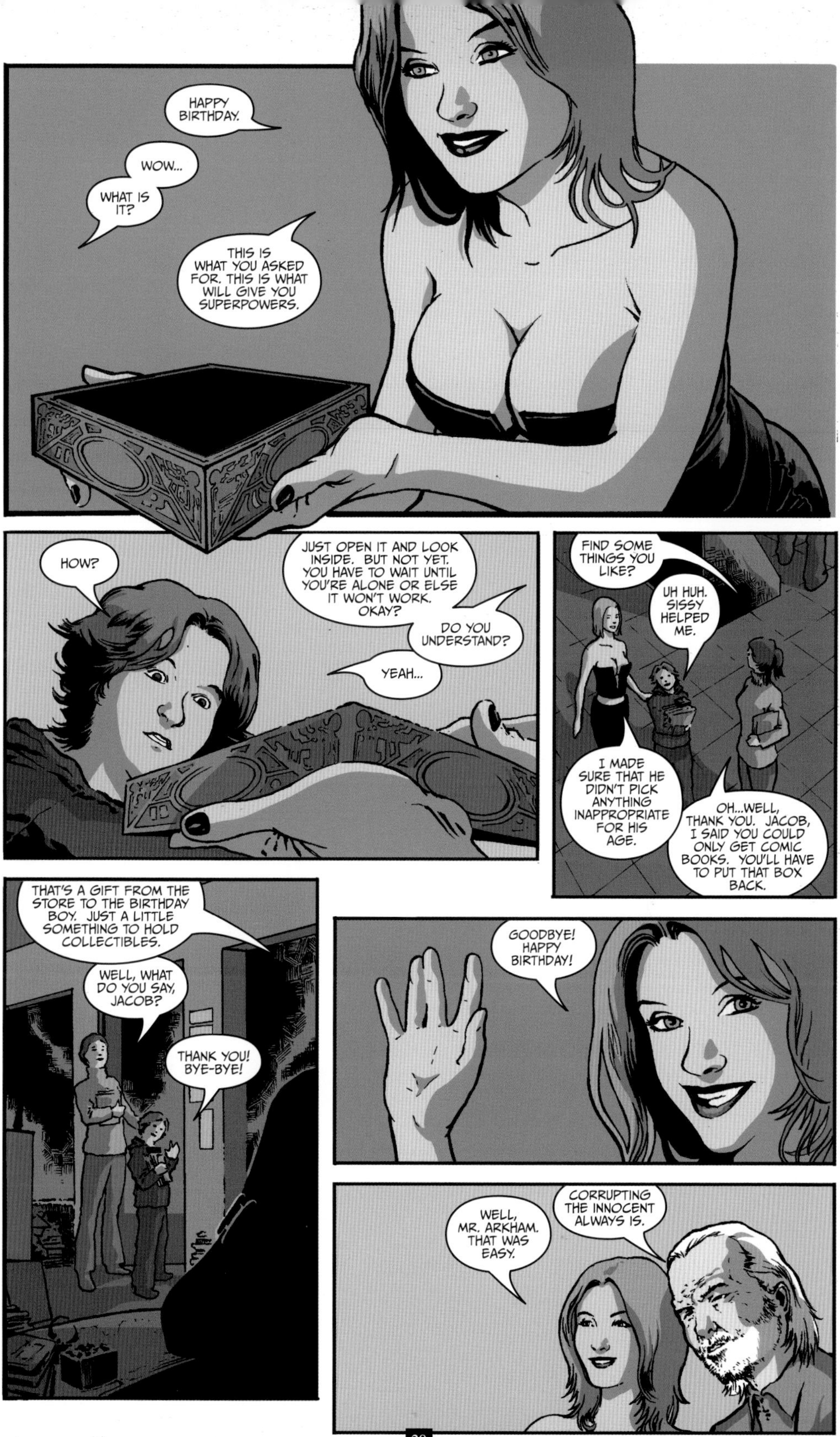
HAPPY BIRTHDAY.
WOW...
WHAT IS IT?
THIS IS WHAT YOU ASKED FOR. THIS IS WHAT WILL GIVE YOU SUPERPOWERS.
HOW?
JUST OPEN IT AND LOOK INSIDE. BUT NOT YET. YOU HAVE TO WAIT UNTIL YOU'RE ALONE OR ELSE IT WON'T WORK. OKAY?
DO YOU UNDERSTAND?
YEAH...
FIND SOME THINGS YOU LIKE?
UH HUH. SISSY HELPED ME.
I MADE SURE THAT HE DIDN'T PICK ANYTHING INAPPROPRIATE FOR HIS AGE.
OH...WELL, THANK YOU. JACOB, I SAID YOU COULD ONLY GET COMIC BOOKS. YOU'LL HAVE TO PUT THAT BOX BACK.
THAT'S A GIFT FROM THE STORE TO THE BIRTHDAY BOY. JUST A LITTLE SOMETHING TO HOLD COLLECTIBLES.
WELL, WHAT DO YOU SAY, JACOB?
THANK YOU! BYE-BYE!
GOODBYE! HAPPY BIRTHDAY!
WELL, MR. ARKHAM. THAT WAS EASY.
CORRUPTING THE INNOCENT ALWAYS IS.

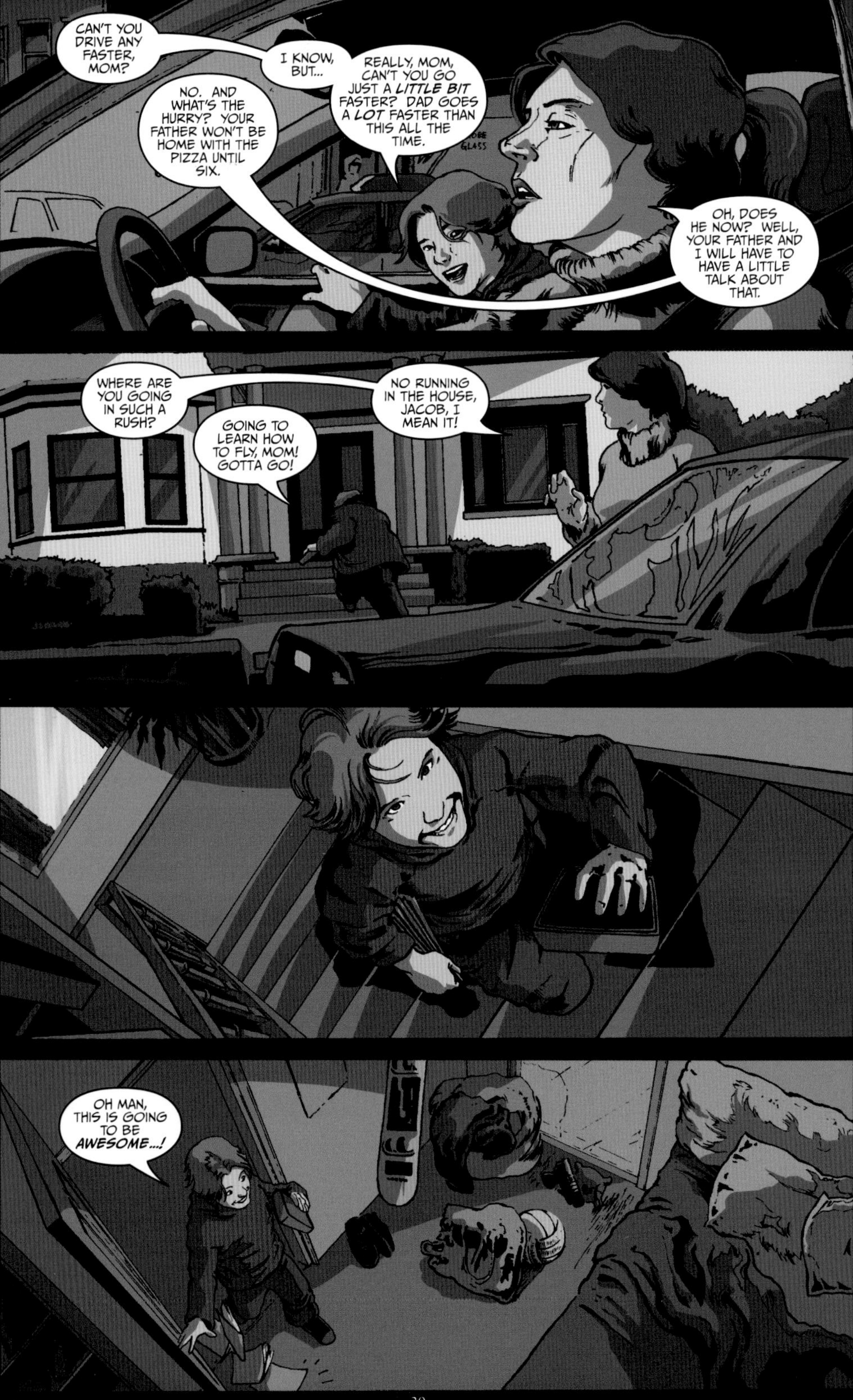
CAN'T YOU DRIVE ANY FASTER, MOM?
NO. AND WHAT'S THE HURRY? YOUR FATHER WON'T BE HOME WITH THE PIZZA UNTIL SIX.
I KNOW, BUT...
REALLY, MOM, CAN'T YOU GO JUST A *LITTLE BIT* FASTER? DAD GOES A *LOT* FASTER THAN THIS ALL THE TIME.
OH, DOES HE NOW? WELL, YOUR FATHER AND I WILL HAVE TO HAVE A LITTLE TALK ABOUT THAT.
WHERE ARE YOU GOING IN SUCH A RUSH?
GOING TO LEARN HOW TO FLY, MOM! GOTTA GO!
NO RUNNING IN THE HOUSE, JACOB, I MEAN IT!
OH MAN, THIS IS GOING TO BE ***AWESOME...!***

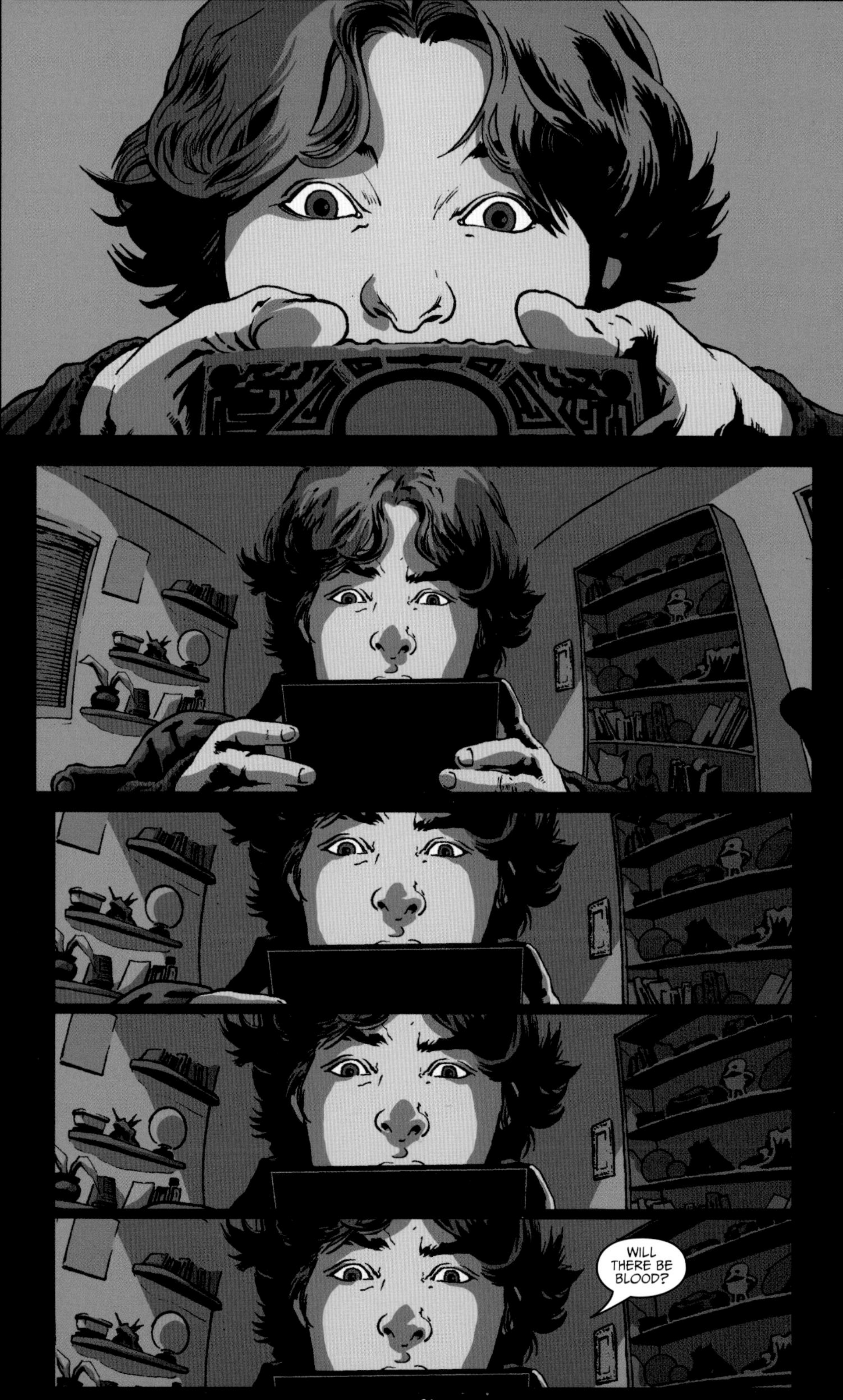
WILL THERE BE BLOOD?

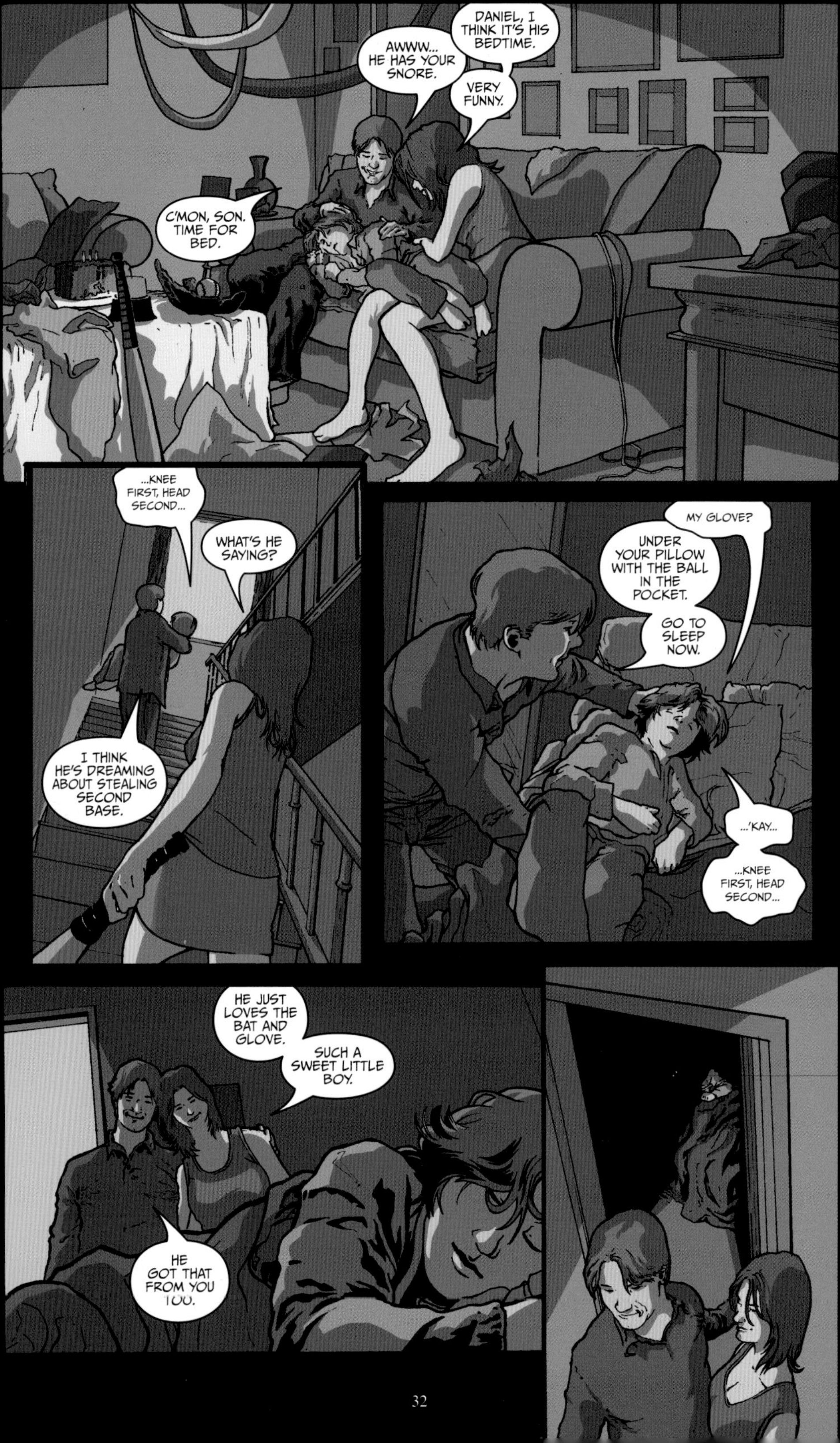
AWWW... HE HAS YOUR SNORE.
DANIEL, I THINK IT'S HIS BEDTIME.
VERY FUNNY.
C'MON, SON. TIME FOR BED.
...KNEE FIRST, HEAD SECOND...
WHAT'S HE SAYING?
I THINK HE'S DREAMING ABOUT STEALING SECOND BASE.
MY GLOVE?
UNDER YOUR PILLOW WITH THE BALL IN THE POCKET.
GO TO SLEEP NOW.
...'KAY...
...KNEE FIRST, HEAD SECOND...
HE JUST LOVES THE BAT AND GLOVE.
SUCH A SWEET LITTLE BOY.
HE GOT THAT FROM YOU TOO.

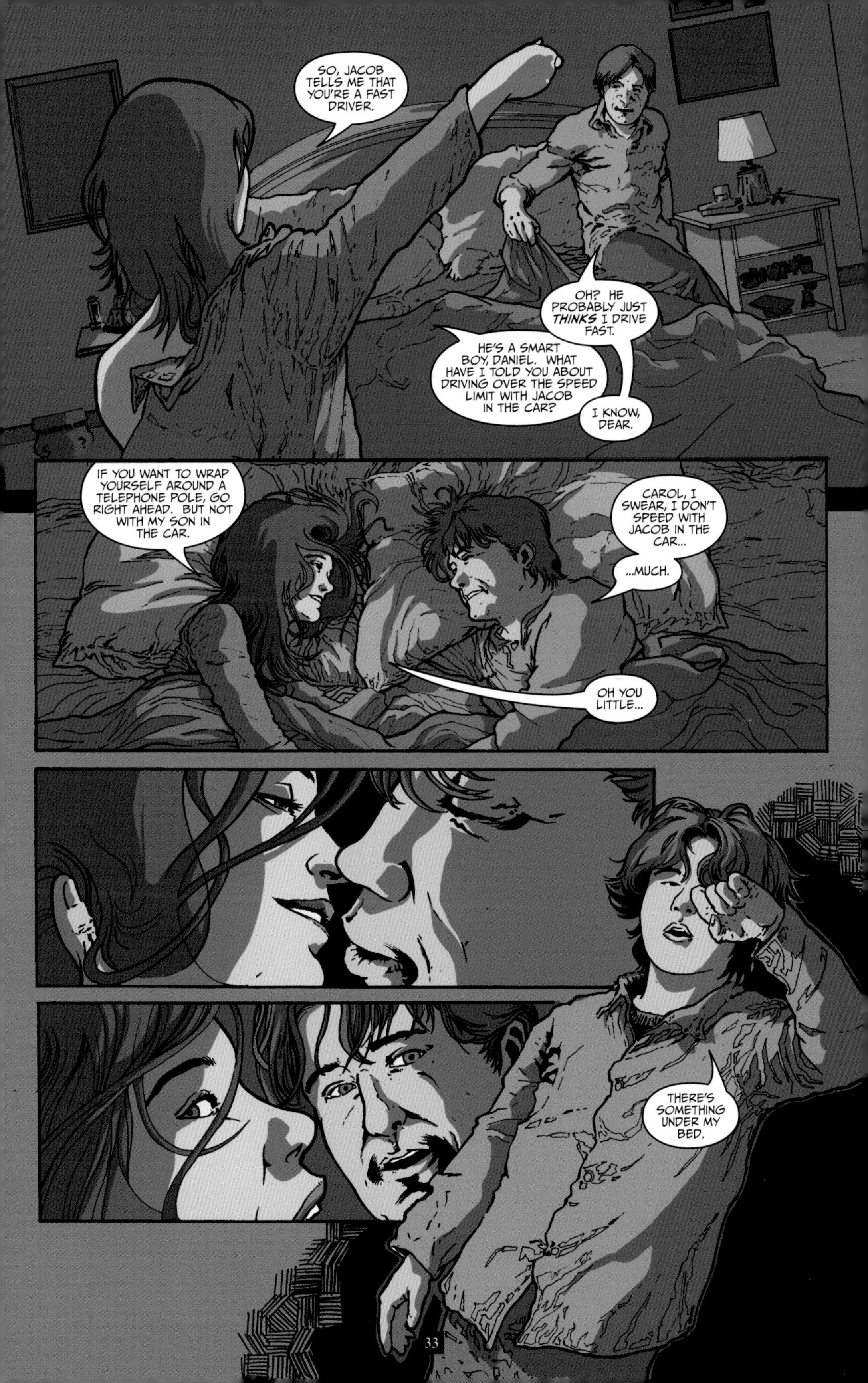
SO, JACOB TELLS ME THAT YOU'RE A FAST DRIVER.
OH? HE PROBABLY JUST *THINKS* I DRIVE FAST.
HE'S A SMART BOY, DANIEL. WHAT HAVE I TOLD YOU ABOUT DRIVING OVER THE SPEED LIMIT WITH JACOB IN THE CAR?
I KNOW, DEAR.
IF YOU WANT TO WRAP YOURSELF AROUND A TELEPHONE POLE, GO RIGHT AHEAD. BUT NOT WITH MY SON IN THE CAR.
CAROL, I SWEAR, I DON'T SPEED WITH JACOB IN THE CAR...
...MUCH.
OH YOU LITTLE...
THERE'S SOMETHING UNDER MY BED.

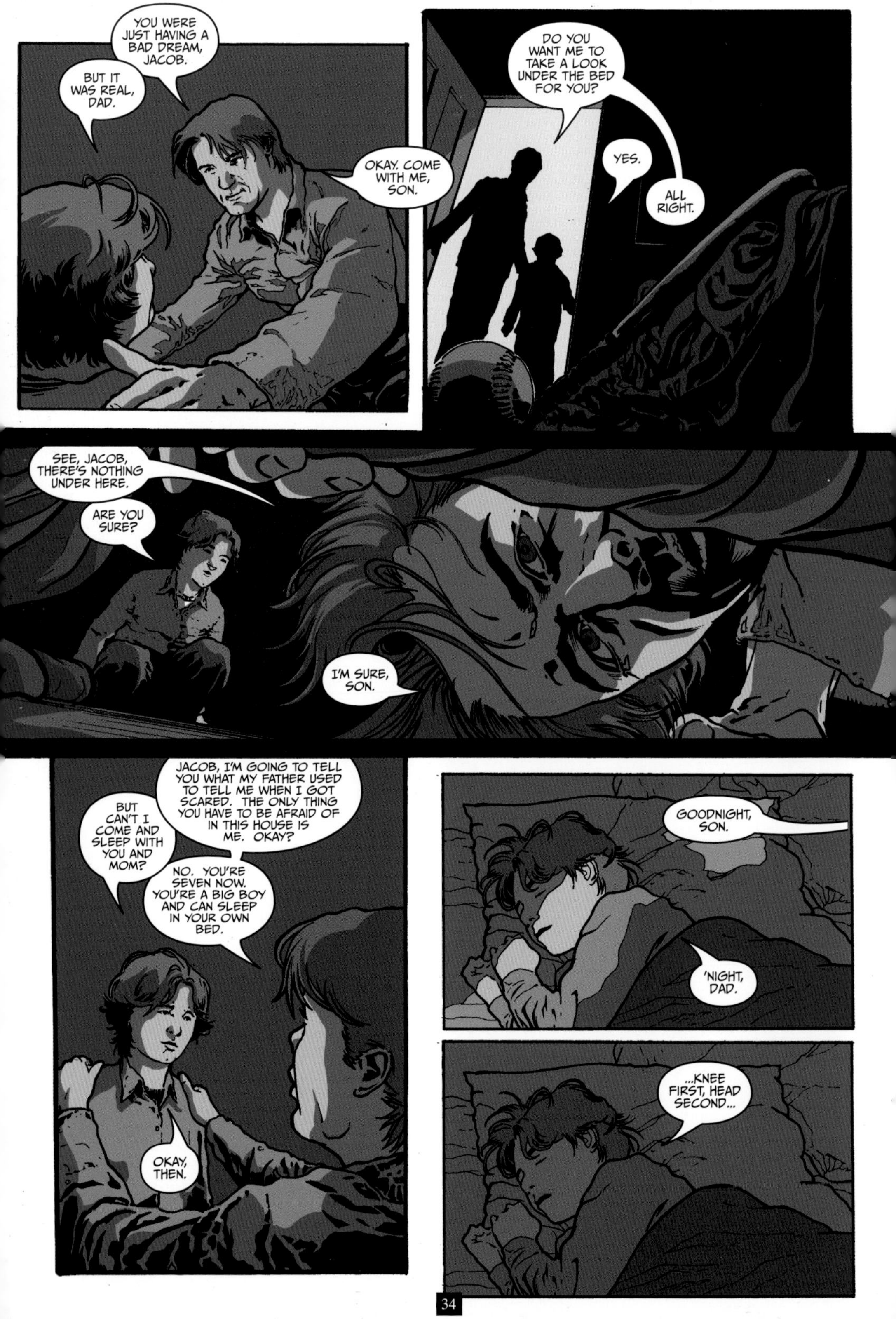
YOU WERE JUST HAVING A BAD DREAM, JACOB.
BUT IT WAS REAL, DAD.
OKAY. COME WITH ME, SON.
DO YOU WANT ME TO TAKE A LOOK UNDER THE BED FOR YOU?
YES.
ALL RIGHT.
SEE, JACOB, THERE'S NOTHING UNDER HERE.
ARE YOU SURE?
I'M SURE, SON.
JACOB, I'M GOING TO TELL YOU WHAT MY FATHER USED TO TELL ME WHEN I GOT SCARED. THE ONLY THING YOU HAVE TO BE AFRAID OF IN THIS HOUSE IS ME. OKAY?
BUT CAN'T I COME AND SLEEP WITH YOU AND MOM?
NO. YOU'RE SEVEN NOW. YOU'RE A BIG BOY AND CAN SLEEP IN YOUR OWN BED.
OKAY, THEN.
GOODNIGHT, SON.
'NIGHT, DAD.
...KNEE FIRST, HEAD SECOND...

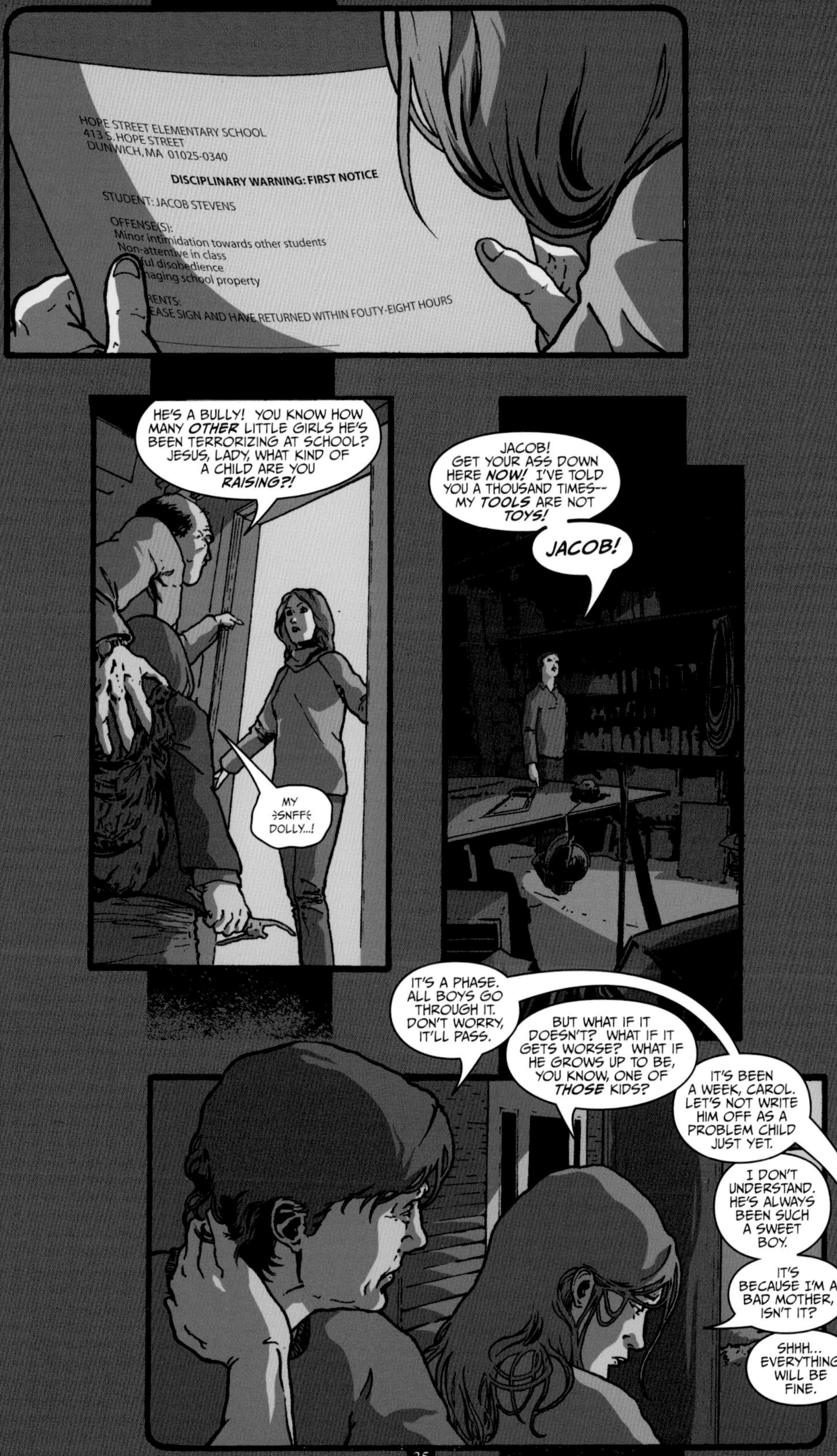
HOPE STREET ELEMENTARY SCHOOL
413 S. HOPE STREET
DUNWICH, MA 01025-0340
DISCIPLINARY WARNING: FIRST NOTICE
STUDENT: JACOB STEVENS
OFFENSE(S):
Minor intimidation towards other students
Non-attentive in class
ful disobedience
aging school property
RENTS:
EASE SIGN AND HAVE RETURNED WITHIN FOUTY-EIGHT HOURS
HE'S A BULLY! YOU KNOW HOW MANY OTHER LITTLE GIRLS HE'S BEEN TERRORIZING AT SCHOOL? JESUS, LADY, WHAT KIND OF A CHILD ARE YOU RAISING?!
MY ∋SNFF∈ DOLLY...!
JACOB! GET YOUR ASS DOWN HERE NOW! I'VE TOLD YOU A THOUSAND TIMES-- MY TOOLS ARE NOT TOYS!
JACOB!
IT'S A PHASE. ALL BOYS GO THROUGH IT. DON'T WORRY, IT'LL PASS.
BUT WHAT IF IT DOESN'T? WHAT IF IT GETS WORSE? WHAT IF HE GROWS UP TO BE, YOU KNOW, ONE OF THOSE KIDS?
IT'S BEEN A WEEK, CAROL. LET'S NOT WRITE HIM OFF AS A PROBLEM CHILD JUST YET.
I DON'T UNDERSTAND. HE'S ALWAYS BEEN SUCH A SWEET BOY.
IT'S BECAUSE I'M A BAD MOTHER, ISN'T IT?
SHHH... EVERYTHING WILL BE FINE.

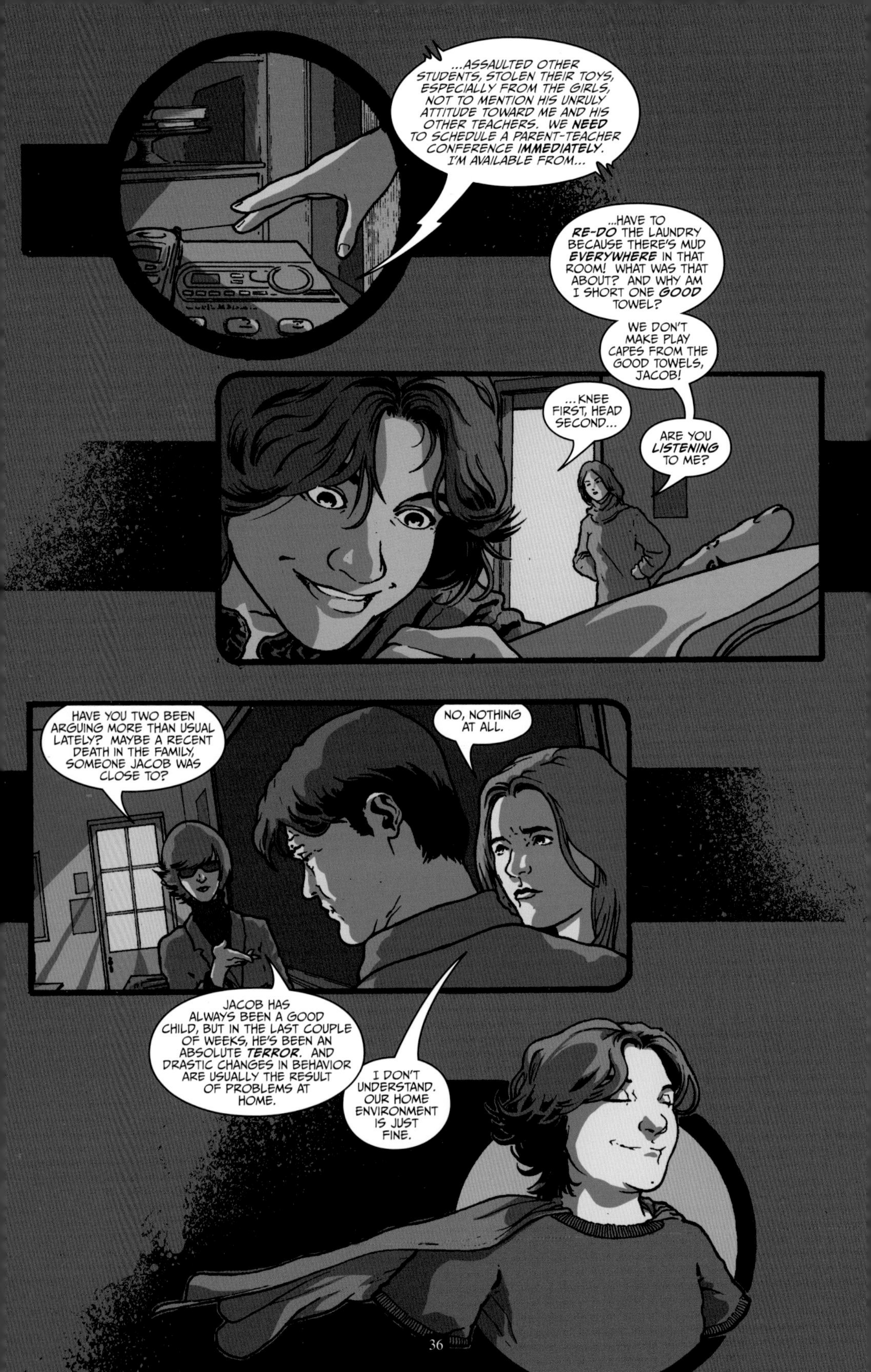
...ASSAULTED OTHER STUDENTS, STOLEN THEIR TOYS, ESPECIALLY FROM THE GIRLS, NOT TO MENTION HIS UNRULY ATTITUDE TOWARD ME AND HIS OTHER TEACHERS. WE NEED TO SCHEDULE A PARENT-TEACHER CONFERENCE IMMEDIATELY. I'M AVAILABLE FROM...
...HAVE TO RE-DO THE LAUNDRY BECAUSE THERE'S MUD EVERYWHERE IN THAT ROOM! WHAT WAS THAT ABOUT? AND WHY AM I SHORT ONE GOOD TOWEL?
WE DON'T MAKE PLAY CAPES FROM THE GOOD TOWELS, JACOB!
...KNEE FIRST, HEAD SECOND...
ARE YOU LISTENING TO ME?
HAVE YOU TWO BEEN ARGUING MORE THAN USUAL LATELY? MAYBE A RECENT DEATH IN THE FAMILY, SOMEONE JACOB WAS CLOSE TO?
NO, NOTHING AT ALL.
JACOB HAS ALWAYS BEEN A GOOD CHILD, BUT IN THE LAST COUPLE OF WEEKS, HE'S BEEN AN ABSOLUTE TERROR. AND DRASTIC CHANGES IN BEHAVIOR ARE USUALLY THE RESULT OF PROBLEMS AT HOME.
I DON'T UNDERSTAND. OUR HOME ENVIRONMENT IS JUST FINE.

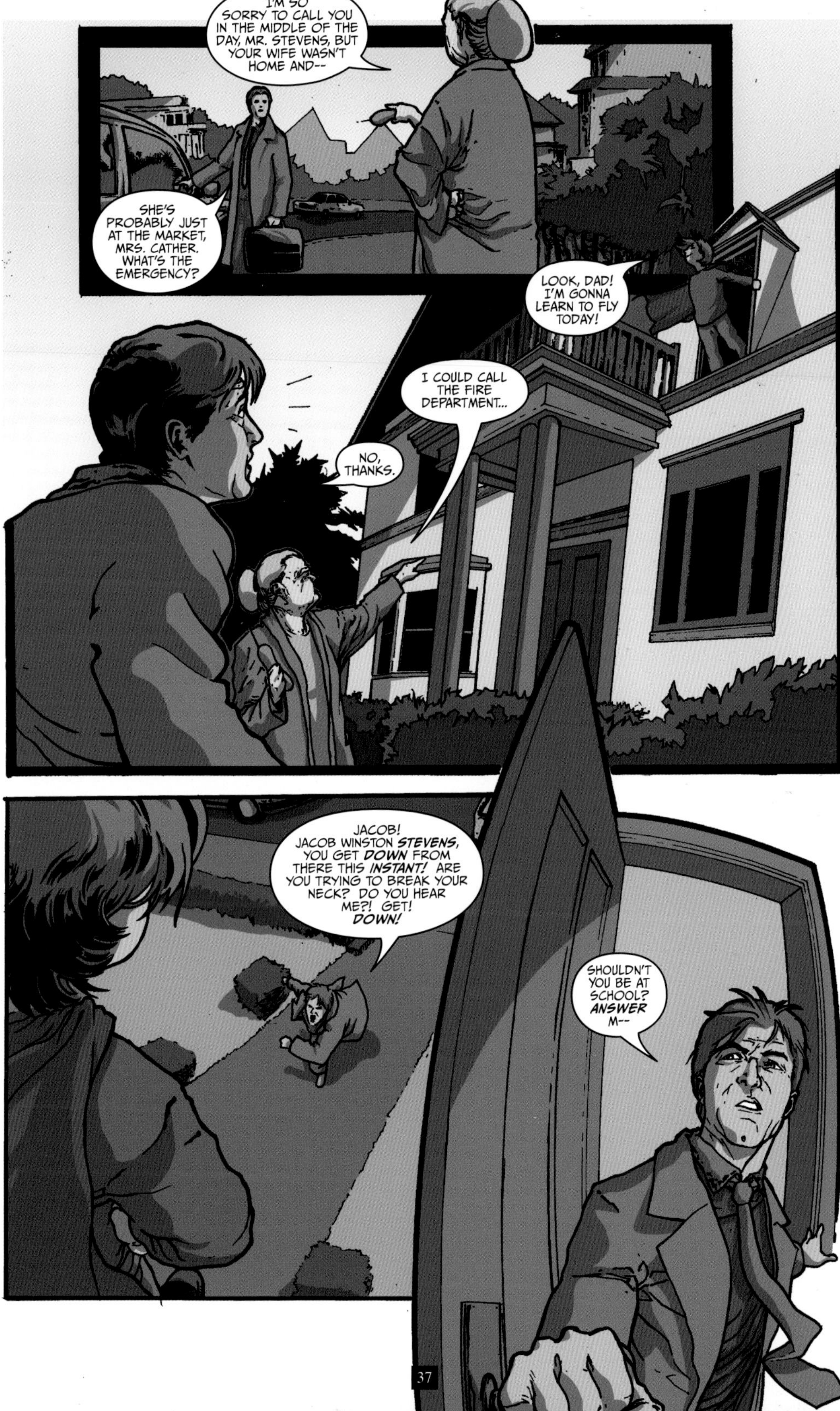
I'M SO SORRY TO CALL YOU IN THE MIDDLE OF THE DAY, MR. STEVENS, BUT YOUR WIFE WASN'T HOME AND--
SHE'S PROBABLY JUST AT THE MARKET, MRS. CATHER. WHAT'S THE EMERGENCY?
LOOK, DAD! I'M GONNA LEARN TO FLY TODAY!
I COULD CALL THE FIRE DEPARTMENT...
NO, THANKS.
JACOB! JACOB WINSTON STEVENS, YOU GET DOWN FROM THERE THIS INSTANT! ARE YOU TRYING TO BREAK YOUR NECK? DO YOU HEAR ME?! GET! DOWN!
SHOULDN'T YOU BE AT SCHOOL? ANSWER M--

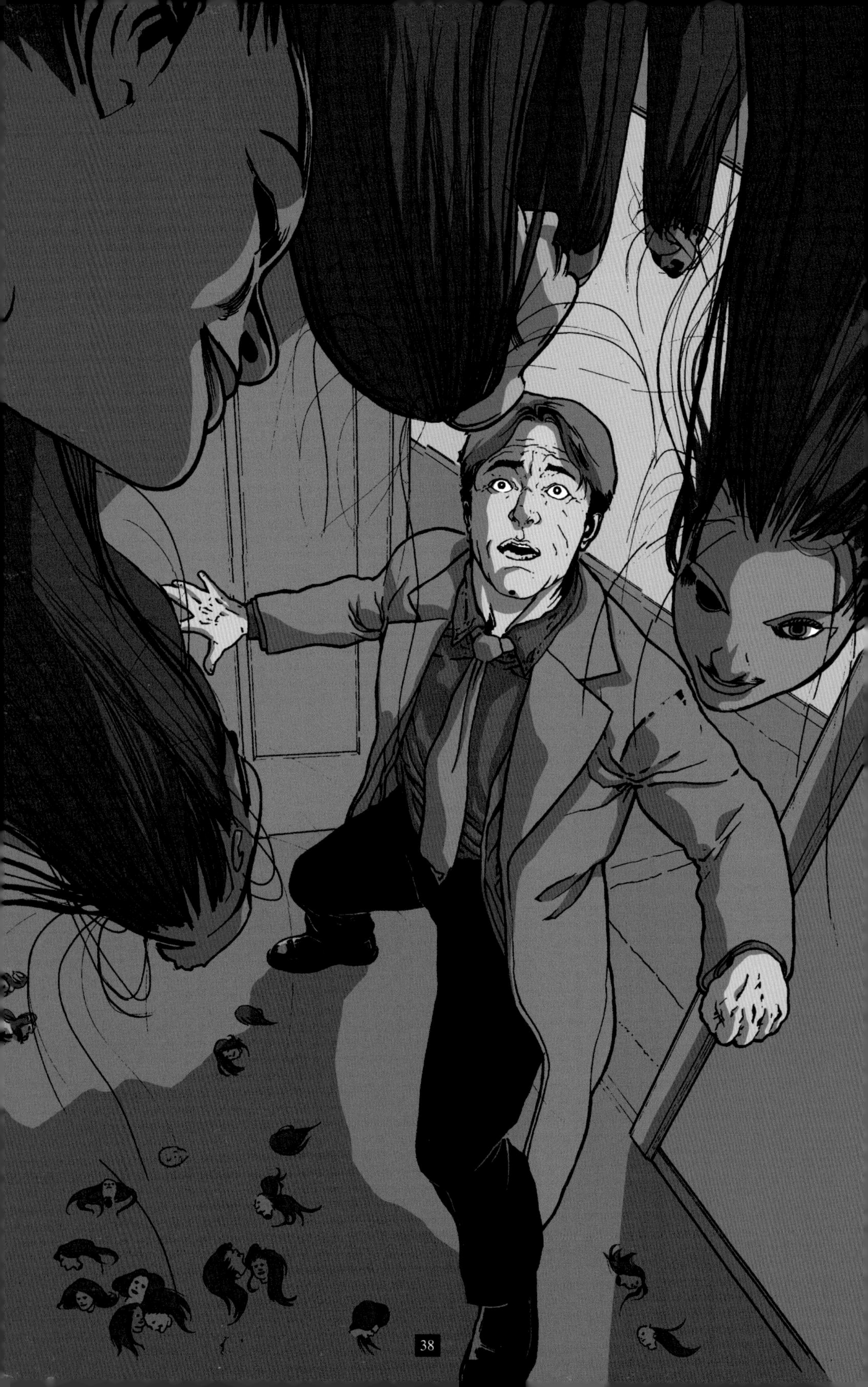

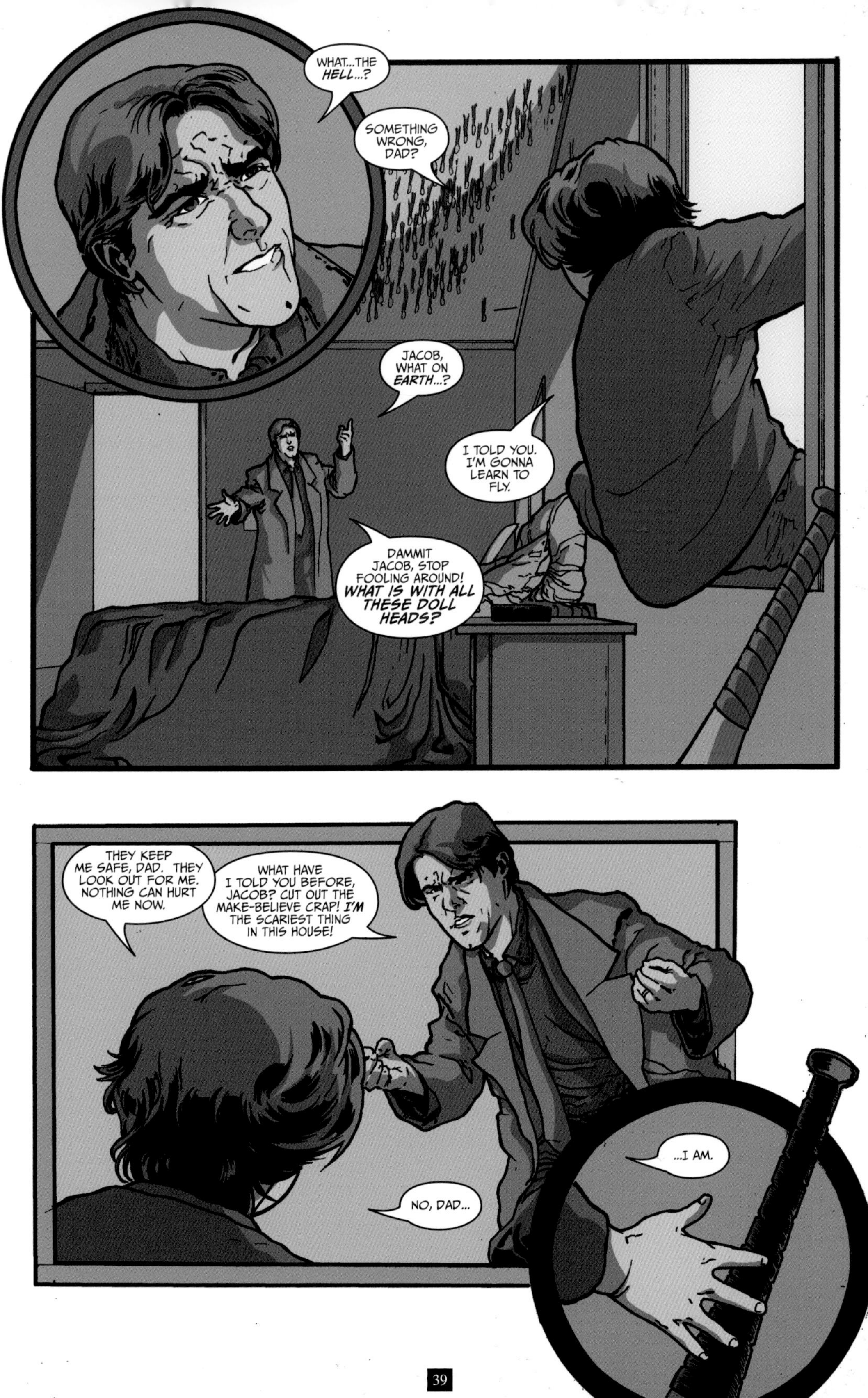
WHAT...THE HELL...?
SOMETHING WRONG, DAD?
JACOB, WHAT ON EARTH...?
I TOLD YOU. I'M GONNA LEARN TO FLY.
DAMMIT JACOB, STOP FOOLING AROUND! WHAT IS WITH ALL THESE DOLL HEADS?
THEY KEEP ME SAFE, DAD. THEY LOOK OUT FOR ME. NOTHING CAN HURT ME NOW.
WHAT HAVE I TOLD YOU BEFORE, JACOB? CUT OUT THE MAKE-BELIEVE CRAP! I'M THE SCARIEST THING IN THIS HOUSE!
NO, DAD...
...I AM.

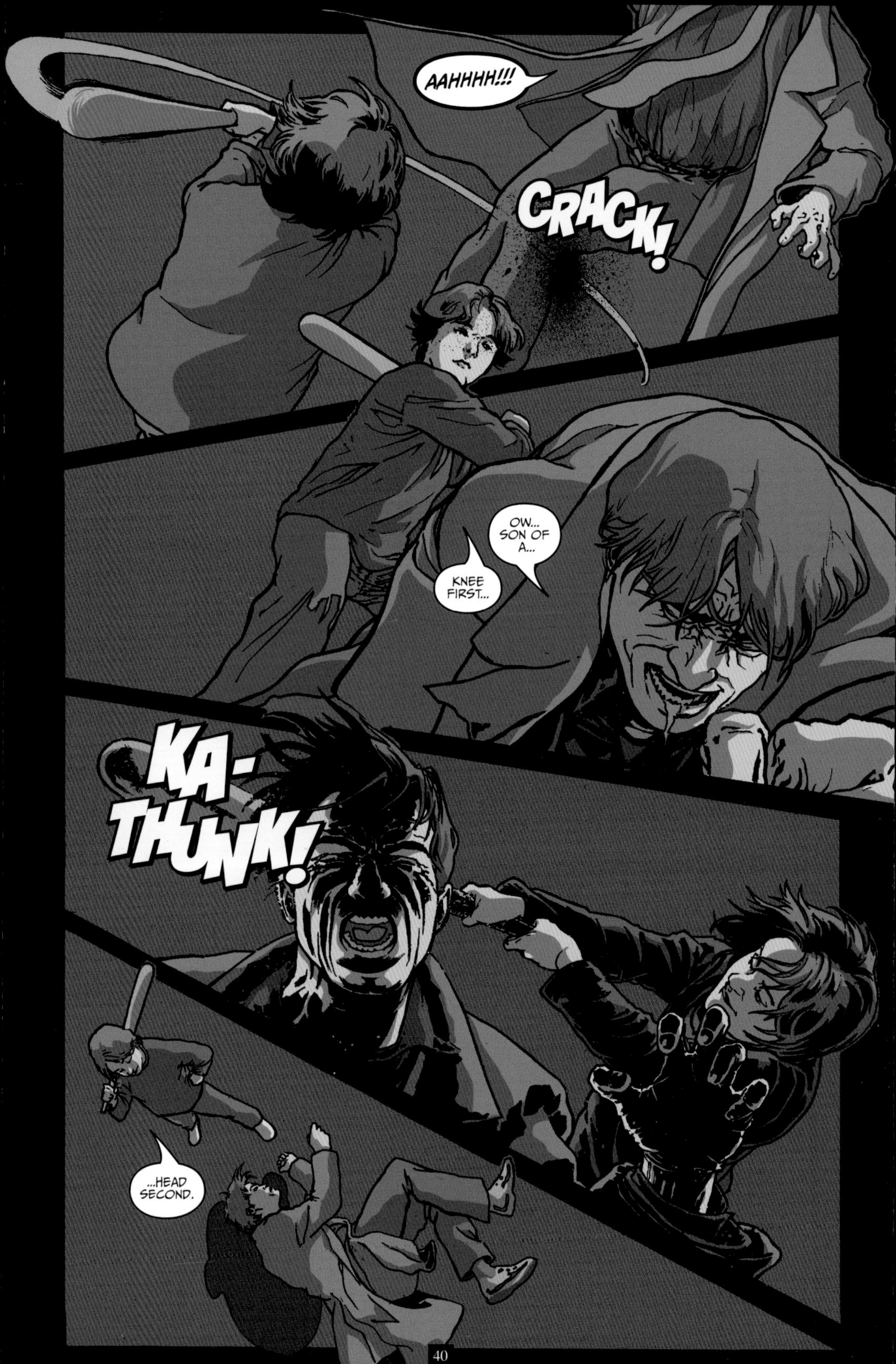
AAHHHH!!!
CRACK!
OW... SON OF A...
KNEE FIRST...
KA-THUNK!
...HEAD SECOND.

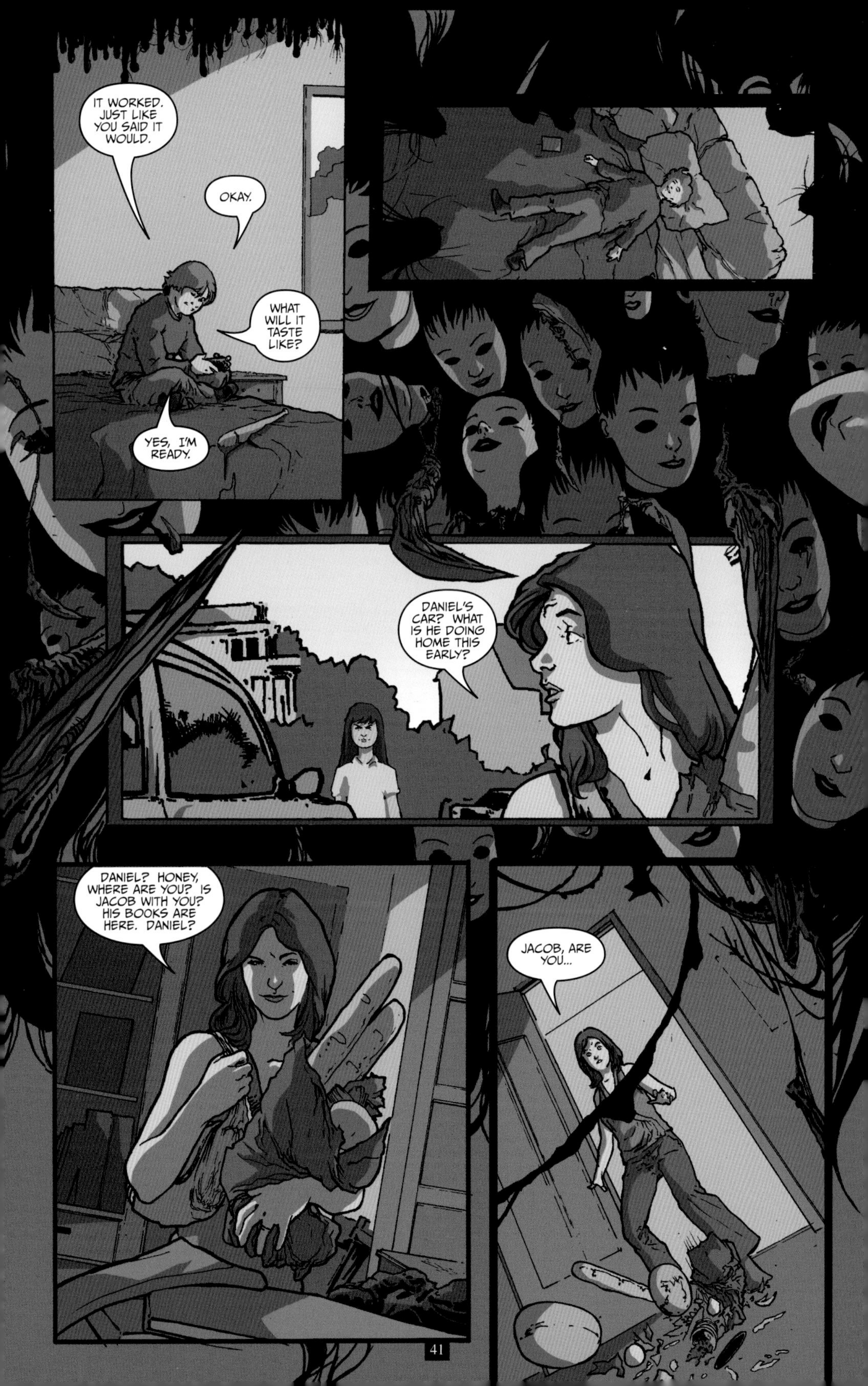
IT WORKED. JUST LIKE YOU SAID IT WOULD.
OKAY.
WHAT WILL IT TASTE LIKE?
YES, I'M READY.
DANIEL'S CAR? WHAT IS HE DOING HOME THIS EARLY?
DANIEL? HONEY, WHERE ARE YOU? IS JACOB WITH YOU? HIS BOOKS ARE HERE. DANIEL?
JACOB, ARE YOU...

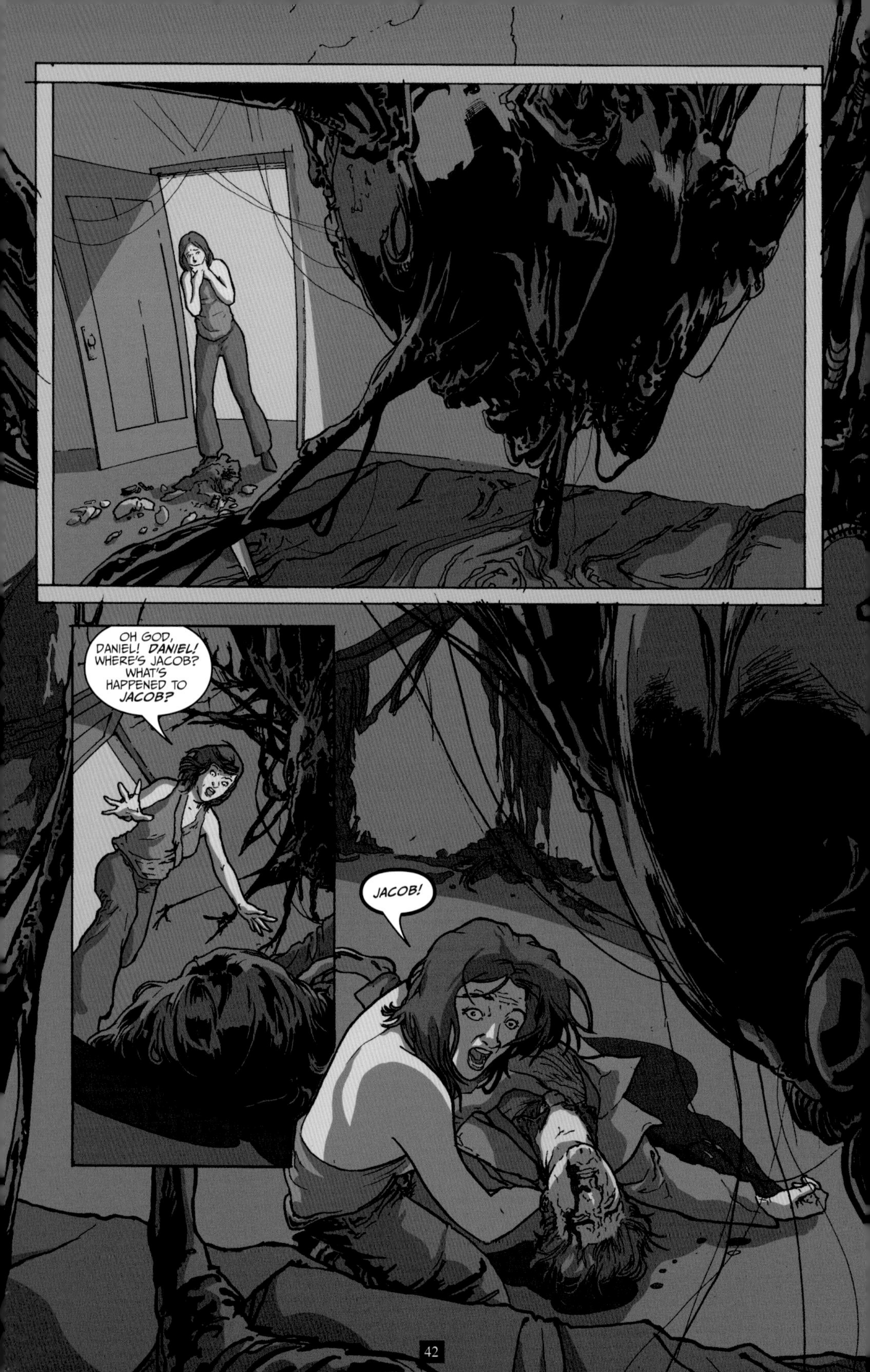
OH GOD, DANIEL! DANIEL! WHERE'S JACOB? WHAT'S HAPPENED TO JACOB?
JACOB!

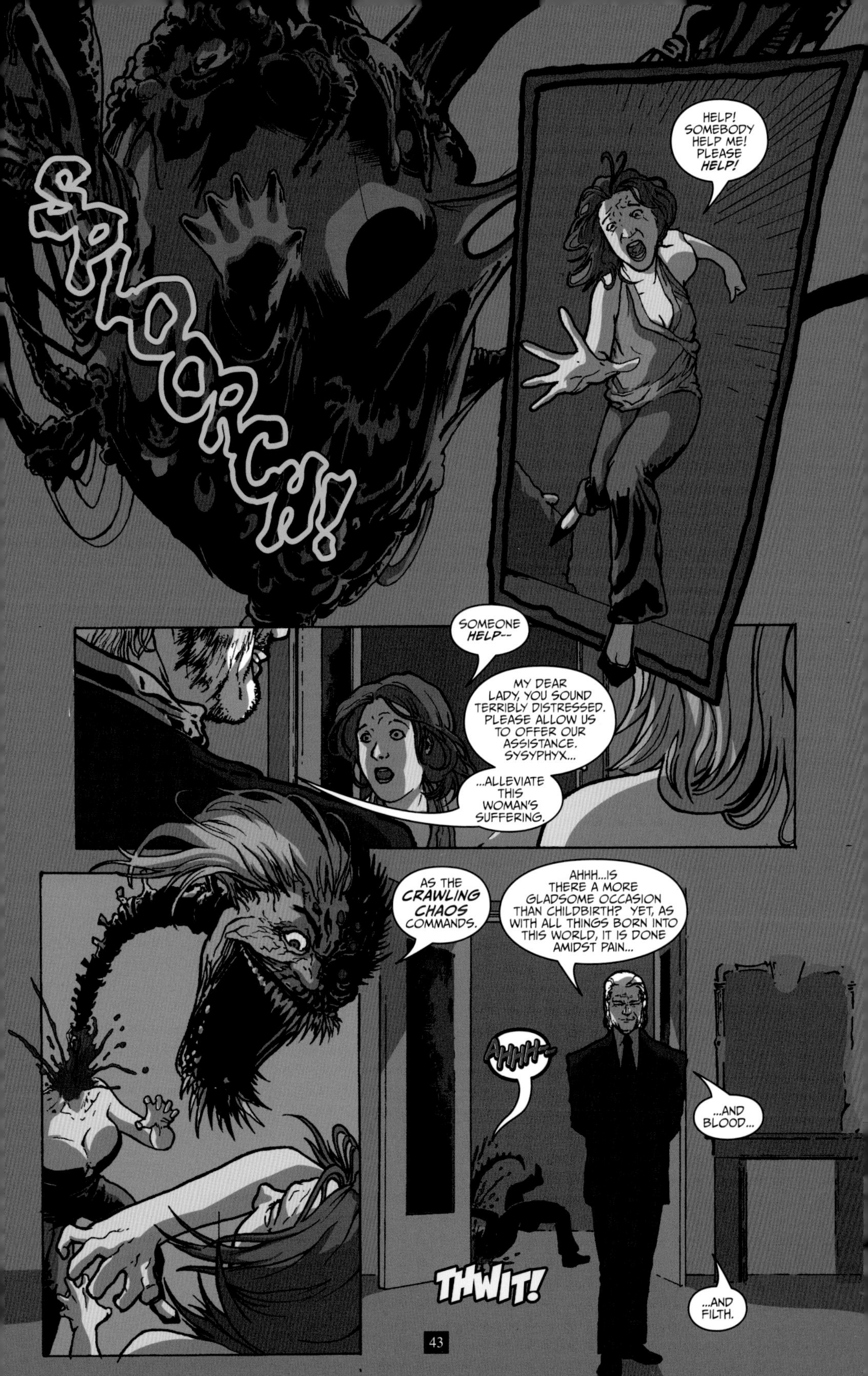
SPLORCH!
HELP! SOMEBODY HELP ME! PLEASE HELP!
SOMEONE HELP--
MY DEAR LADY, YOU SOUND TERRIBLY DISTRESSED. PLEASE ALLOW US TO OFFER OUR ASSISTANCE. SYSYPHYX...
...ALLEVIATE THIS WOMAN'S SUFFERING.
AS THE CRAWLING CHAOS COMMANDS.
AHHH...IS THERE A MORE GLADSOME OCCASION THAN CHILDBIRTH? YET, AS WITH ALL THINGS BORN INTO THIS WORLD, IT IS DONE AMIDST PAIN...
AHHH--
...AND BLOOD...
THWIT!
...AND FILTH.

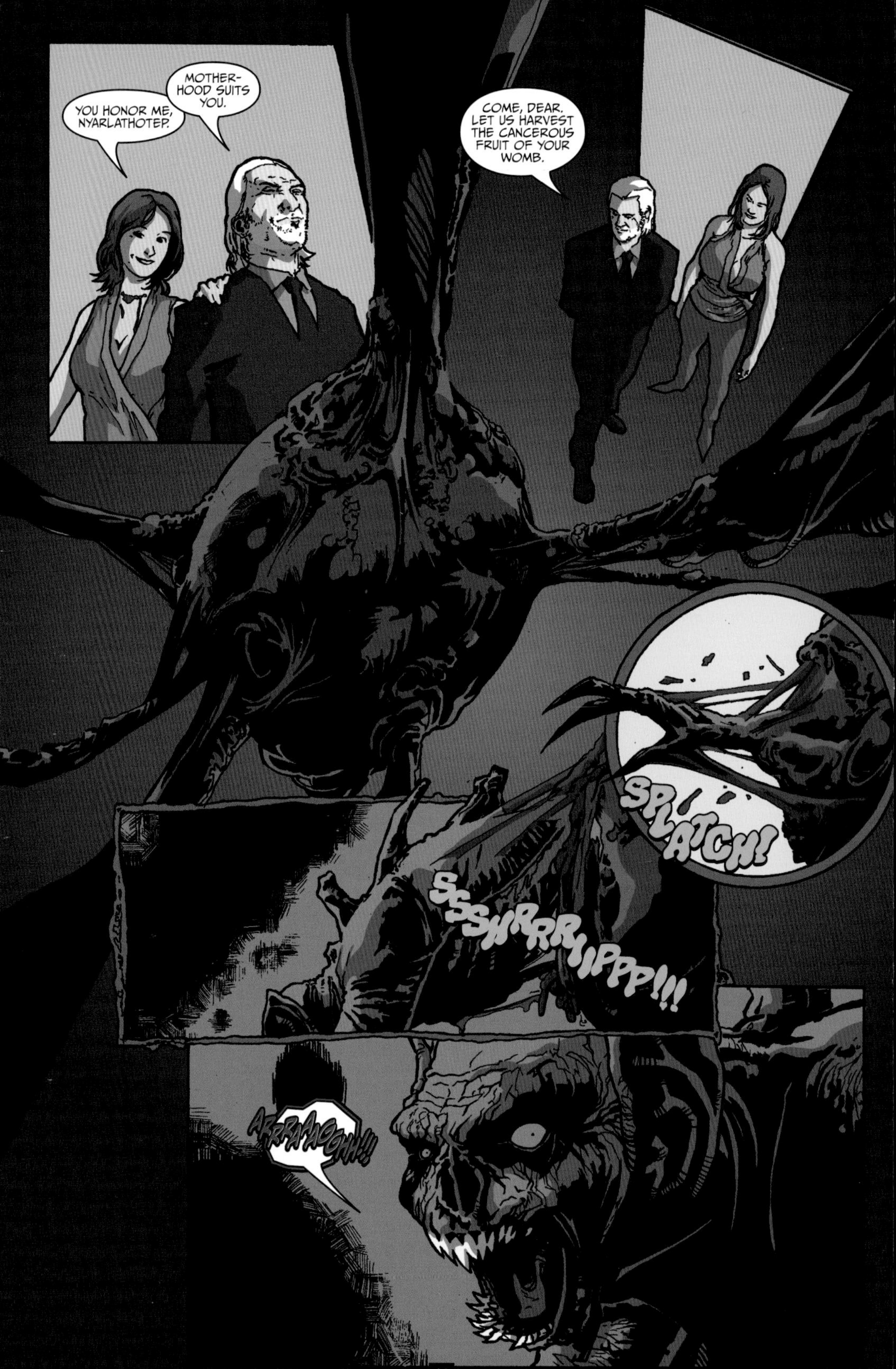
YOU HONOR ME, NYARLATHOTEP.
MOTHER-HOOD SUITS YOU.
COME, DEAR. LET US HARVEST THE CANCEROUS FRUIT OF YOUR WOMB.
SPLATCH!
SSSHRRRRIPPPP!!!
AHRRAAAOOHH!!!

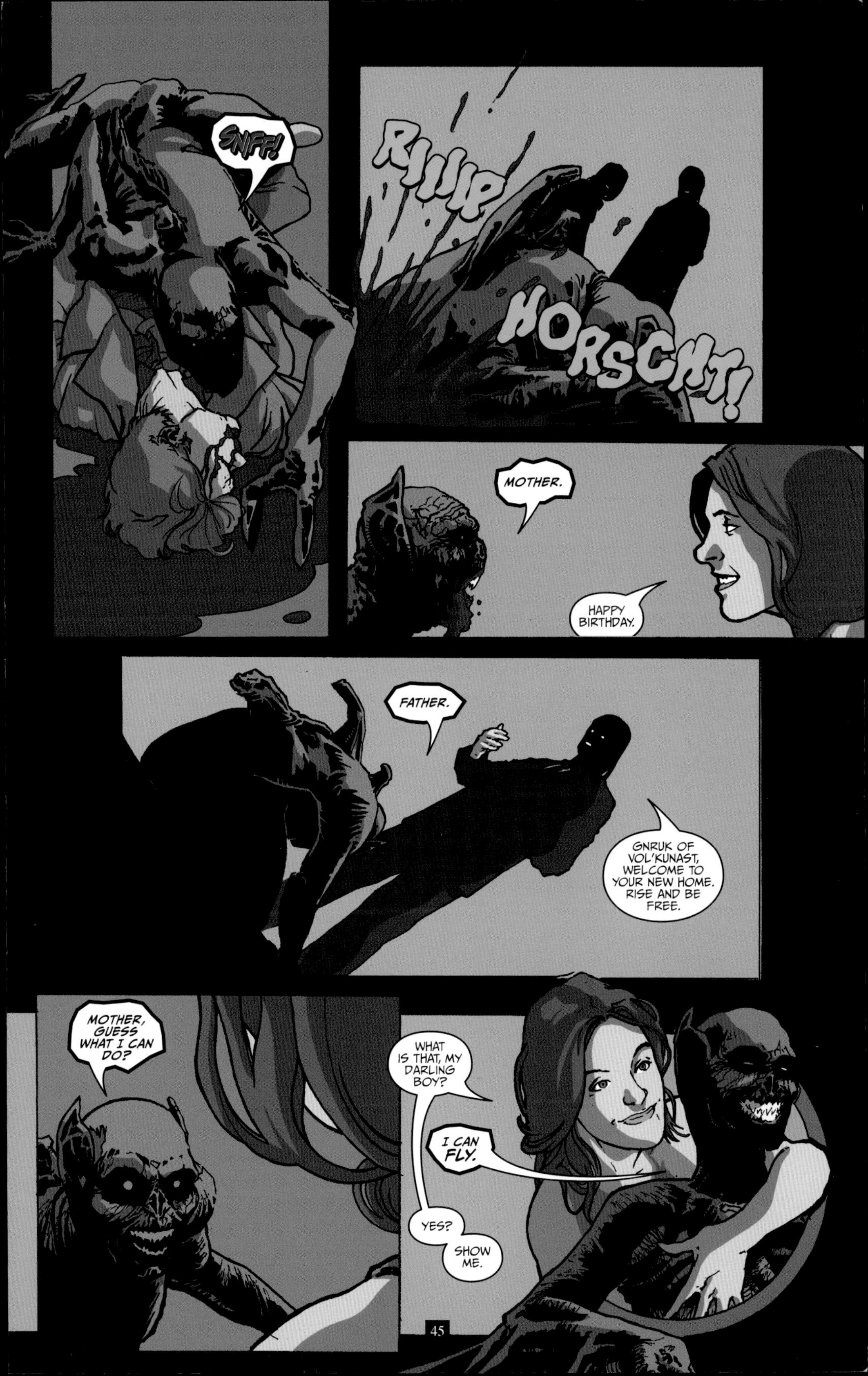
SNIFF!
RIIIIR
HORSCHT!
MOTHER.
HAPPY BIRTHDAY.
FATHER.
GNRUK OF VOL'KUNAST, WELCOME TO YOUR NEW HOME. RISE AND BE FREE.
MOTHER, GUESS WHAT I CAN DO?
WHAT IS THAT, MY DARLING BOY?
I CAN FLY.
YES?
SHOW ME.

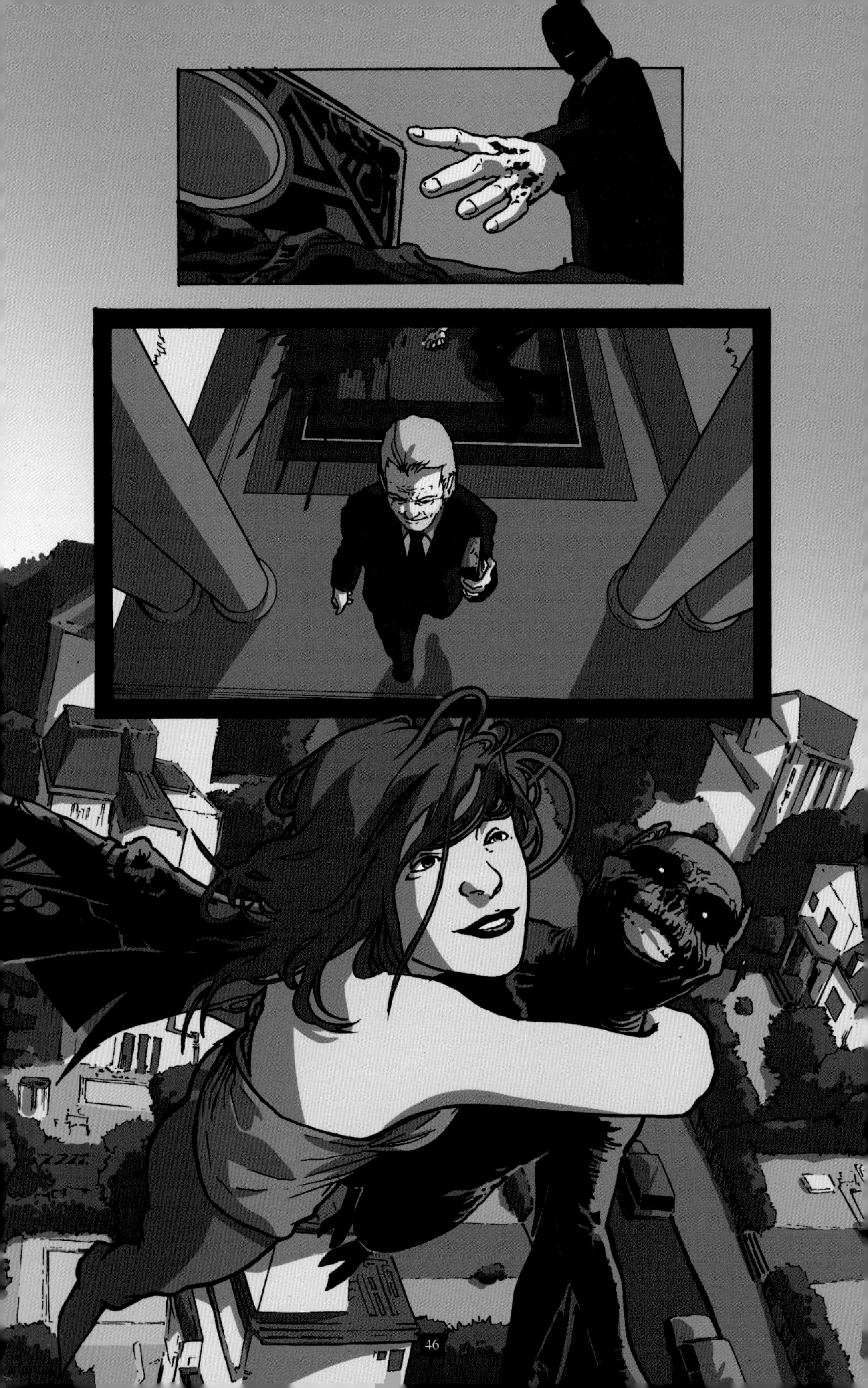

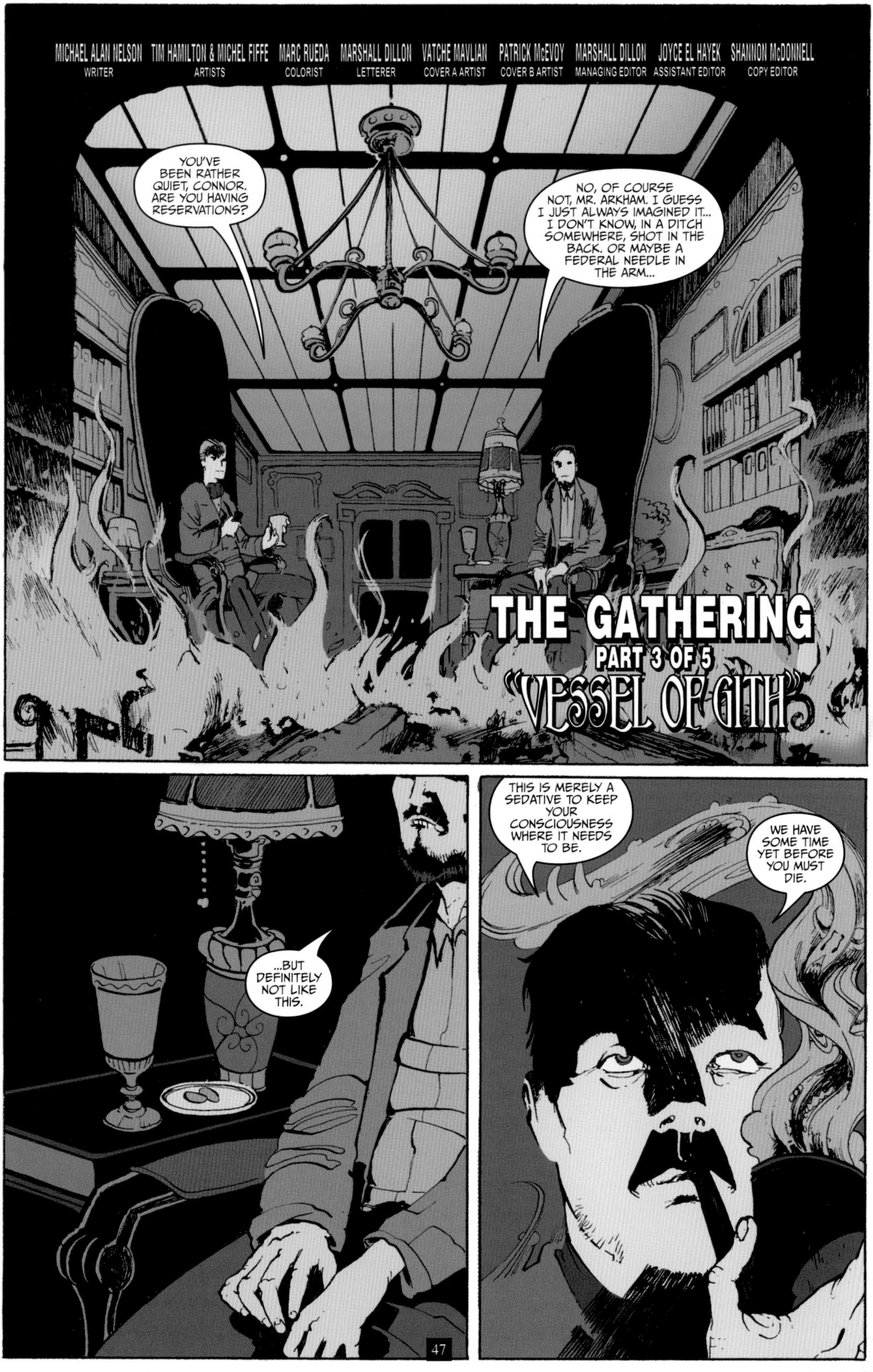
MICHAEL ALAN NELSON WRITER
TIM HAMILTON & MICHEL FIFFE ARTISTS
MARC RUEDA COLORIST
MARSHALL DILLON LETTERER
VATCHE MAVLIAN COVER A ARTIST
PATRICK McEVOY COVER B ARTIST
MARSHALL DILLON MANAGING EDITOR
JOYCE EL HAYEK ASSISTANT EDITOR
SHANNON McDONNELL COPY EDITOR
YOU'VE BEEN RATHER QUIET, CONNOR. ARE YOU HAVING RESERVATIONS?
NO, OF COURSE NOT, MR. ARKHAM. I GUESS I JUST ALWAYS IMAGINED IT... I DON'T KNOW, IN A DITCH SOMEWHERE, SHOT IN THE BACK. OR MAYBE A FEDERAL NEEDLE IN THE ARM...
THE GATHERING
PART 3 OF 5
"VESSEL OF GITH"
...BUT DEFINITELY NOT LIKE THIS.
THIS IS MERELY A SEDATIVE TO KEEP YOUR CONSCIOUSNESS WHERE IT NEEDS TO BE.
WE HAVE SOME TIME YET BEFORE YOU MUST DIE.

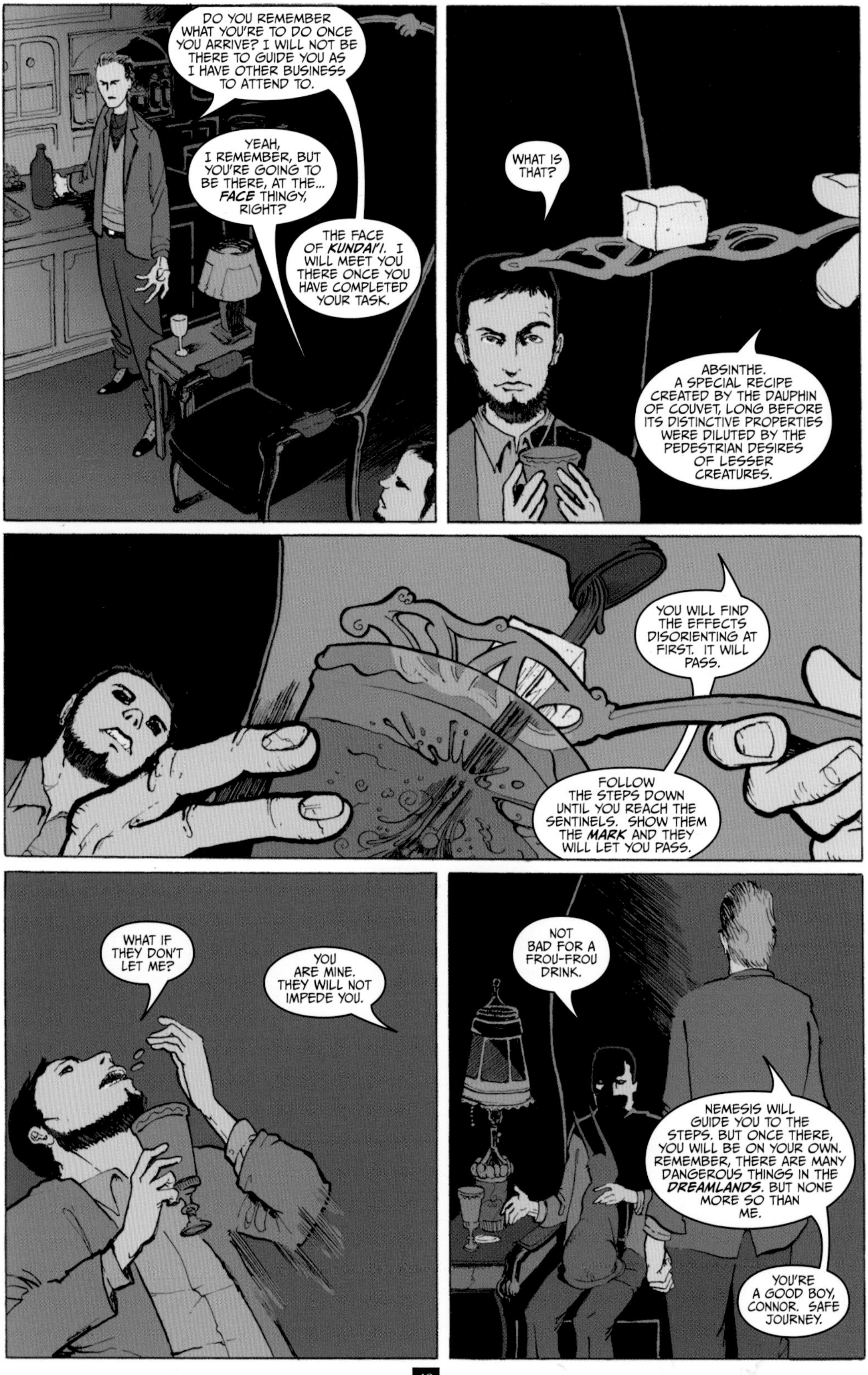
DO YOU REMEMBER WHAT YOU'RE TO DO ONCE YOU ARRIVE? I WILL NOT BE THERE TO GUIDE YOU AS I HAVE OTHER BUSINESS TO ATTEND TO.
YEAH, I REMEMBER, BUT YOU'RE GOING TO BE THERE, AT THE... FACE THINGY, RIGHT?
THE FACE OF KUNDAI'I. I WILL MEET YOU THERE ONCE YOU HAVE COMPLETED YOUR TASK.
WHAT IS THAT?
ABSINTHE. A SPECIAL RECIPE CREATED BY THE DAUPHIN OF COUVET, LONG BEFORE ITS DISTINCTIVE PROPERTIES WERE DILUTED BY THE PEDESTRIAN DESIRES OF LESSER CREATURES.
YOU WILL FIND THE EFFECTS DISORIENTING AT FIRST. IT WILL PASS.
FOLLOW THE STEPS DOWN UNTIL YOU REACH THE SENTINELS. SHOW THEM THE MARK AND THEY WILL LET YOU PASS.
WHAT IF THEY DON'T LET ME?
YOU ARE MINE. THEY WILL NOT IMPEDE YOU.
NOT BAD FOR A FROU-FROU DRINK.
NEMESIS WILL GUIDE YOU TO THE STEPS. BUT ONCE THERE, YOU WILL BE ON YOUR OWN. REMEMBER, THERE ARE MANY DANGEROUS THINGS IN THE DREAMLANDS. BUT NONE MORE SO THAN ME.
YOU'RE A GOOD BOY, CONNOR. SAFE JOURNEY.

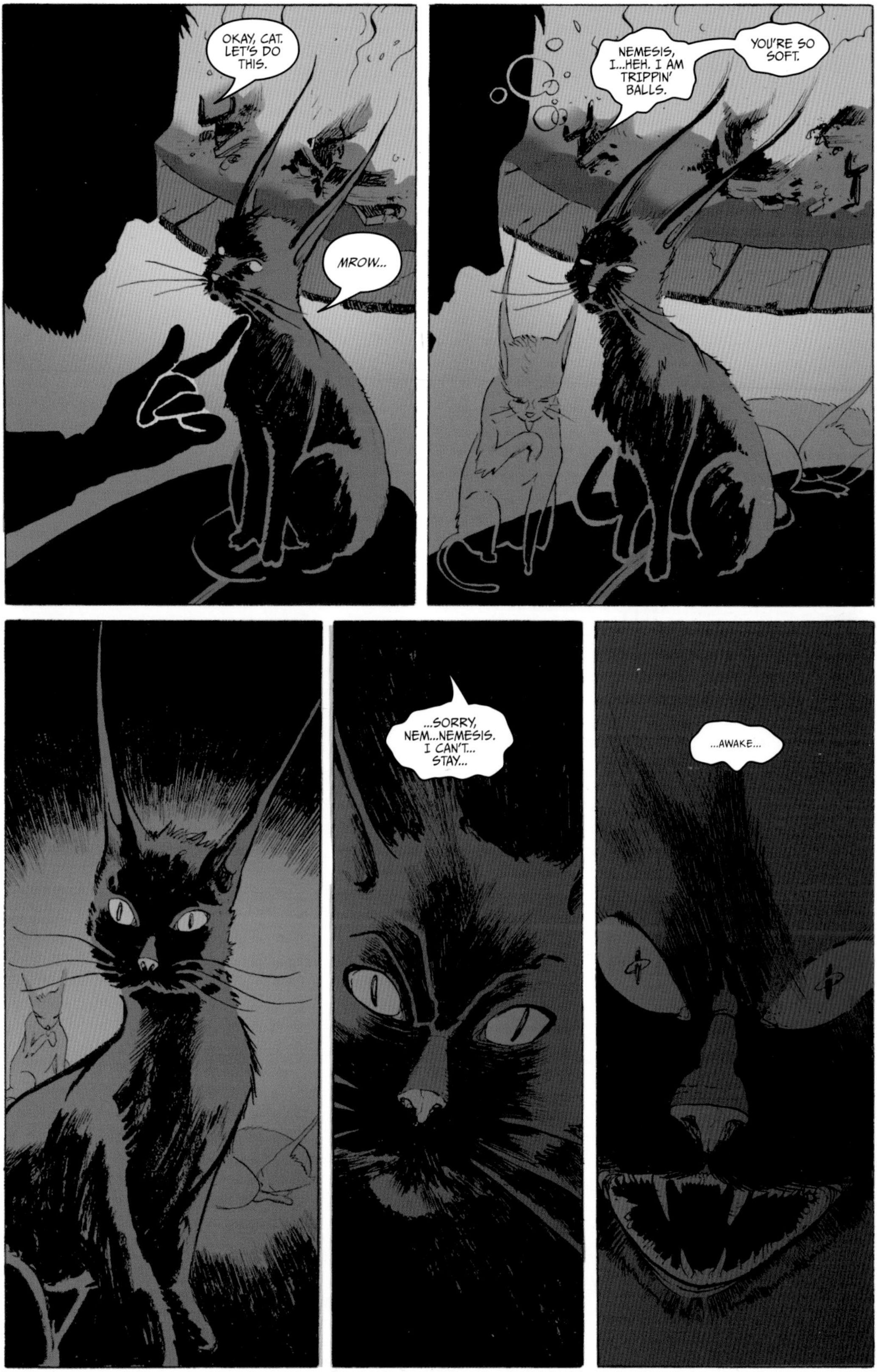
OKAY, CAT. LET'S DO THIS.
MROW...
NEMESIS, I...HEH. I AM TRIPPIN' BALLS.
YOU'RE SO SOFT.
...SORRY, NEM...NEMESIS. I CAN'T... STAY...
...AWAKE...

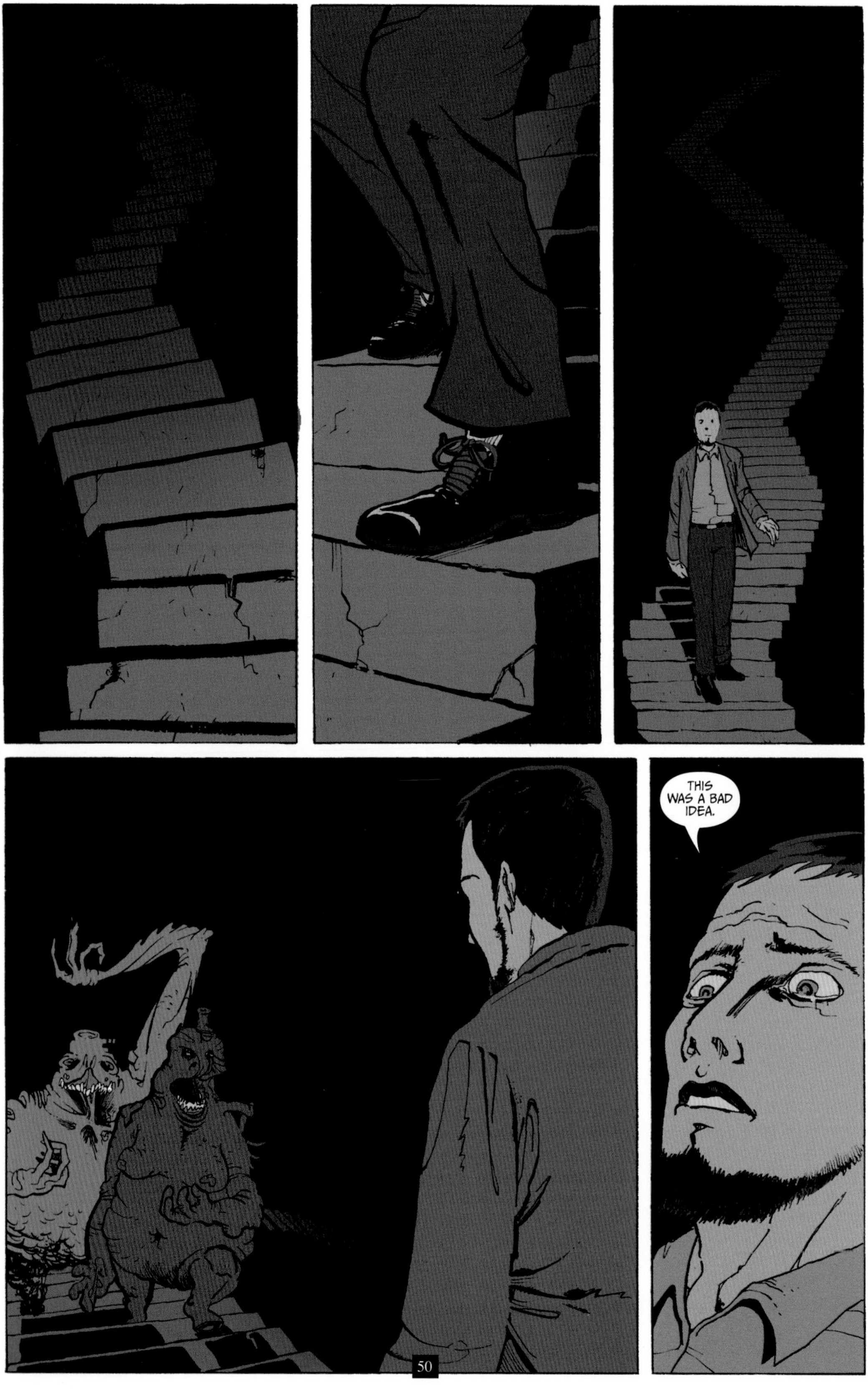
THIS WAS A BAD IDEA.

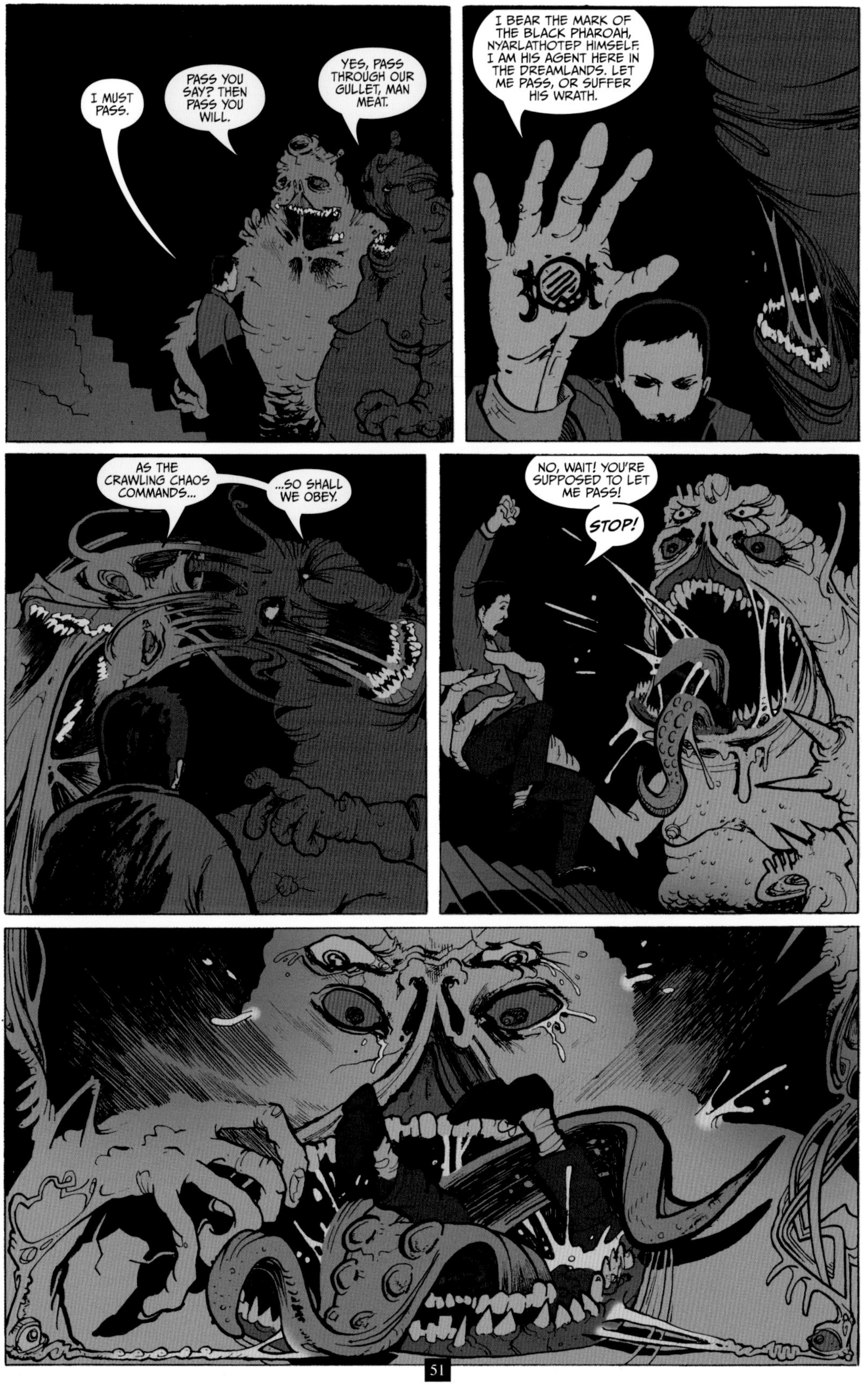
I MUST PASS.
PASS YOU SAY? THEN PASS YOU WILL.
YES, PASS THROUGH OUR GULLET, MAN MEAT.
I BEAR THE MARK OF THE BLACK PHAROAH, NYARLATHOTEP HIMSELF. I AM HIS AGENT HERE IN THE DREAMLANDS. LET ME PASS, OR SUFFER HIS WRATH.
AS THE CRAWLING CHAOS COMMANDS...
...SO SHALL WE OBEY.
NO, WAIT! YOU'RE SUPPOSED TO LET ME PASS!
STOP!

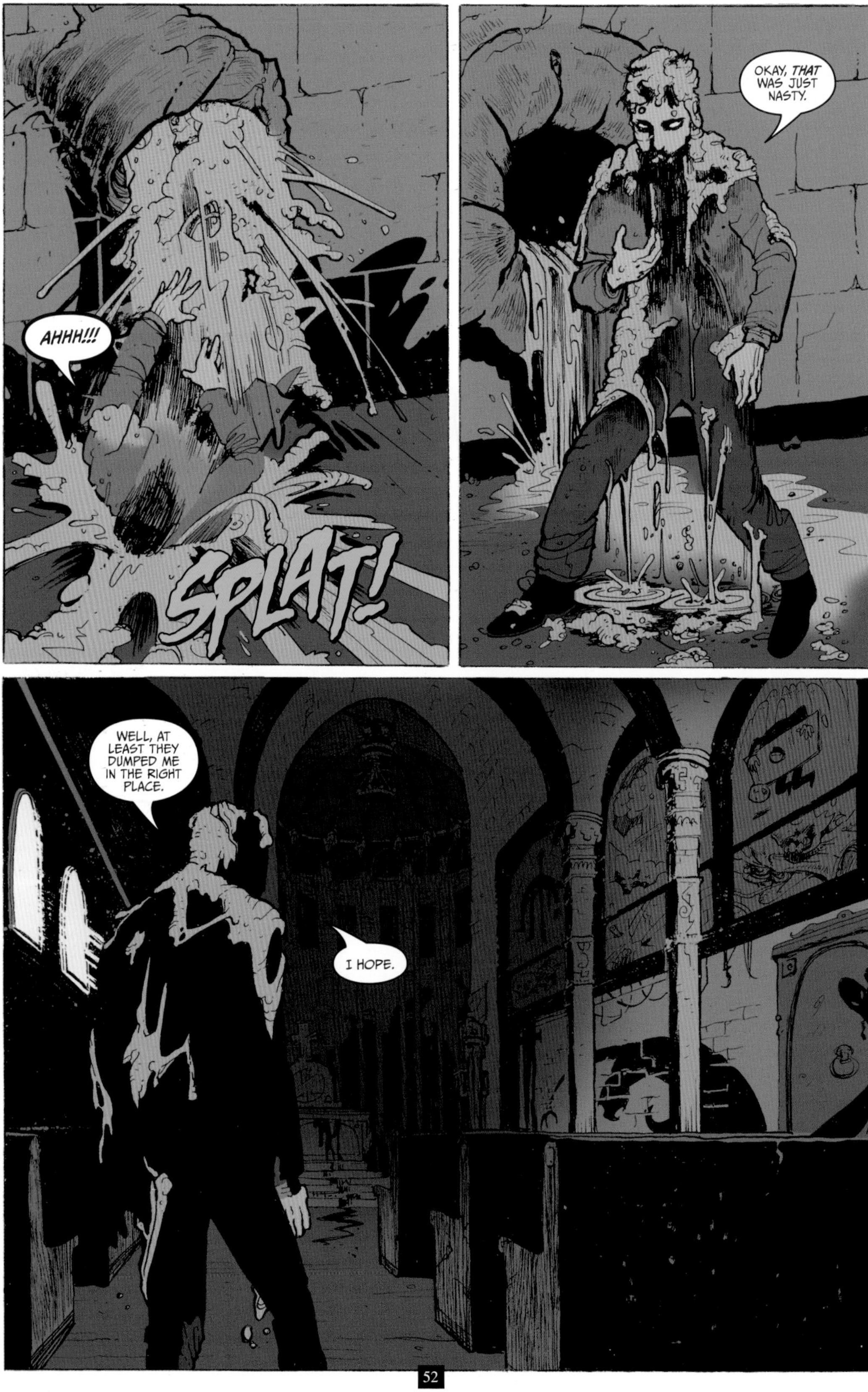
AHHH!!!
SPLAT!
OKAY, THAT WAS JUST NASTY.
WELL, AT LEAST THEY DUMPED ME IN THE RIGHT PLACE.
I HOPE.

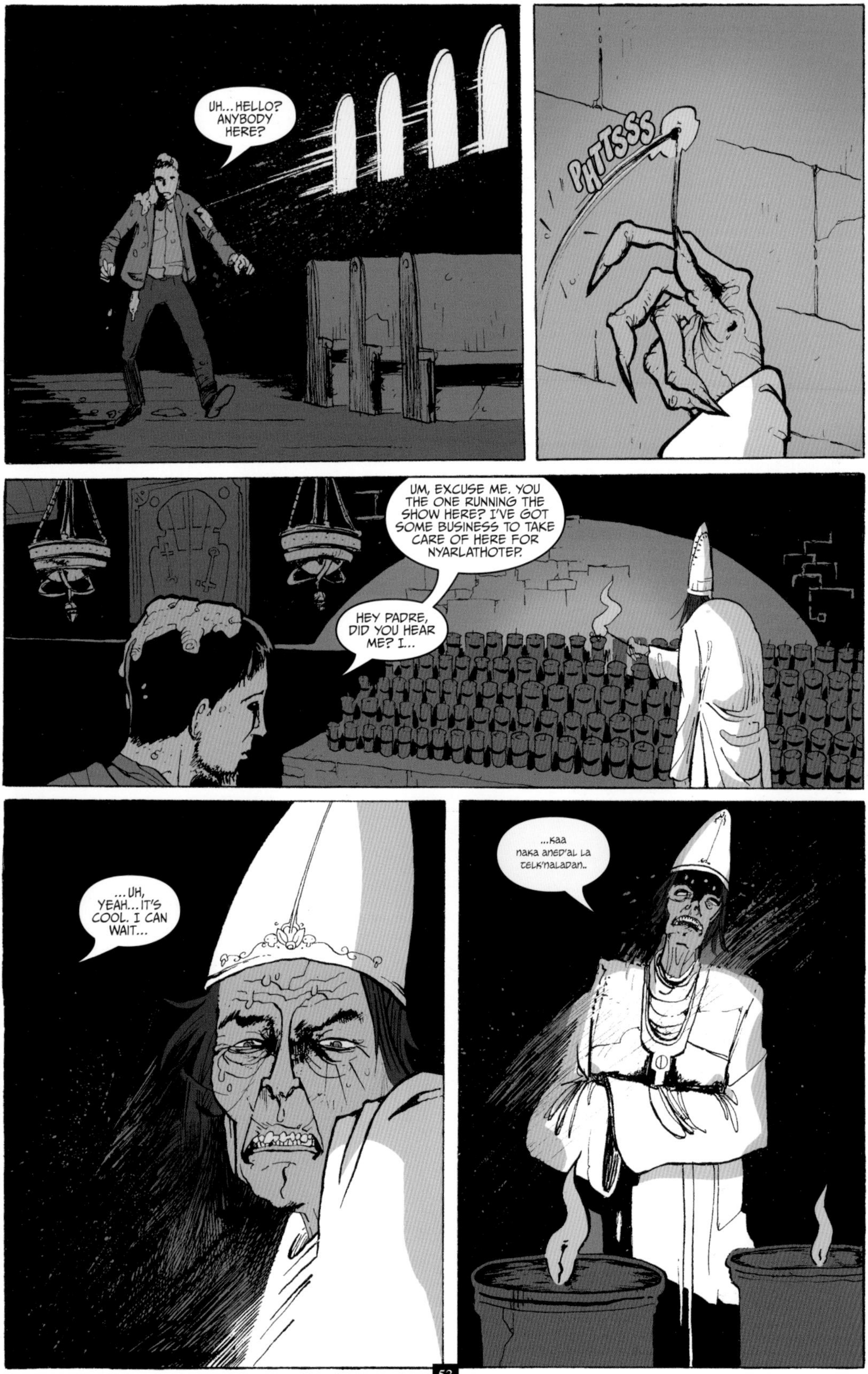
UH...HELLO? ANYBODY HERE?
PHTTSSS
UM, EXCUSE ME. YOU THE ONE RUNNING THE SHOW HERE? I'VE GOT SOME BUSINESS TO TAKE CARE OF HERE FOR NYARLATHOTEP.
HEY PADRE, DID YOU HEAR ME? I...
...UH, YEAH...IT'S COOL. I CAN WAIT...
...kaa naka aned'al la telk'naladan..

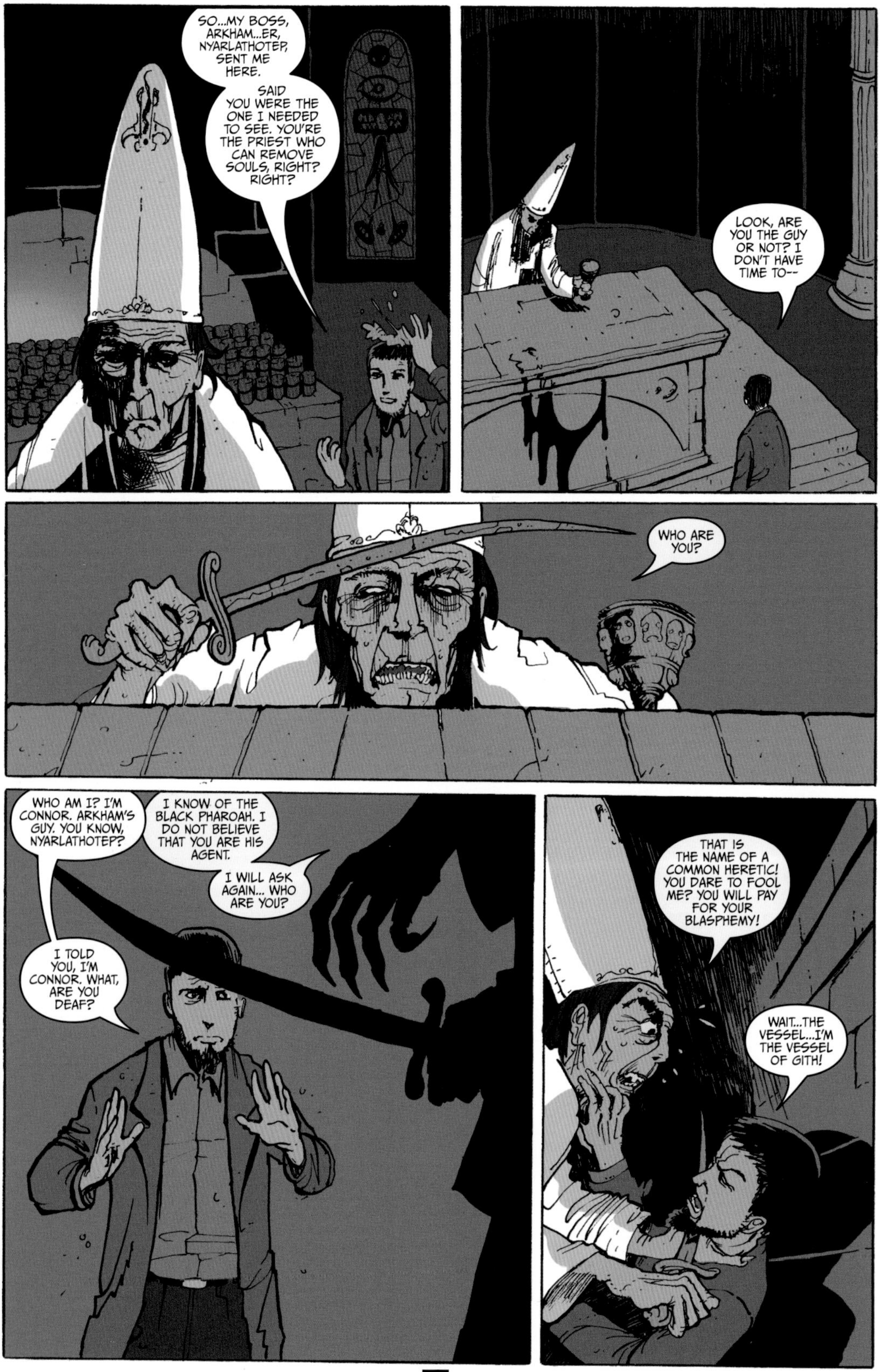
SO...MY BOSS, ARKHAM...ER, NYARLATHOTEP, SENT ME HERE.
SAID YOU WERE THE ONE I NEEDED TO SEE. YOU'RE THE PRIEST WHO CAN REMOVE SOULS, RIGHT? RIGHT?
LOOK, ARE YOU THE GUY OR NOT? I DON'T HAVE TIME TO--
WHO ARE YOU?
WHO AM I? I'M CONNOR. ARKHAM'S GUY. YOU KNOW, NYARLATHOTEP?
I KNOW OF THE BLACK PHAROAH. I DO NOT BELIEVE THAT YOU ARE HIS AGENT.
I WILL ASK AGAIN... WHO ARE YOU?
I TOLD YOU, I'M CONNOR. WHAT, ARE YOU DEAF?
THAT IS THE NAME OF A COMMON HERETIC! YOU DARE TO FOOL ME? YOU WILL PAY FOR YOUR BLASPHEMY!
WAIT...THE VESSEL...I'M THE VESSEL OF GITH!

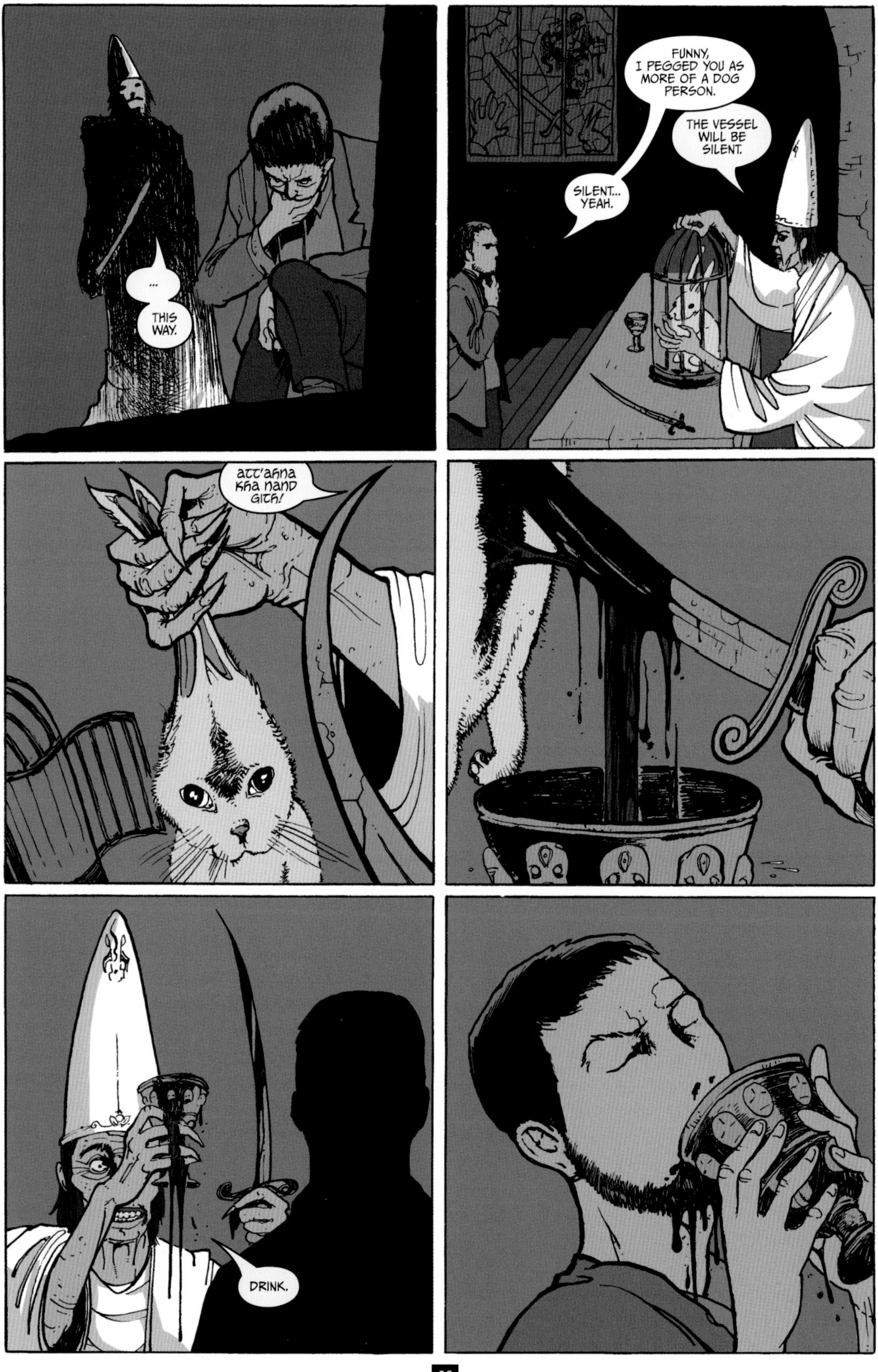
...
THIS WAY.
FUNNY, I PEGGED YOU AS MORE OF A DOG PERSON.
THE VESSEL WILL BE SILENT.
SILENT... YEAH.
ATT'AHNA KHA NAND GITH!
DRINK.

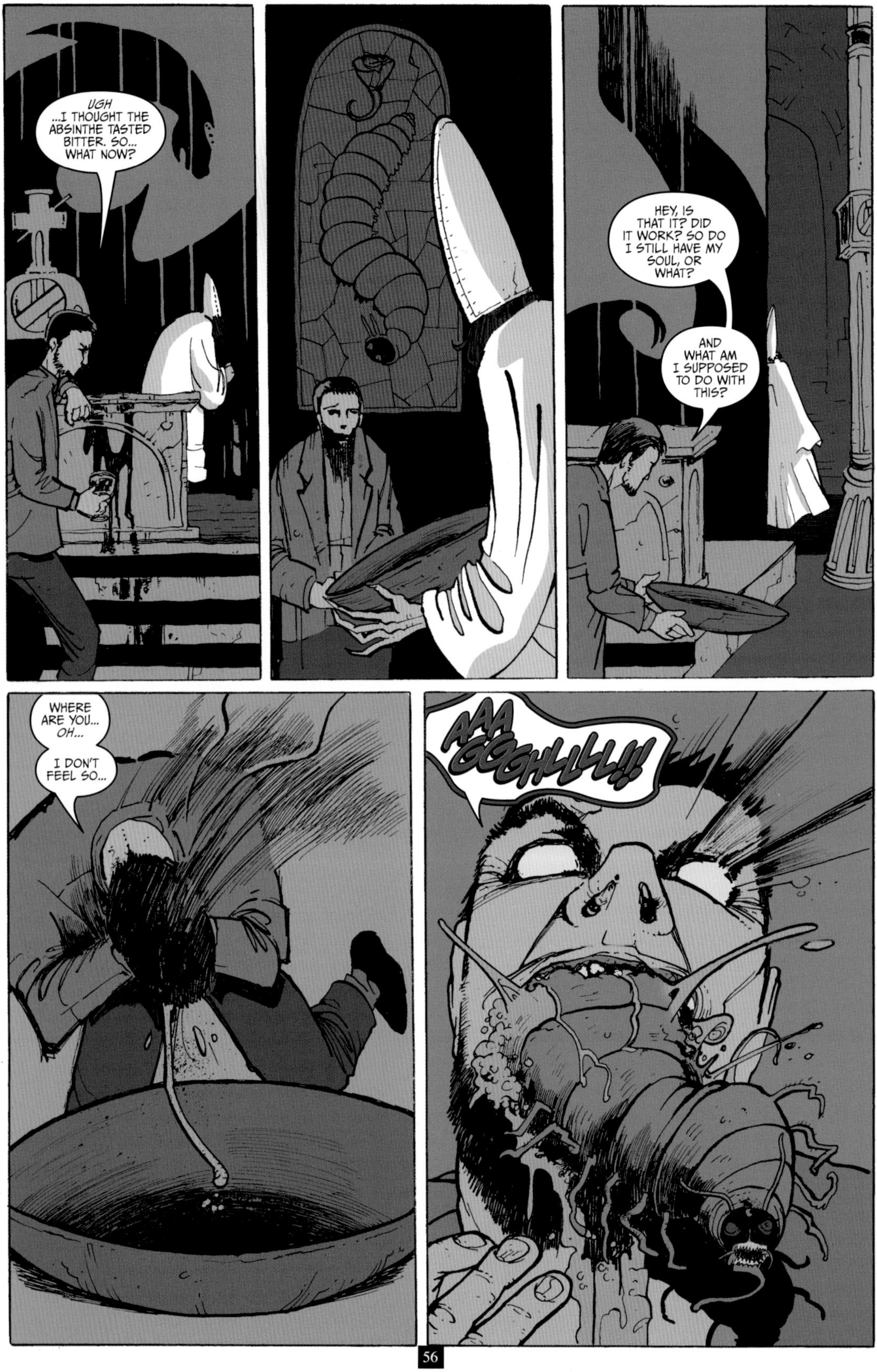
UGH ...I THOUGHT THE ABSINTHE TASTED BITTER. SO... WHAT NOW?
HEY, IS THAT IT? DID IT WORK? SO DO I STILL HAVE MY SOUL, OR WHAT?
AND WHAT AM I SUPPOSED TO DO WITH THIS?
WHERE ARE YOU... OH...
I DON'T FEEL SO...
AAAGGGHLLLL!!

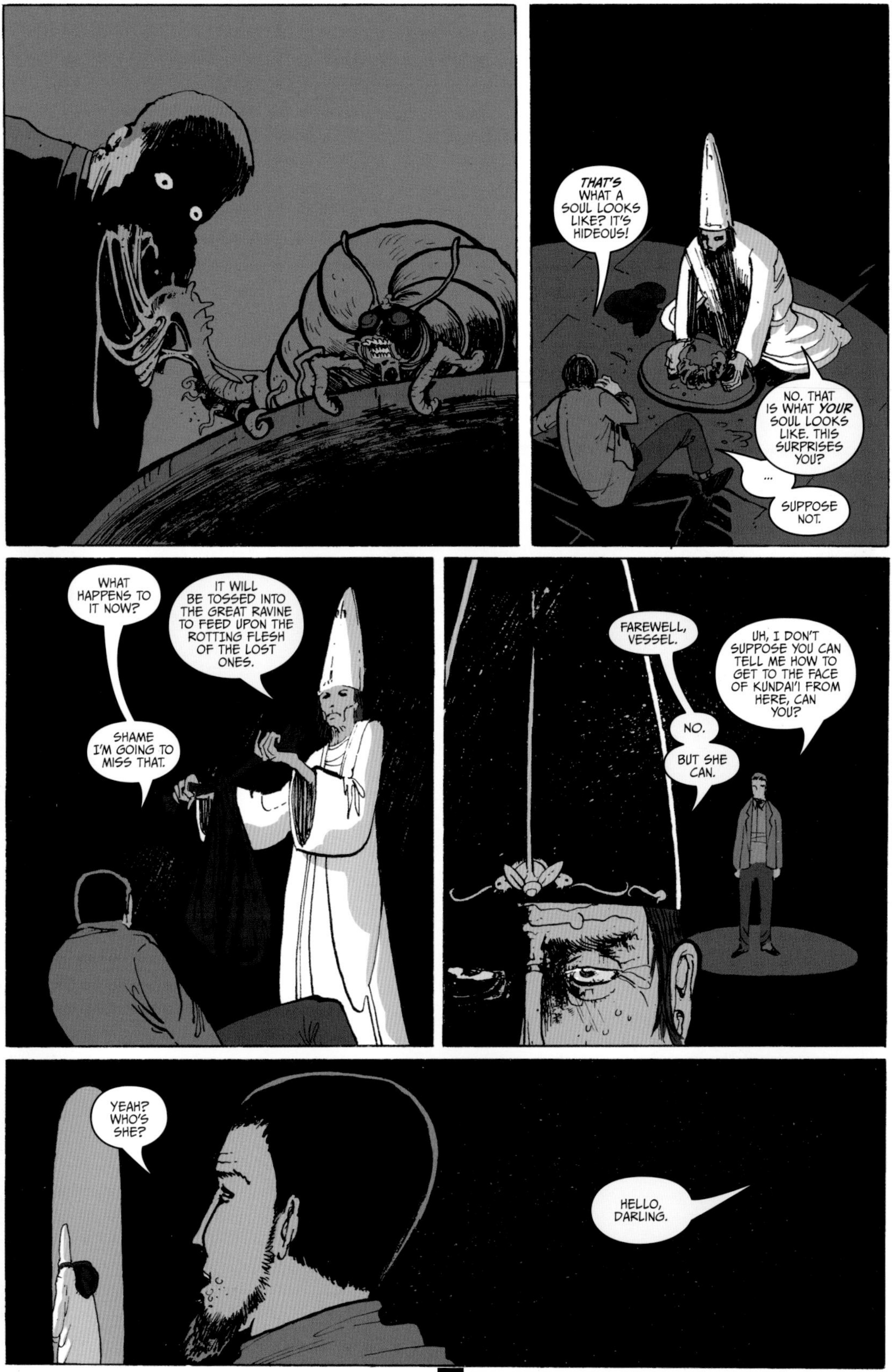
THAT'S WHAT A SOUL LOOKS LIKE? IT'S HIDEOUS!
NO. THAT IS WHAT YOUR SOUL LOOKS LIKE. THIS SURPRISES YOU?
...
SUPPOSE NOT.
WHAT HAPPENS TO IT NOW?
IT WILL BE TOSSED INTO THE GREAT RAVINE TO FEED UPON THE ROTTING FLESH OF THE LOST ONES.
SHAME I'M GOING TO MISS THAT.
FAREWELL, VESSEL.
UH, I DON'T SUPPOSE YOU CAN TELL ME HOW TO GET TO THE FACE OF KUNDAI'I FROM HERE, CAN YOU?
NO.
BUT SHE CAN.
YEAH? WHO'S SHE?
HELLO, DARLING.

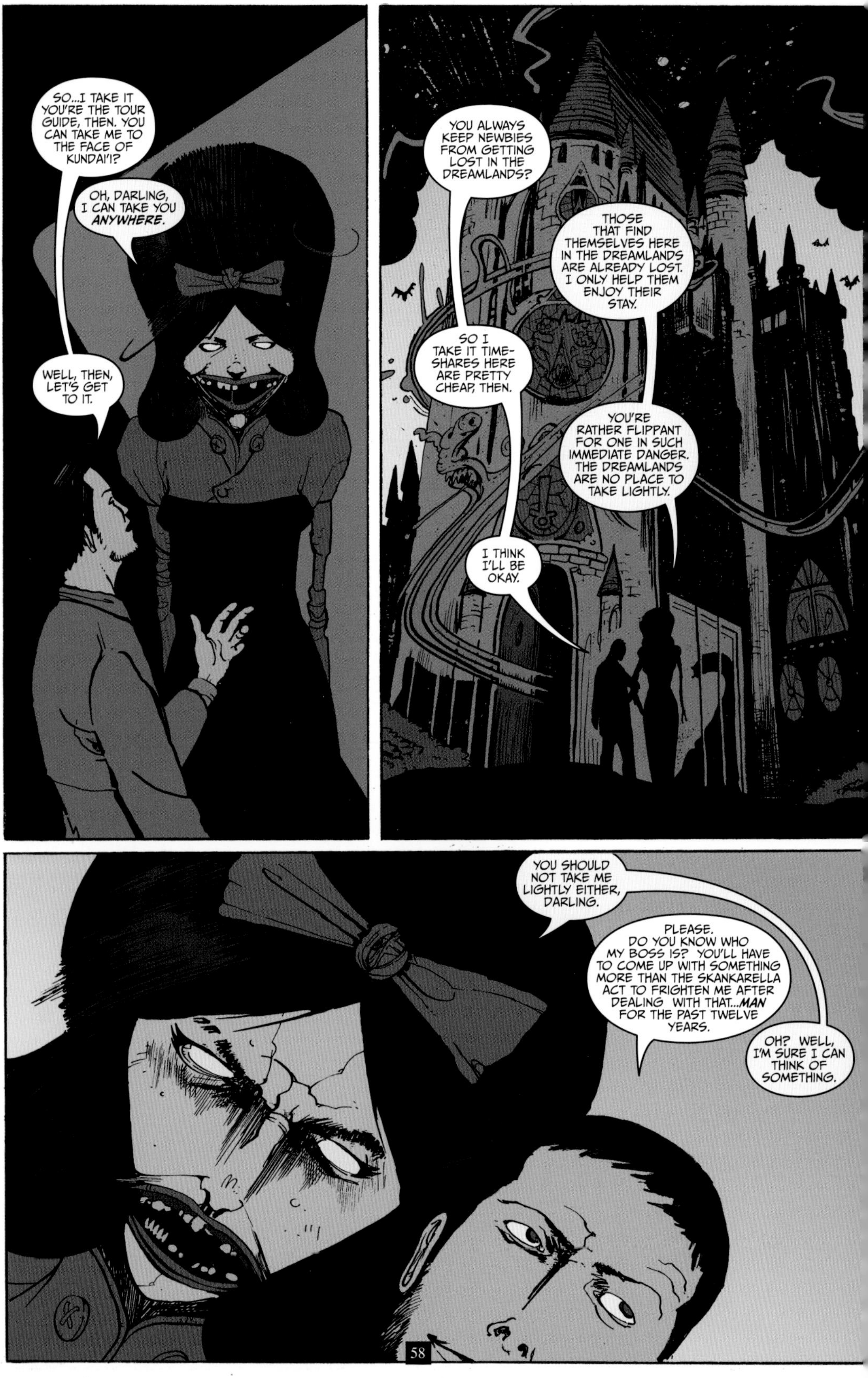

SO...I TAKE IT YOU'RE THE TOUR GUIDE, THEN. YOU CAN TAKE ME TO THE FACE OF KUNDAI'I?
OH, DARLING, I CAN TAKE YOU *ANYWHERE*.
WELL, THEN, LET'S GET TO IT.
YOU ALWAYS KEEP NEWBIES FROM GETTING LOST IN THE DREAMLANDS?
THOSE THAT FIND THEMSELVES HERE IN THE DREAMLANDS ARE ALREADY LOST. I ONLY HELP THEM ENJOY THEIR STAY.
SO I TAKE IT TIME-SHARES HERE ARE PRETTY CHEAP, THEN.
YOU'RE RATHER FLIPPANT FOR ONE IN SUCH IMMEDIATE DANGER. THE DREAMLANDS ARE NO PLACE TO TAKE LIGHTLY.
I THINK I'LL BE OKAY.
YOU SHOULD NOT TAKE ME LIGHTLY EITHER, DARLING.
PLEASE. DO YOU KNOW WHO MY BOSS IS? YOU'LL HAVE TO COME UP WITH SOMETHING MORE THAN THE SKANKARELLA ACT TO FRIGHTEN ME AFTER DEALING WITH THAT...*MAN* FOR THE PAST TWELVE YEARS.
OH? WELL, I'M SURE I CAN THINK OF SOMETHING.

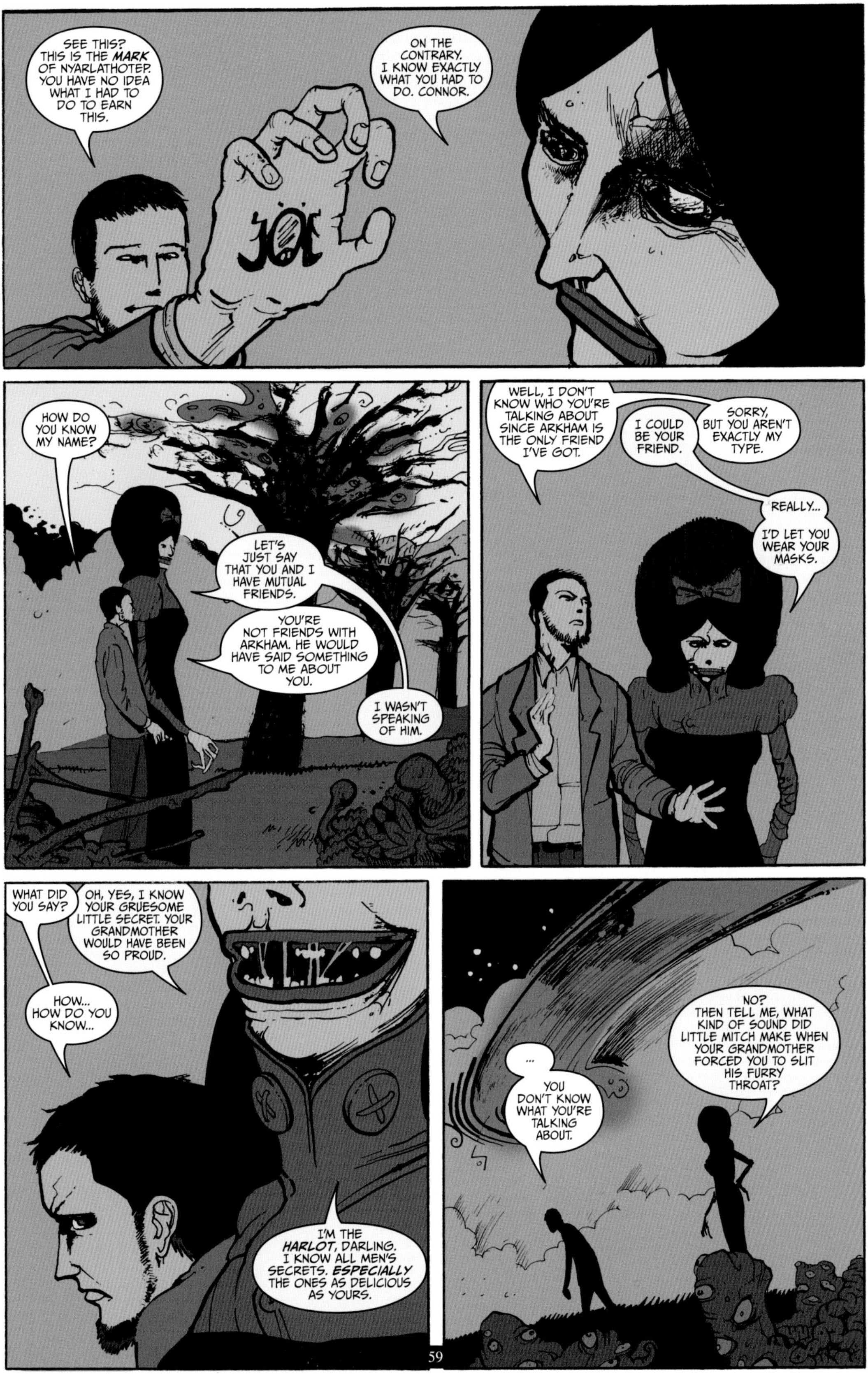
SEE THIS? THIS IS THE MARK OF NYARLATHOTEP. YOU HAVE NO IDEA WHAT I HAD TO DO TO EARN THIS.
ON THE CONTRARY. I KNOW EXACTLY WHAT YOU HAD TO DO. CONNOR.
HOW DO YOU KNOW MY NAME?
LET'S JUST SAY THAT YOU AND I HAVE MUTUAL FRIENDS.
YOU'RE NOT FRIENDS WITH ARKHAM. HE WOULD HAVE SAID SOMETHING TO ME ABOUT YOU.
I WASN'T SPEAKING OF HIM.
WELL, I DON'T KNOW WHO YOU'RE TALKING ABOUT SINCE ARKHAM IS THE ONLY FRIEND I'VE GOT.
I COULD BE YOUR FRIEND.
SORRY, BUT YOU AREN'T EXACTLY MY TYPE.
REALLY...
I'D LET YOU WEAR YOUR MASKS.
WHAT DID YOU SAY?
OH, YES, I KNOW YOUR GRUESOME LITTLE SECRET. YOUR GRANDMOTHER WOULD HAVE BEEN SO PROUD.
HOW... HOW DO YOU KNOW...
I'M THE HARLOT, DARLING. I KNOW ALL MEN'S SECRETS. ESPECIALLY THE ONES AS DELICIOUS AS YOURS.
...
YOU DON'T KNOW WHAT YOU'RE TALKING ABOUT.
NO? THEN TELL ME, WHAT KIND OF SOUND DID LITTLE MITCH MAKE WHEN YOUR GRANDMOTHER FORCED YOU TO SLIT HIS FURRY THROAT?

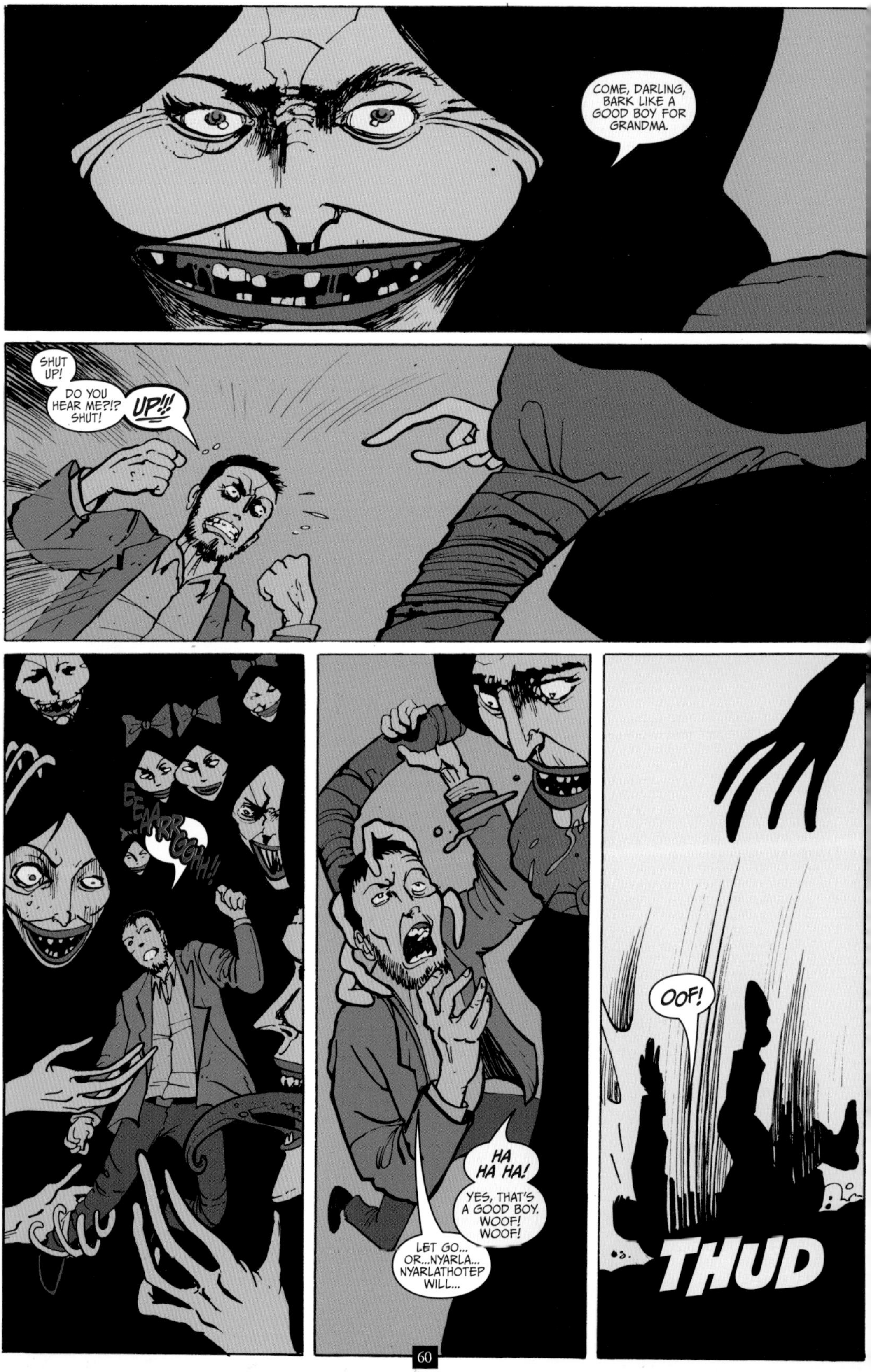
COME, DARLING, BARK LIKE A GOOD BOY FOR GRANDMA.
SHUT UP!
DO YOU HEAR ME?!? SHUT!
UP!!!
EEAARRGGHH!!
HA HA HA!
YES, THAT'S A GOOD BOY. WOOF! WOOF!
LET GO... OR...NYARLA... NYARLATHOTEP WILL...
OOF!
THUD

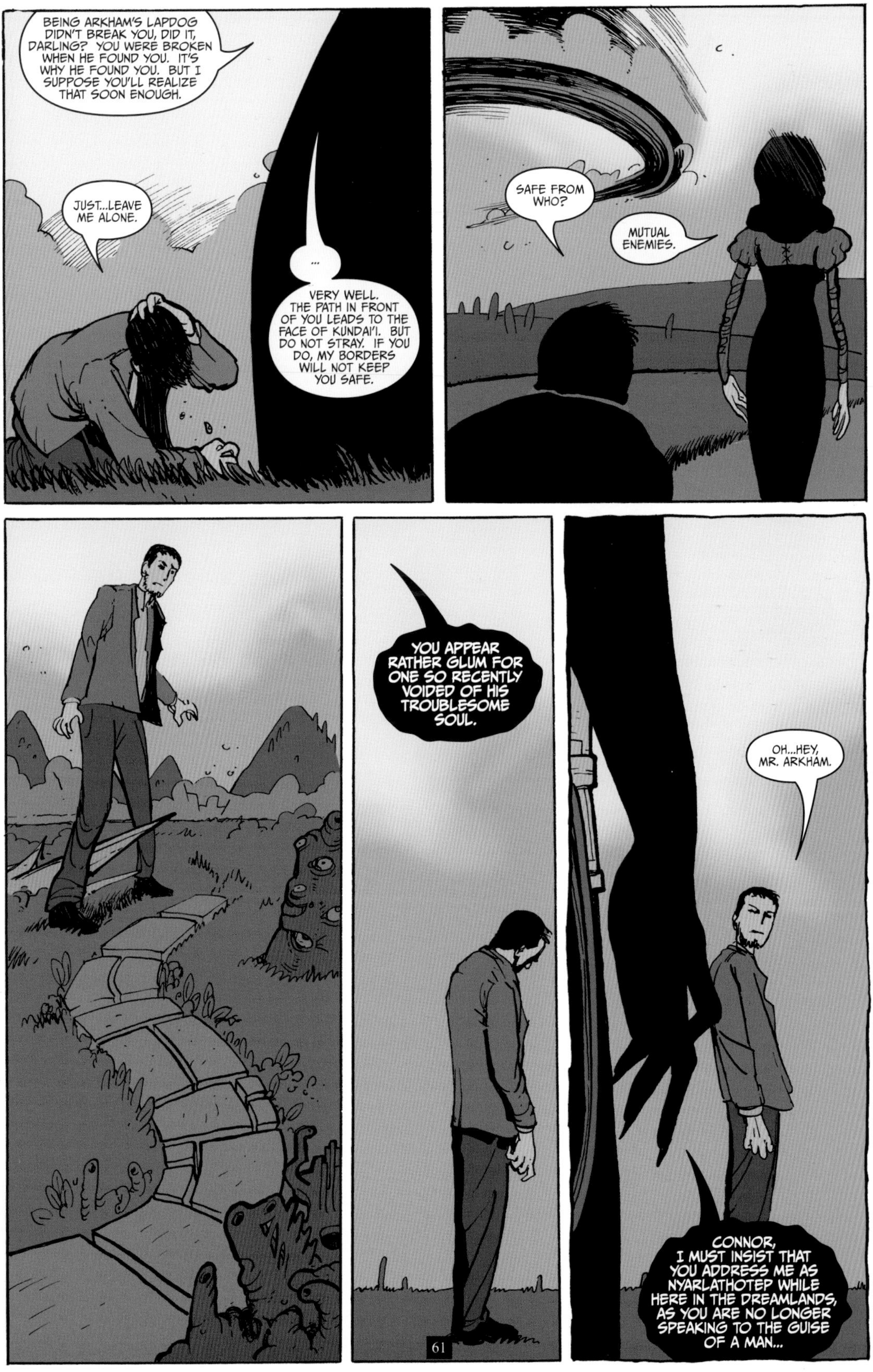
BEING ARKHAM'S LAPDOG DIDN'T BREAK YOU, DID IT, DARLING? YOU WERE BROKEN WHEN HE FOUND YOU. IT'S WHY HE FOUND YOU. BUT I SUPPOSE YOU'LL REALIZE THAT SOON ENOUGH.
JUST...LEAVE ME ALONE.
...
VERY WELL. THE PATH IN FRONT OF YOU LEADS TO THE FACE OF KUNDAI'I. BUT DO NOT STRAY. IF YOU DO, MY BORDERS WILL NOT KEEP YOU SAFE.
SAFE FROM WHO?
MUTUAL ENEMIES.
YOU APPEAR RATHER GLUM FOR ONE SO RECENTLY VOIDED OF HIS TROUBLESOME SOUL.
OH...HEY, MR. ARKHAM.
CONNOR, I MUST INSIST THAT YOU ADDRESS ME AS NYARLATHOTEP WHILE HERE IN THE DREAMLANDS, AS YOU ARE NO LONGER SPEAKING TO THE GUISE OF A MAN...

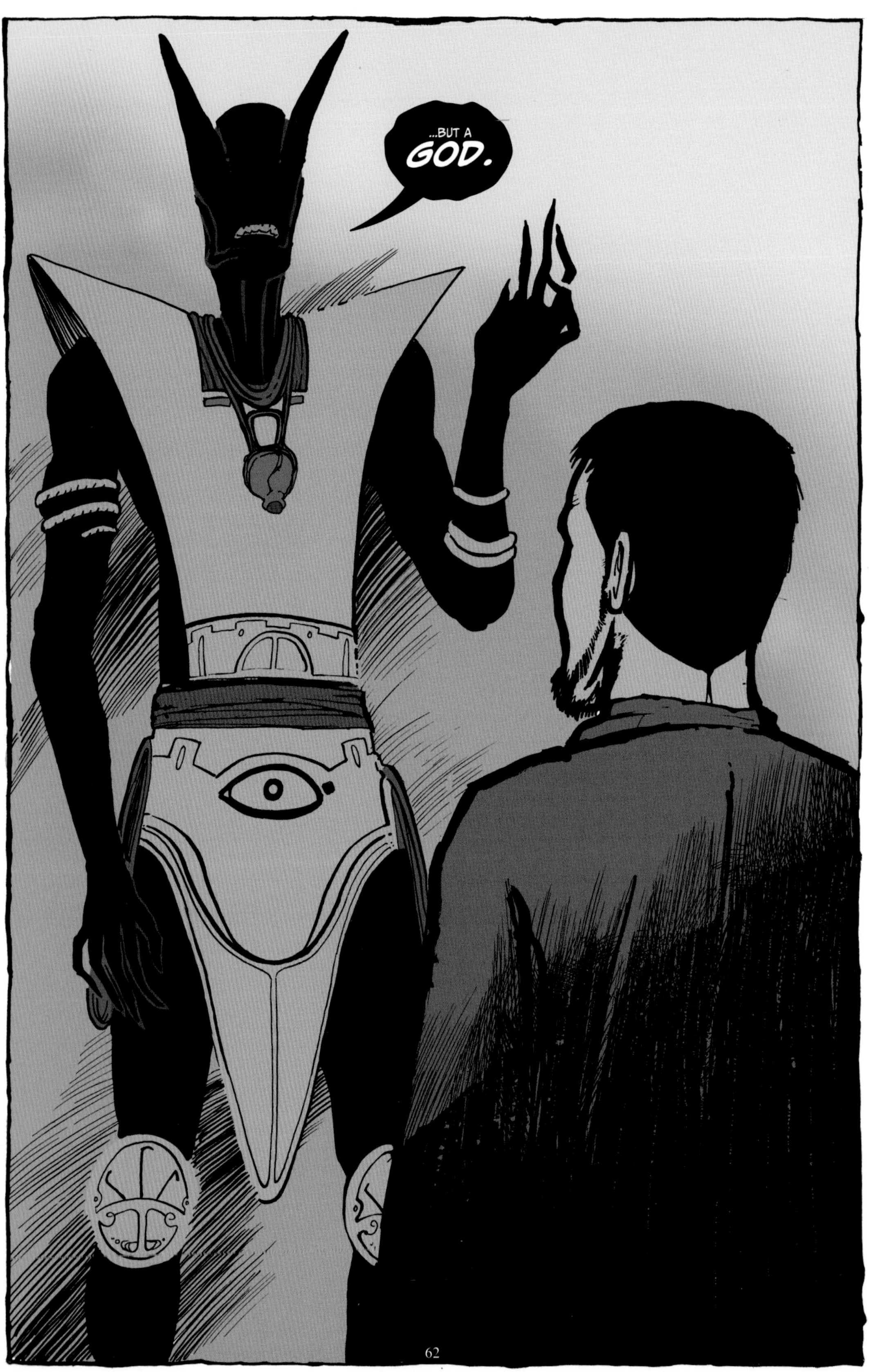
...BUT A GOD.

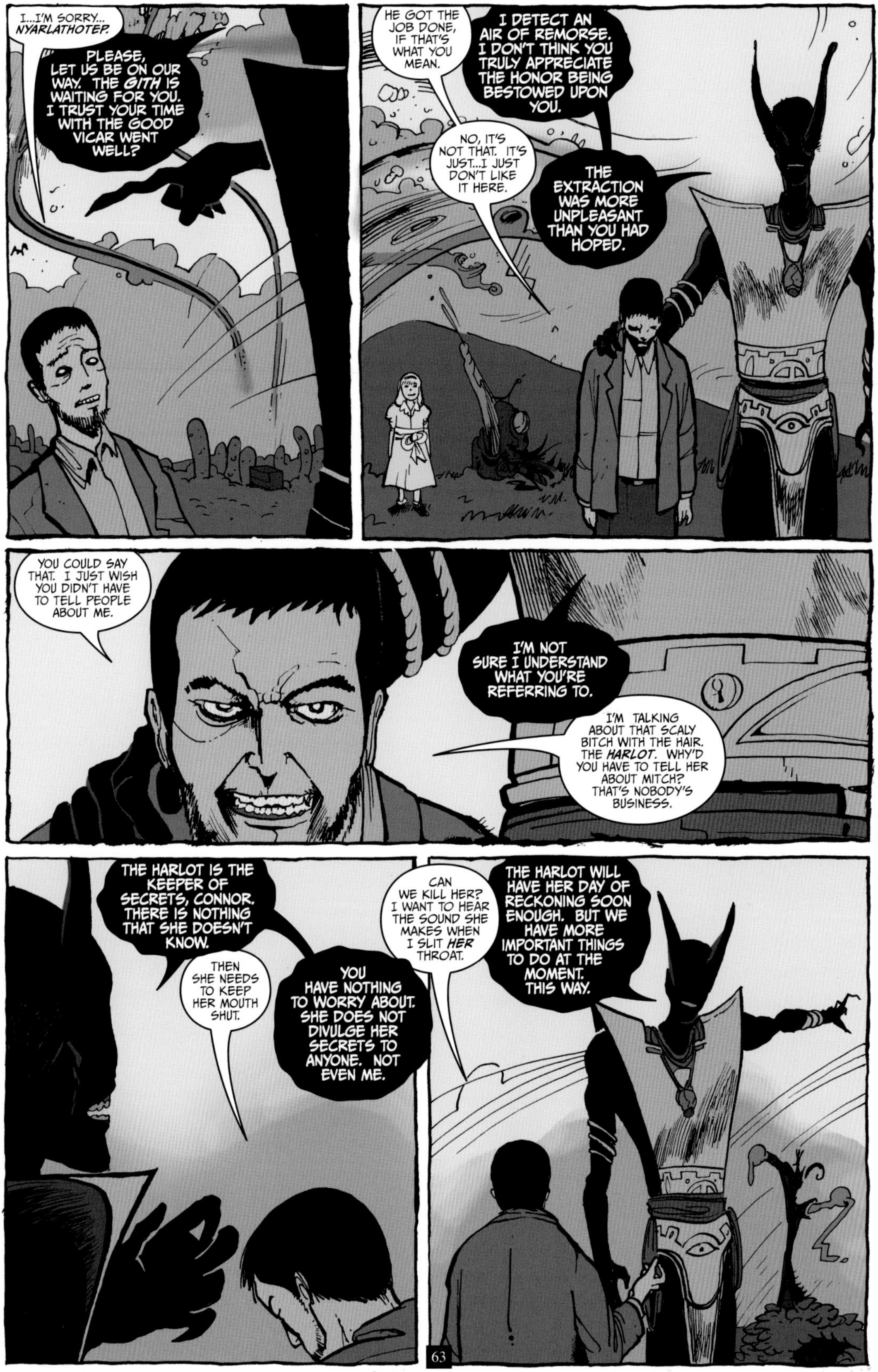
I...I'M SORRY... NYARLATHOTEP.
PLEASE, LET US BE ON OUR WAY. THE GITH IS WAITING FOR YOU. I TRUST YOUR TIME WITH THE GOOD VICAR WENT WELL?
HE GOT THE JOB DONE, IF THAT'S WHAT YOU MEAN.
I DETECT AN AIR OF REMORSE. I DON'T THINK YOU TRULY APPRECIATE THE HONOR BEING BESTOWED UPON YOU.
NO, IT'S NOT THAT. IT'S JUST...I JUST DON'T LIKE IT HERE.
THE EXTRACTION WAS MORE UNPLEASANT THAN YOU HAD HOPED.
YOU COULD SAY THAT. I JUST WISH YOU DIDN'T HAVE TO TELL PEOPLE ABOUT ME.
I'M NOT SURE I UNDERSTAND WHAT YOU'RE REFERRING TO.
I'M TALKING ABOUT THAT SCALY BITCH WITH THE HAIR. THE HARLOT. WHY'D YOU HAVE TO TELL HER ABOUT MITCH? THAT'S NOBODY'S BUSINESS.
THE HARLOT IS THE KEEPER OF SECRETS, CONNOR. THERE IS NOTHING THAT SHE DOESN'T KNOW.
THEN SHE NEEDS TO KEEP HER MOUTH SHUT.
YOU HAVE NOTHING TO WORRY ABOUT. SHE DOES NOT DIVULGE HER SECRETS TO ANYONE. NOT EVEN ME.
CAN WE KILL HER? I WANT TO HEAR THE SOUND SHE MAKES WHEN I SLIT HER THROAT.
THE HARLOT WILL HAVE HER DAY OF RECKONING SOON ENOUGH. BUT WE HAVE MORE IMPORTANT THINGS TO DO AT THE MOMENT. THIS WAY.

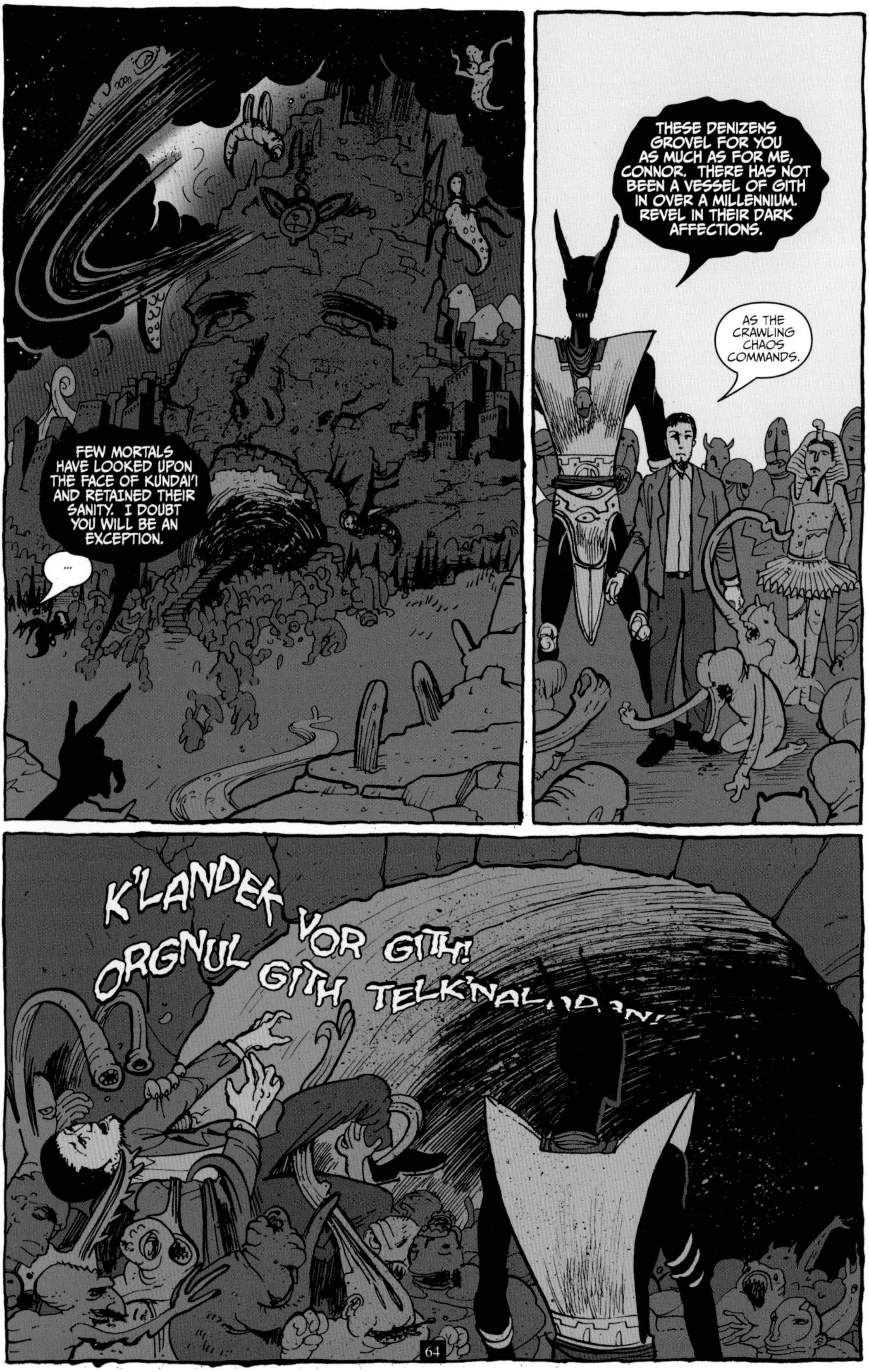
FEW MORTALS HAVE LOOKED UPON THE FACE OF KUNDAI'I AND RETAINED THEIR SANITY. I DOUBT YOU WILL BE AN EXCEPTION.
...
THESE DENIZENS GROVEL FOR YOU AS MUCH AS FOR ME, CONNOR. THERE HAS NOT BEEN A VESSEL OF GITH IN OVER A MILLENNIUM. REVEL IN THEIR DARK AFFECTIONS.
AS THE CRAWLING CHAOS COMMANDS.
K'LANDEK VOR GITH!
ORGNUL GITH TELK'NALADAN!

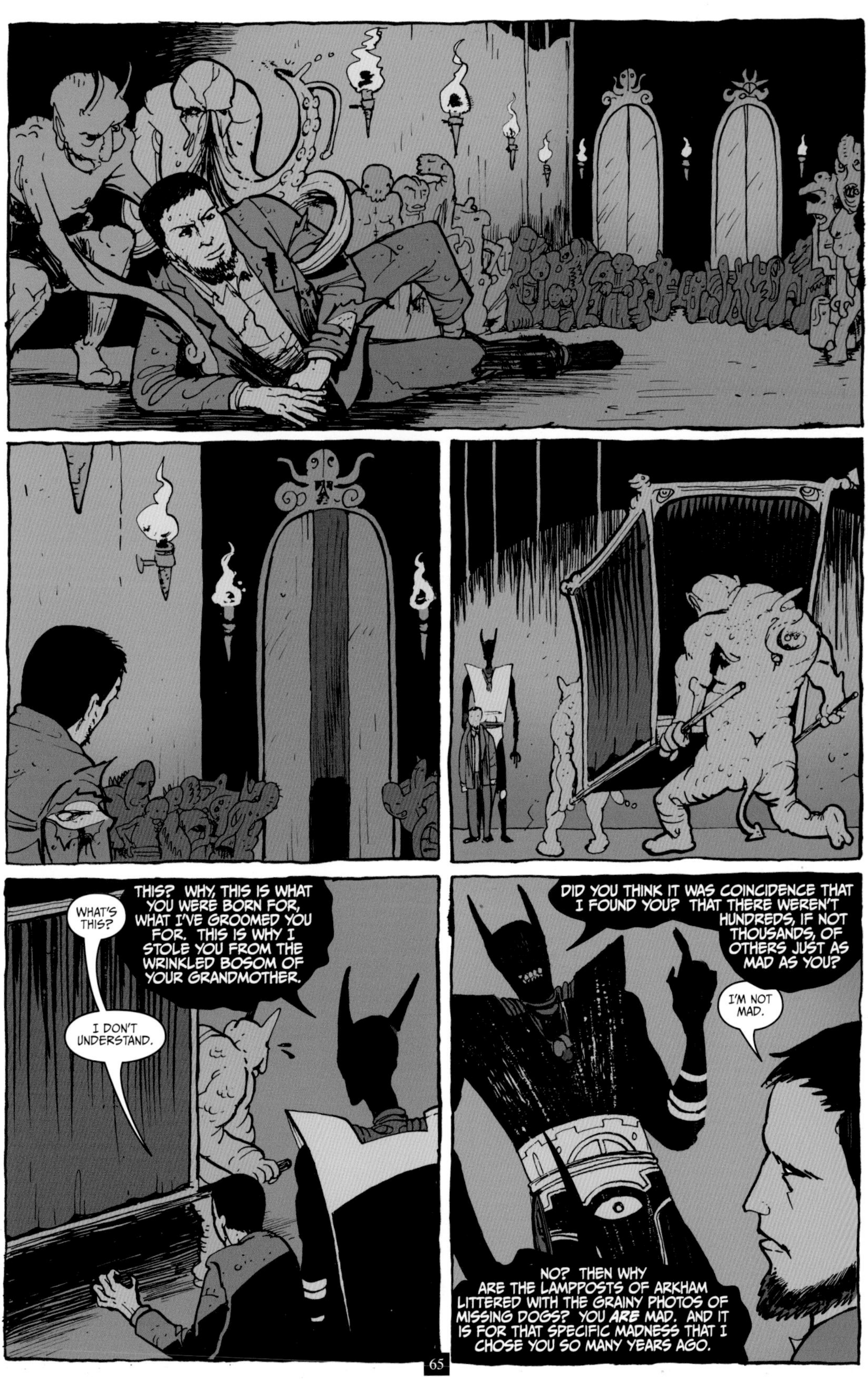

WHAT'S THIS?
THIS? WHY, THIS IS WHAT YOU WERE BORN FOR, WHAT I'VE GROOMED YOU FOR. THIS IS WHY I STOLE YOU FROM THE WRINKLED BOSOM OF YOUR GRANDMOTHER.
I DON'T UNDERSTAND.
DID YOU THINK IT WAS COINCIDENCE THAT I FOUND YOU? THAT THERE WEREN'T HUNDREDS, IF NOT THOUSANDS, OF OTHERS JUST AS MAD AS YOU?
I'M NOT MAD.
NO? THEN WHY ARE THE LAMPPOSTS OF ARKHAM LITTERED WITH THE GRAINY PHOTOS OF MISSING DOGS? YOU ARE MAD. AND IT IS FOR THAT SPECIFIC MADNESS THAT I CHOSE YOU SO MANY YEARS AGO.

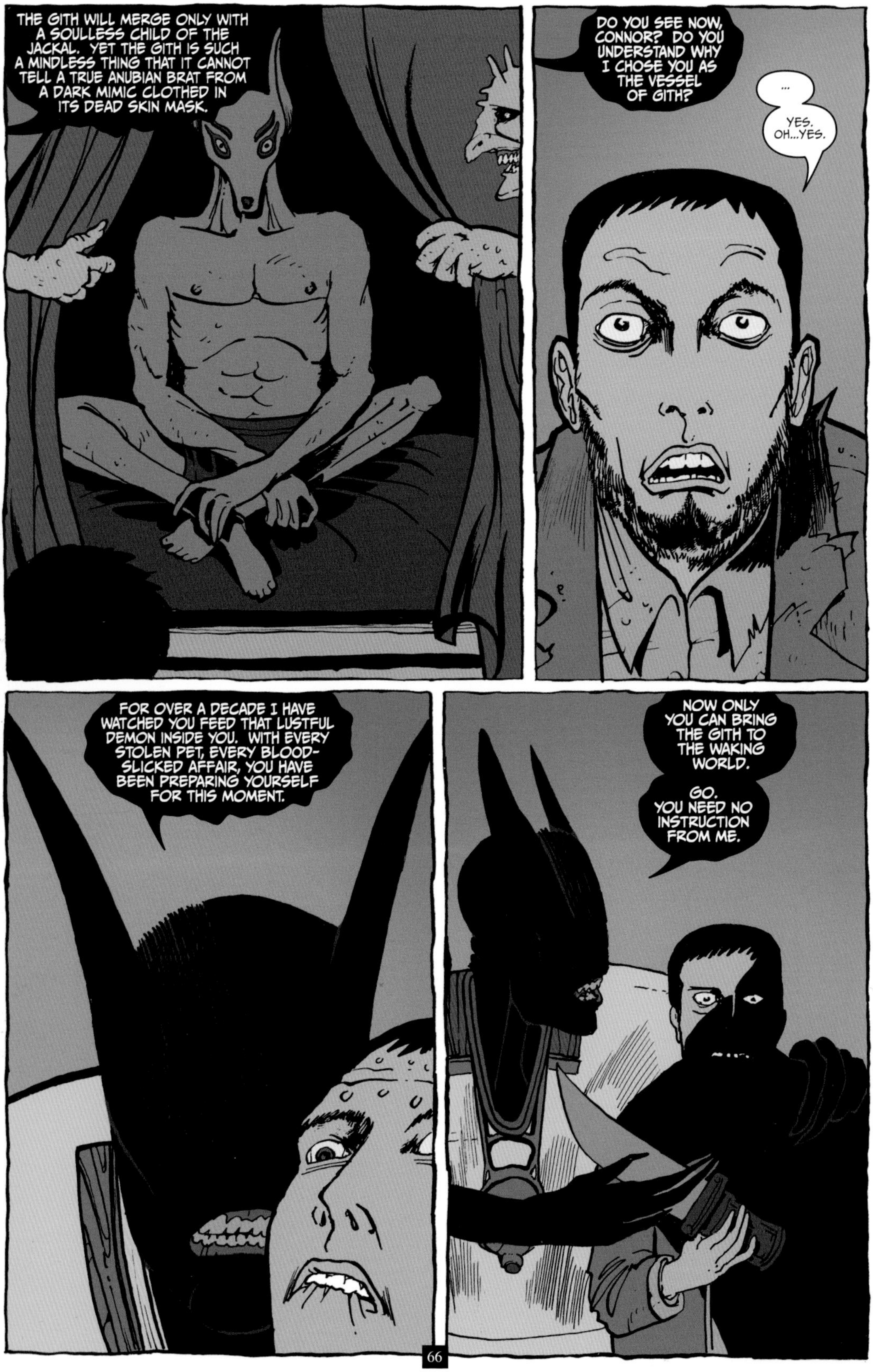
THE GITH WILL MERGE ONLY WITH A SOULLESS CHILD OF THE JACKAL. YET THE GITH IS SUCH A MINDLESS THING THAT IT CANNOT TELL A TRUE ANUBIAN BRAT FROM A DARK MIMIC CLOTHED IN ITS DEAD SKIN MASK.
DO YOU SEE NOW, CONNOR? DO YOU UNDERSTAND WHY I CHOSE YOU AS THE VESSEL OF GITH?
...
YES. OH...YES.
FOR OVER A DECADE I HAVE WATCHED YOU FEED THAT LUSTFUL DEMON INSIDE YOU. WITH EVERY STOLEN PET, EVERY BLOOD-SLICKED AFFAIR, YOU HAVE BEEN PREPARING YOURSELF FOR THIS MOMENT.
NOW ONLY YOU CAN BRING THE GITH TO THE WAKING WORLD.
GO. YOU NEED NO INSTRUCTION FROM ME.

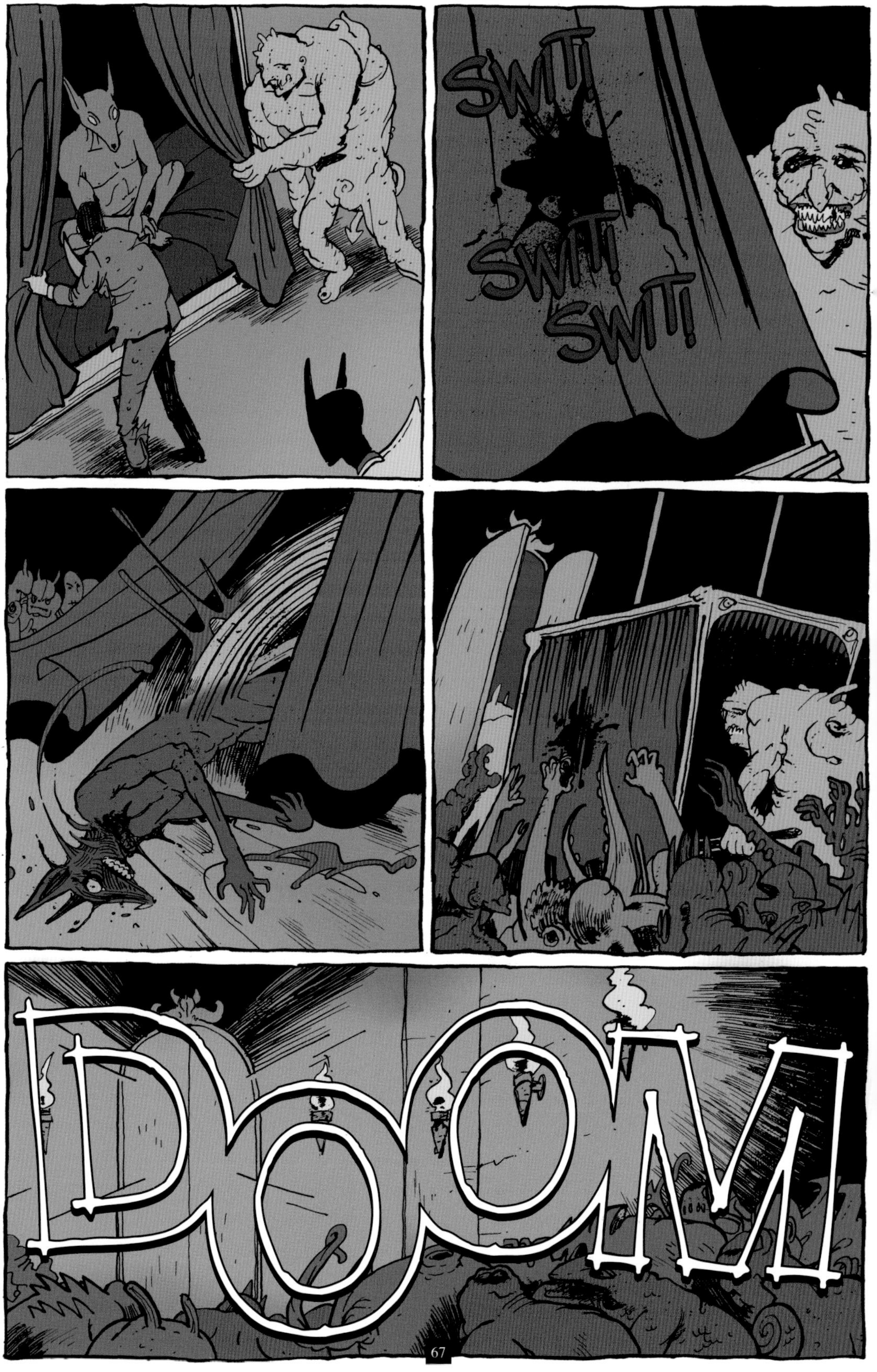
SWIT!
SWIT!
SWIT!
DOOM

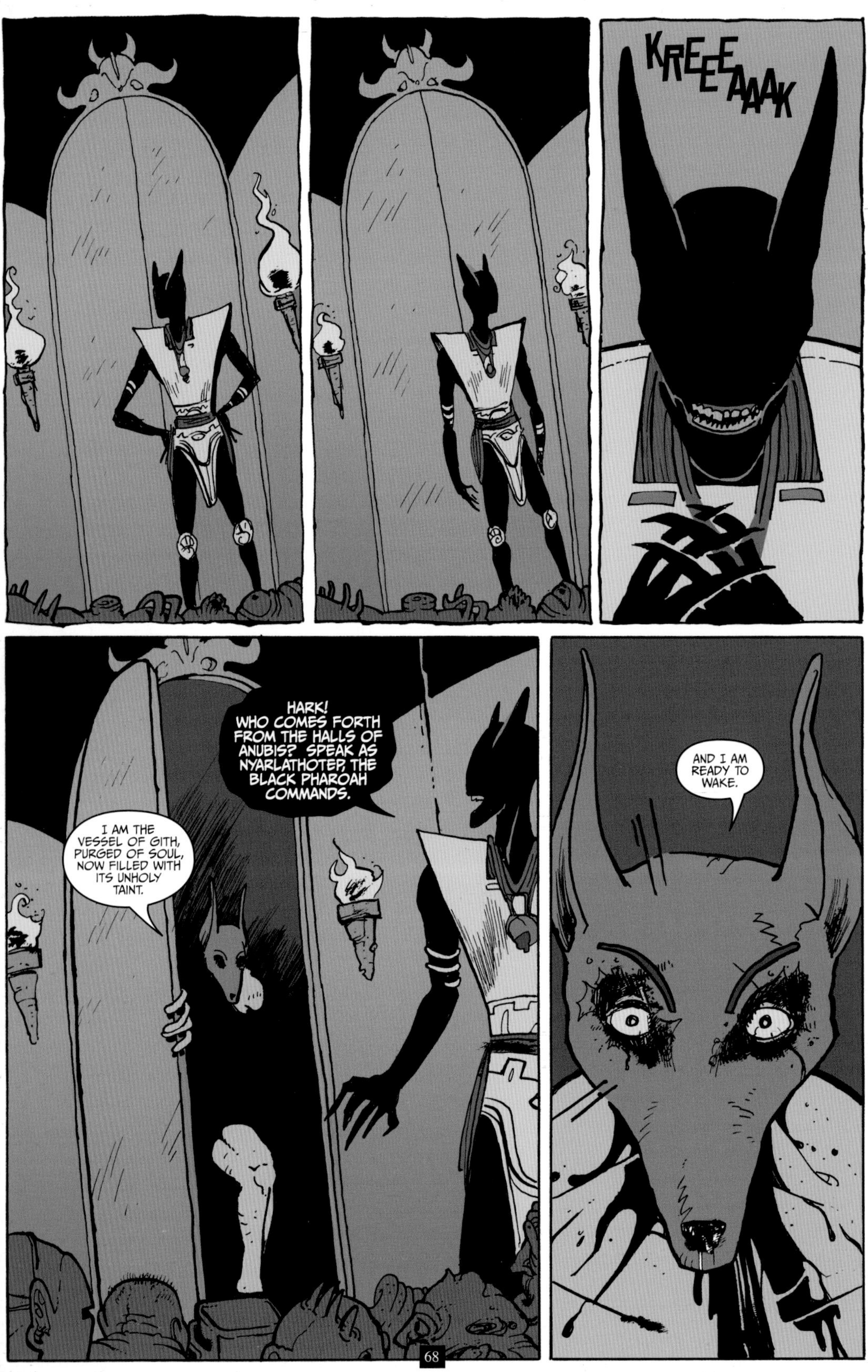
KREEEAAAK
HARK! WHO COMES FORTH FROM THE HALLS OF ANUBIS? SPEAK AS NYARLATHOTEP, THE BLACK PHAROAH COMMANDS.
I AM THE VESSEL OF GITH, PURGED OF SOUL, NOW FILLED WITH ITS UNHOLY TAINT.
AND I AM READY TO WAKE.

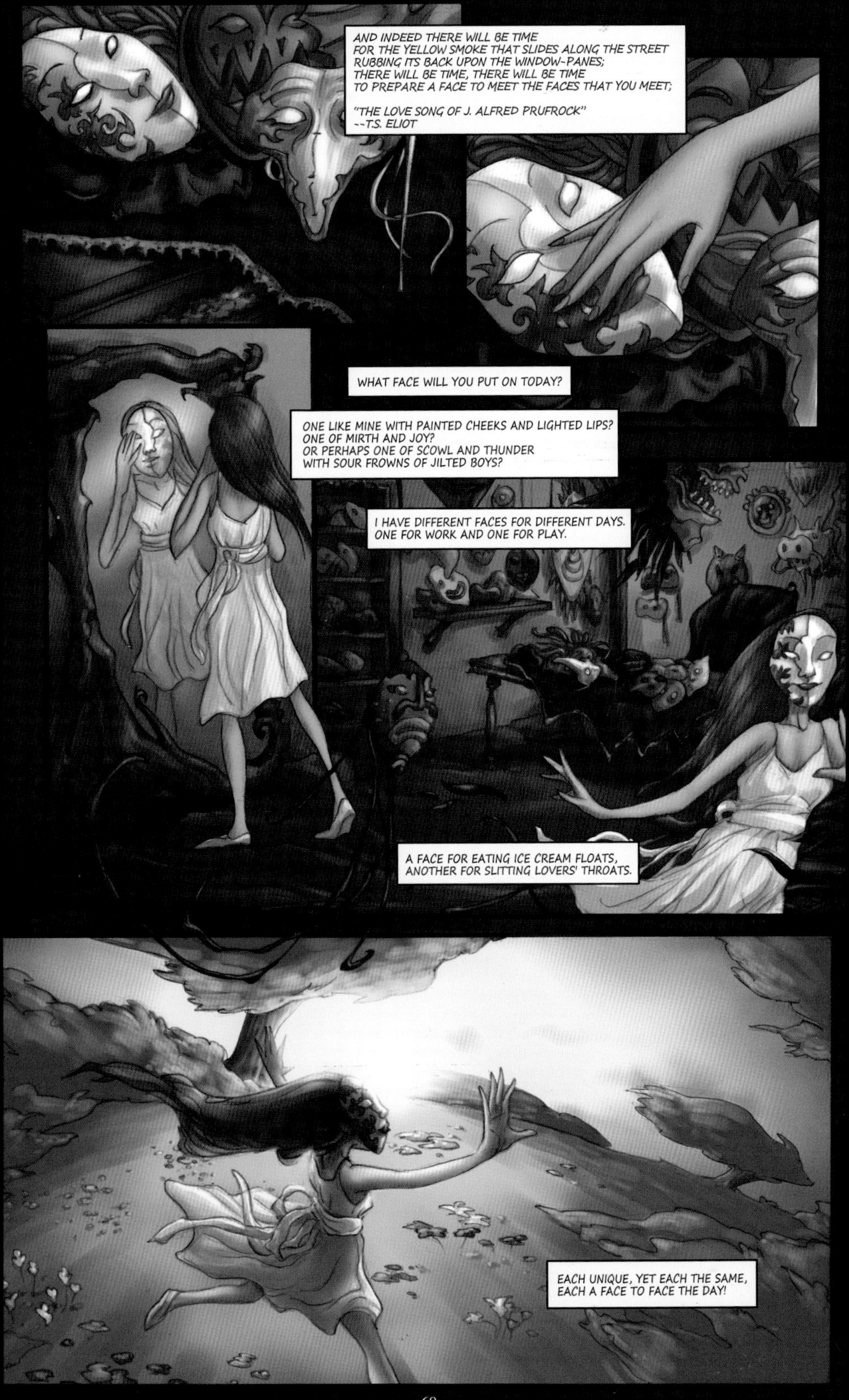
AND INDEED THERE WILL BE TIME
FOR THE YELLOW SMOKE THAT SLIDES ALONG THE STREET
RUBBING ITS BACK UPON THE WINDOW-PANES;
THERE WILL BE TIME, THERE WILL BE TIME
TO PREPARE A FACE TO MEET THE FACES THAT YOU MEET;
"THE LOVE SONG OF J. ALFRED PRUFROCK"
--T.S. ELIOT
WHAT FACE WILL YOU PUT ON TODAY?
ONE LIKE MINE WITH PAINTED CHEEKS AND LIGHTED LIPS?
ONE OF MIRTH AND JOY?
OR PERHAPS ONE OF SCOWL AND THUNDER
WITH SOUR FROWNS OF JILTED BOYS?
I HAVE DIFFERENT FACES FOR DIFFERENT DAYS.
ONE FOR WORK AND ONE FOR PLAY.
A FACE FOR EATING ICE CREAM FLOATS,
ANOTHER FOR SLITTING LOVERS' THROATS.
EACH UNIQUE, YET EACH THE SAME,
EACH A FACE TO FACE THE DAY!

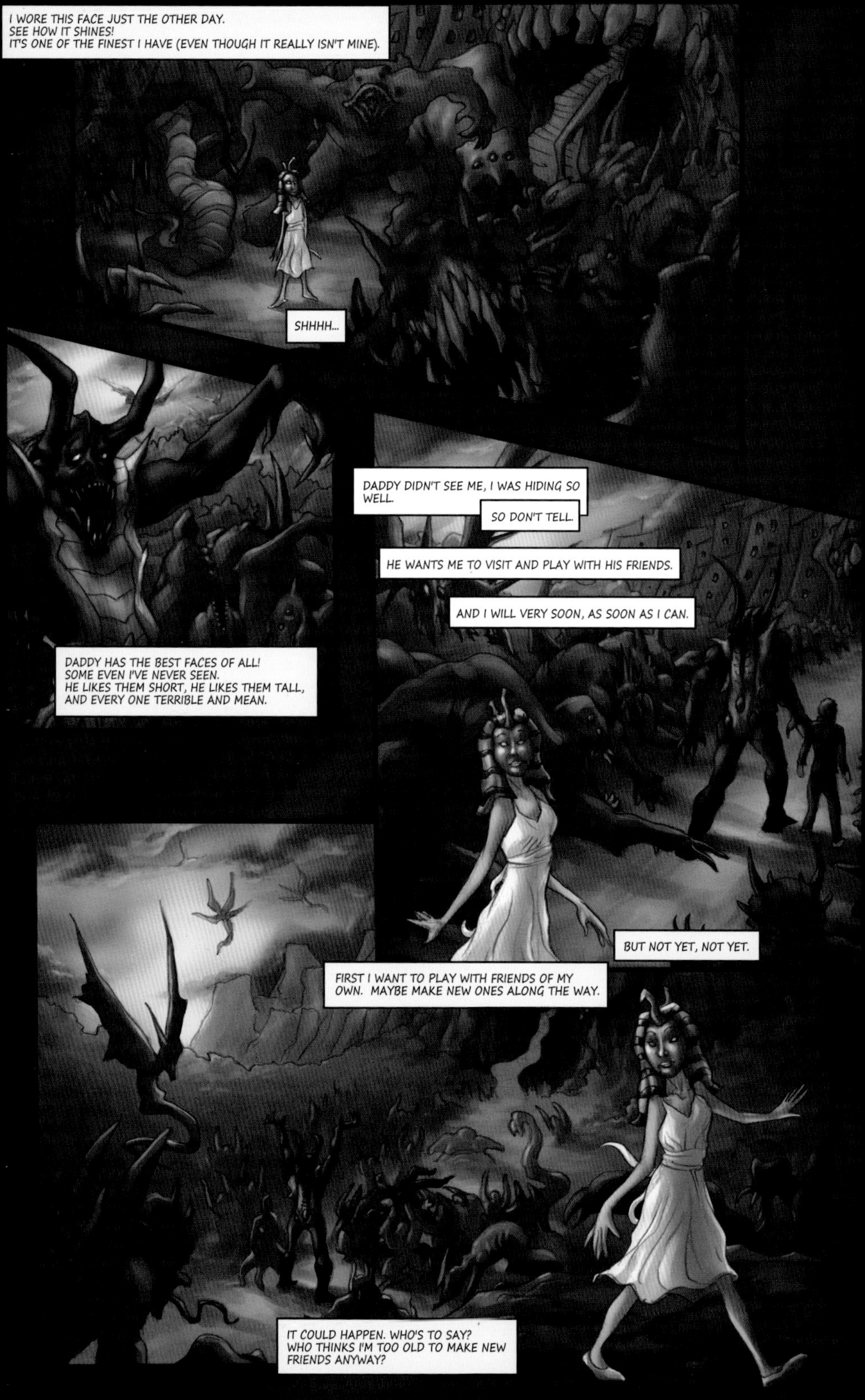
I WORE THIS FACE JUST THE OTHER DAY. SEE HOW IT SHINES! IT'S ONE OF THE FINEST I HAVE (EVEN THOUGH IT REALLY ISN'T MINE).
SHHHH...
DADDY HAS THE BEST FACES OF ALL! SOME EVEN I'VE NEVER SEEN. HE LIKES THEM SHORT, HE LIKES THEM TALL, AND EVERY ONE TERRIBLE AND MEAN.
DADDY DIDN'T SEE ME, I WAS HIDING SO WELL.
SO DON'T TELL.
HE WANTS ME TO VISIT AND PLAY WITH HIS FRIENDS.
AND I WILL VERY SOON, AS SOON AS I CAN.
BUT NOT YET, NOT YET.
FIRST I WANT TO PLAY WITH FRIENDS OF MY OWN. MAYBE MAKE NEW ONES ALONG THE WAY.
IT COULD HAPPEN. WHO'S TO SAY? WHO THINKS I'M TOO OLD TO MAKE NEW FRIENDS ANYWAY?

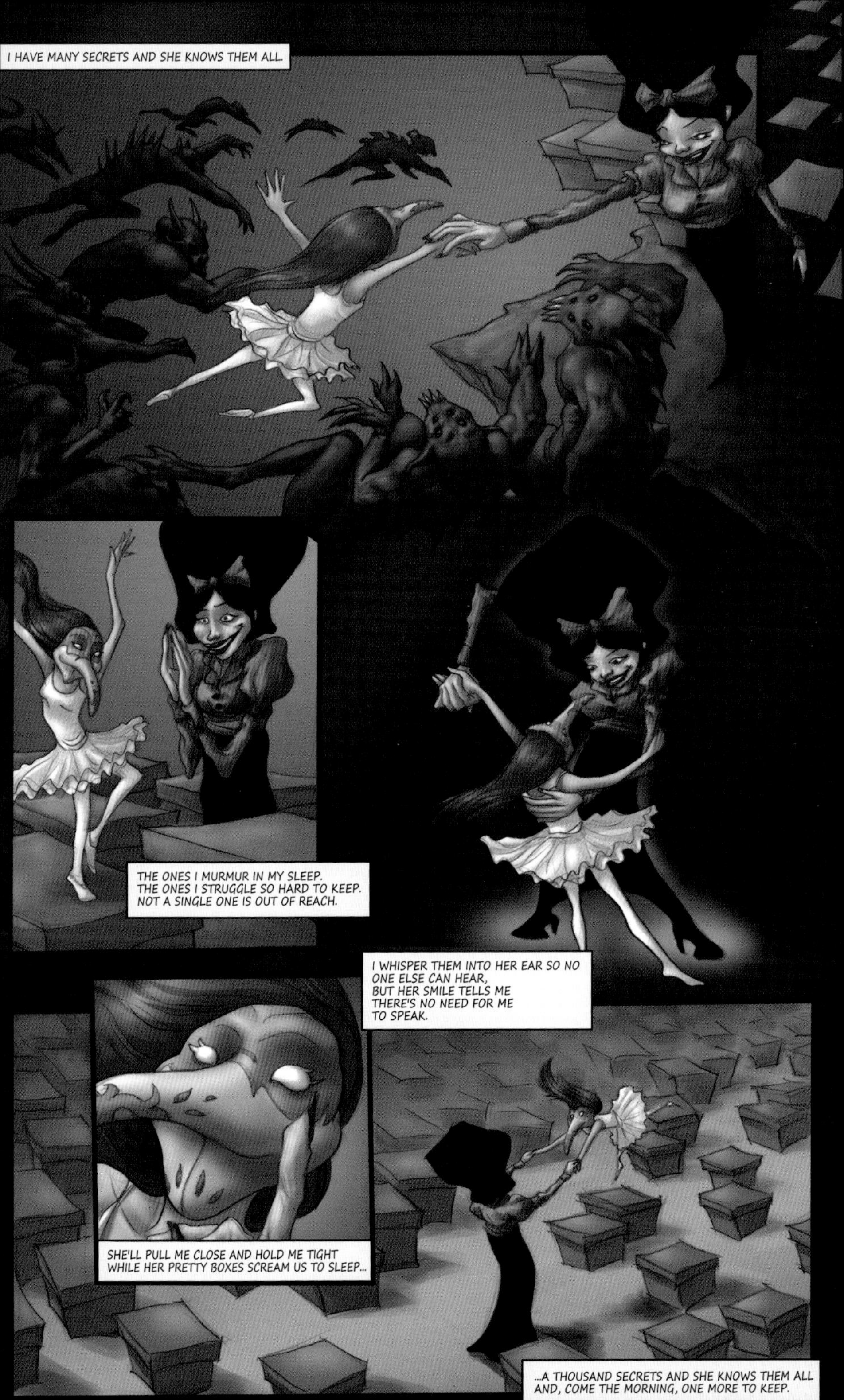
I HAVE MANY SECRETS AND SHE KNOWS THEM ALL.
THE ONES I MURMUR IN MY SLEEP. THE ONES I STRUGGLE SO HARD TO KEEP. NOT A SINGLE ONE IS OUT OF REACH.
I WHISPER THEM INTO HER EAR SO NO ONE ELSE CAN HEAR, BUT HER SMILE TELLS ME THERE'S NO NEED FOR ME TO SPEAK.
SHE'LL PULL ME CLOSE AND HOLD ME TIGHT WHILE HER PRETTY BOXES SCREAM US TO SLEEP...
...A THOUSAND SECRETS AND SHE KNOWS THEM ALL AND, COME THE MORNING, ONE MORE TO KEEP.

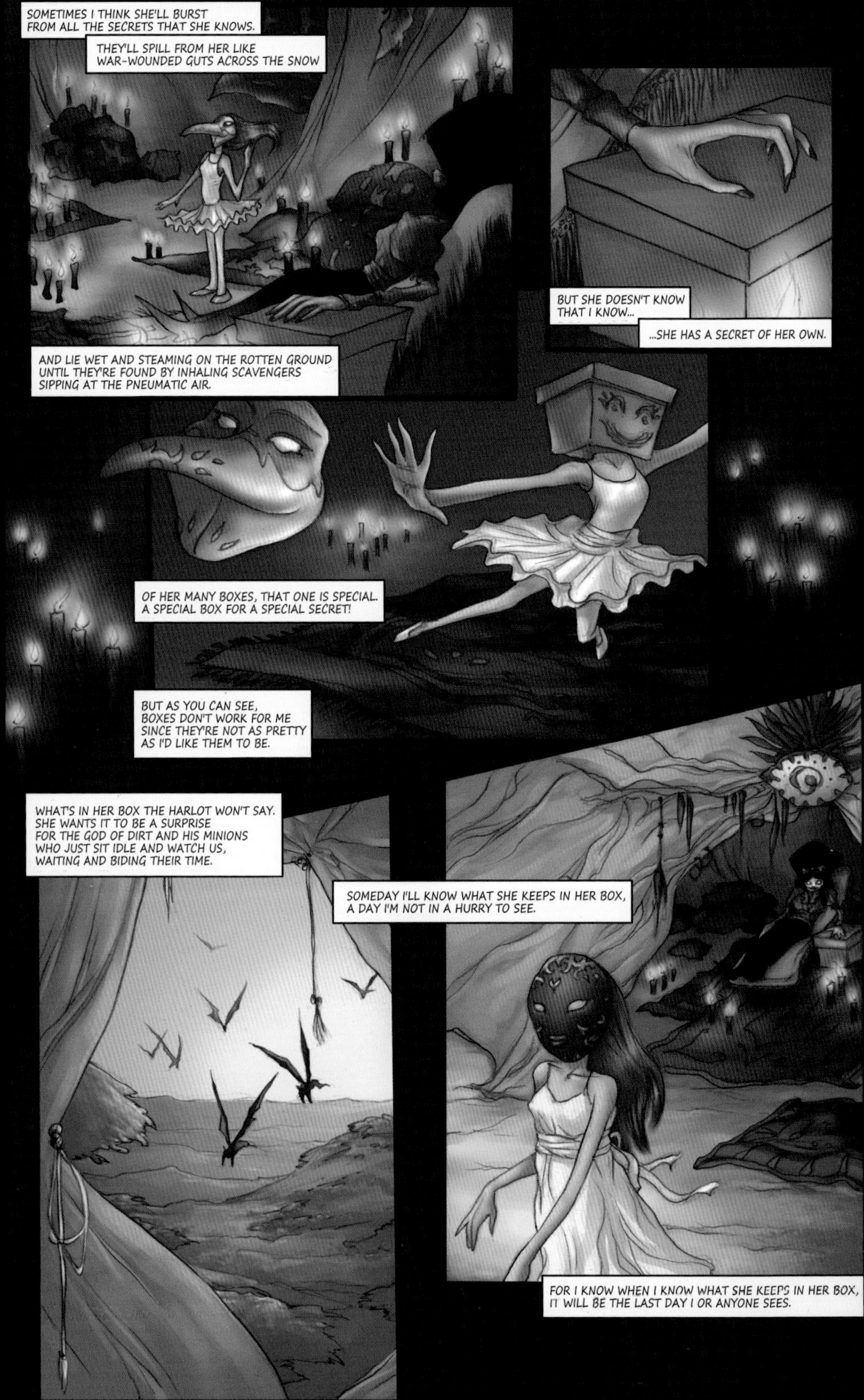
SOMETIMES I THINK SHE'LL BURST FROM ALL THE SECRETS THAT SHE KNOWS.
THEY'LL SPILL FROM HER LIKE WAR-WOUNDED GUTS ACROSS THE SNOW
AND LIE WET AND STEAMING ON THE ROTTEN GROUND UNTIL THEY'RE FOUND BY INHALING SCAVENGERS SIPPING AT THE PNEUMATIC AIR.
BUT SHE DOESN'T KNOW THAT I KNOW...
...SHE HAS A SECRET OF HER OWN.
OF HER MANY BOXES, THAT ONE IS SPECIAL. A SPECIAL BOX FOR A SPECIAL SECRET!
BUT AS YOU CAN SEE, BOXES DON'T WORK FOR ME SINCE THEY'RE NOT AS PRETTY AS I'D LIKE THEM TO BE.
WHAT'S IN HER BOX THE HARLOT WON'T SAY. SHE WANTS IT TO BE A SURPRISE FOR THE GOD OF DIRT AND HIS MINIONS WHO JUST SIT IDLE AND WATCH US, WAITING AND BIDING THEIR TIME.
SOMEDAY I'LL KNOW WHAT SHE KEEPS IN HER BOX, A DAY I'M NOT IN A HURRY TO SEE.
FOR I KNOW WHEN I KNOW WHAT SHE KEEPS IN HER BOX, IT WILL BE THE LAST DAY I OR ANYONE SEES.

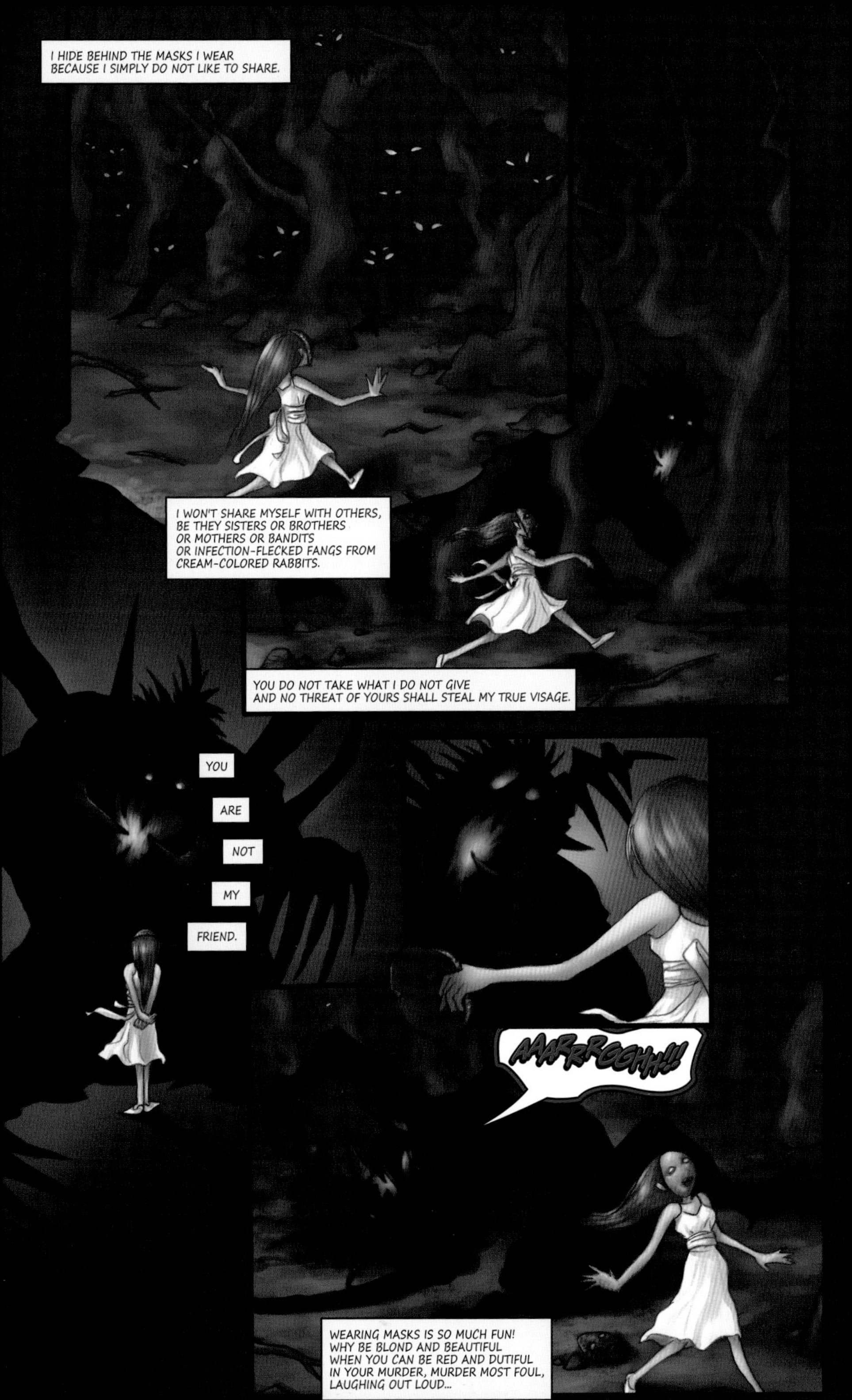
I HIDE BEHIND THE MASKS I WEAR
BECAUSE I SIMPLY DO NOT LIKE TO SHARE.
I WON'T SHARE MYSELF WITH OTHERS,
BE THEY SISTERS OR BROTHERS
OR MOTHERS OR BANDITS
OR INFECTION-FLECKED FANGS FROM
CREAM-COLORED RABBITS.
YOU DO NOT TAKE WHAT I DO NOT GIVE
AND NO THREAT OF YOURS SHALL STEAL MY TRUE VISAGE.
YOU
ARE
NOT
MY
FRIEND.
AAARRRGGHH!!!
WEARING MASKS IS SO MUCH FUN!
WHY BE BLOND AND BEAUTIFUL
WHEN YOU CAN BE RED AND DUTIFUL
IN YOUR MURDER, MURDER MOST FOUL,
LAUGHING OUT LOUD...

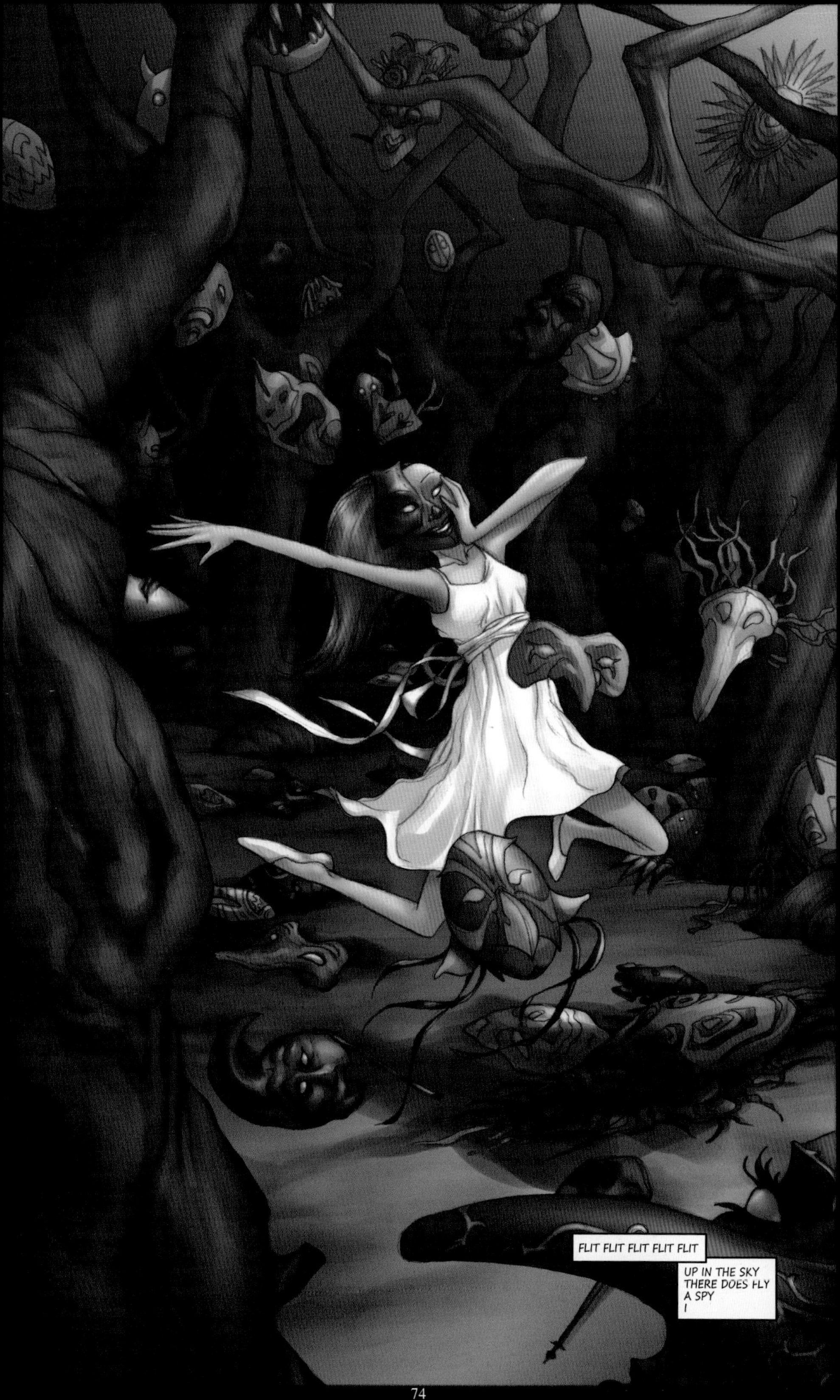
FLIT FLIT FLIT FLIT FLIT
UP IN THE SKY THERE DOES FLY A SPY I

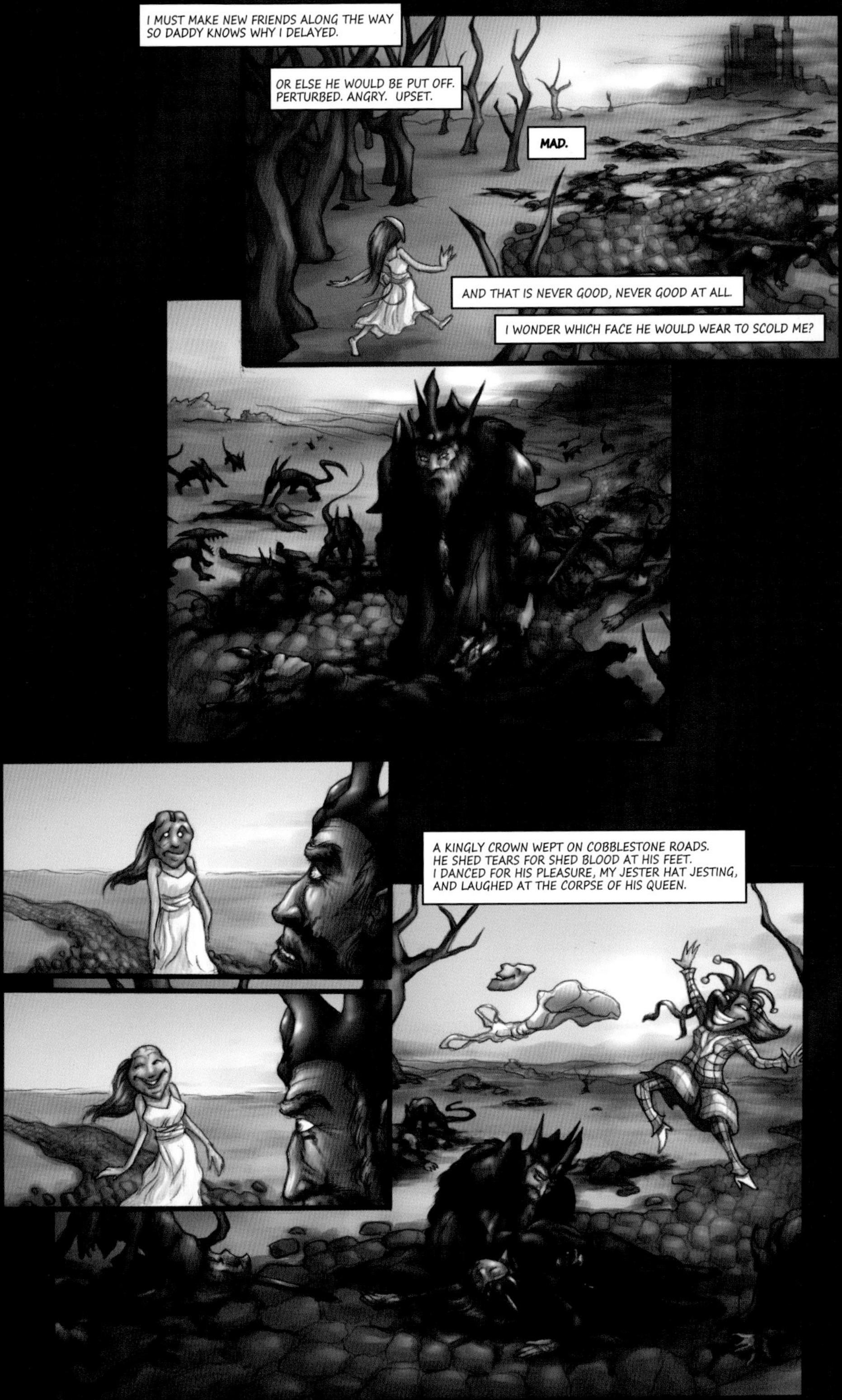
I MUST MAKE NEW FRIENDS ALONG THE WAY SO DADDY KNOWS WHY I DELAYED.
OR ELSE HE WOULD BE PUT OFF. PERTURBED. ANGRY. UPSET.
MAD.
AND THAT IS NEVER GOOD, NEVER GOOD AT ALL.
I WONDER WHICH FACE HE WOULD WEAR TO SCOLD ME?
A KINGLY CROWN WEPT ON COBBLESTONE ROADS.
HE SHED TEARS FOR SHED BLOOD AT HIS FEET.
I DANCED FOR HIS PLEASURE, MY JESTER HAT JESTING,
AND LAUGHED AT THE CORPSE OF HIS QUEEN.

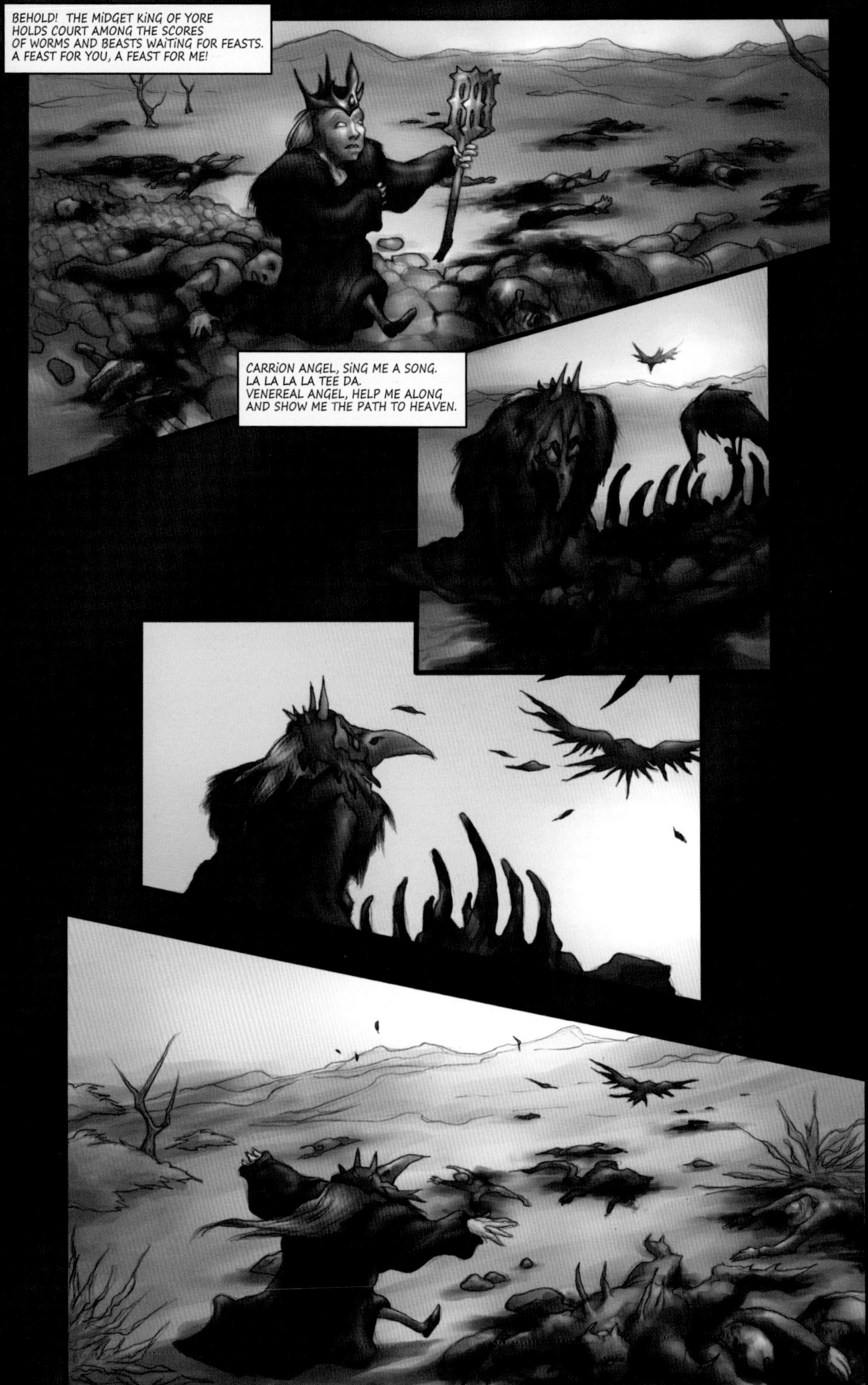
BEHOLD! THE MIDGET KING OF YORE
HOLDS COURT AMONG THE SCORES
OF WORMS AND BEASTS WAITING FOR FEASTS.
A FEAST FOR YOU, A FEAST FOR ME!
CARRION ANGEL, SING ME A SONG.
LA LA LA LA TEE DA.
VENEREAL ANGEL, HELP ME ALONG
AND SHOW ME THE PATH TO HEAVEN.

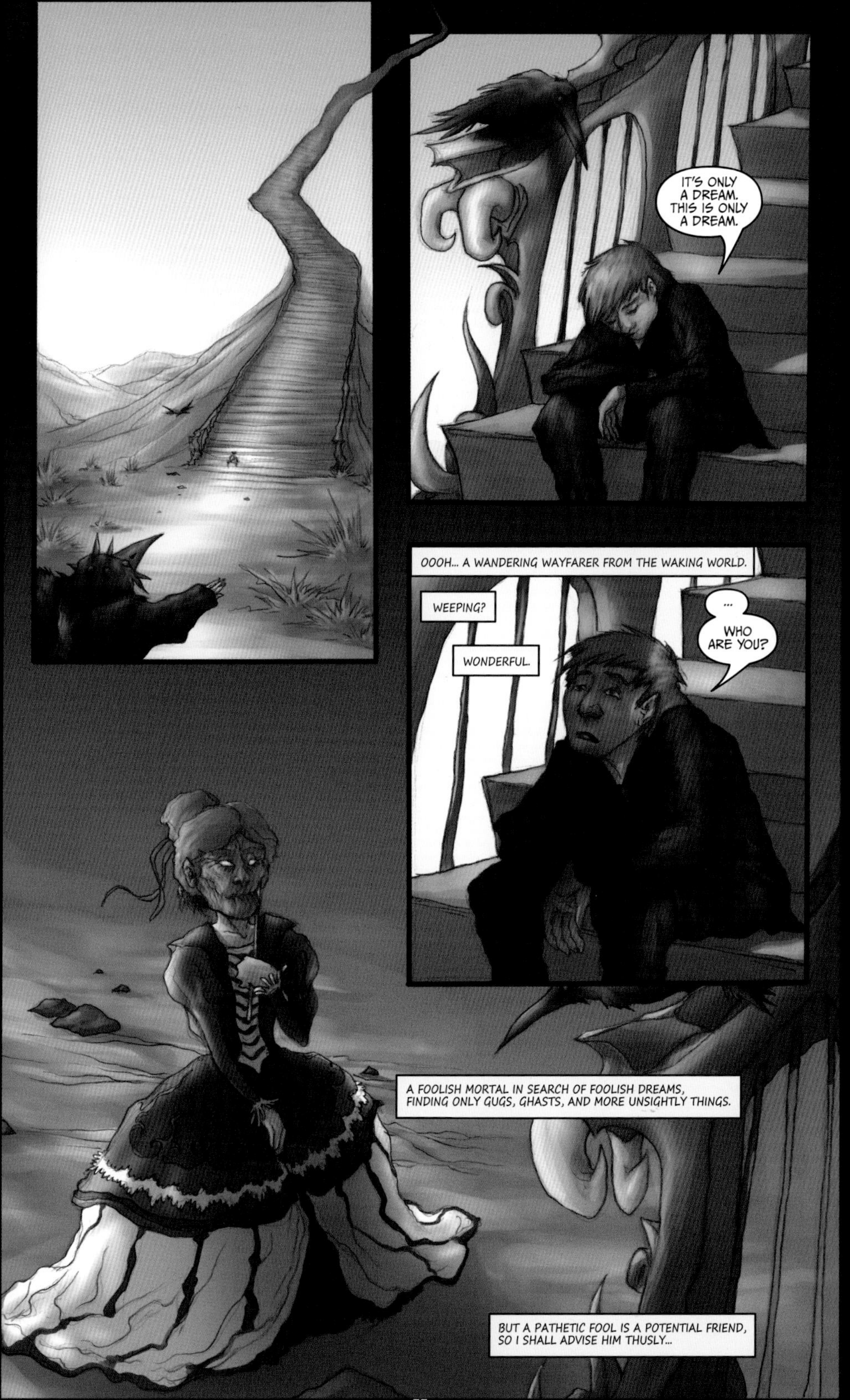
IT'S ONLY A DREAM. THIS IS ONLY A DREAM.
OOOH... A WANDERING WAYFARER FROM THE WAKING WORLD.
WEEPING?
WONDERFUL.
...
WHO ARE YOU?
A FOOLISH MORTAL IN SEARCH OF FOOLISH DREAMS, FINDING ONLY GUGS, GHASTS, AND MORE UNSIGHTLY THINGS.
BUT A PATHETIC FOOL IS A POTENTIAL FRIEND, SO I SHALL ADVISE HIM THUSLY...

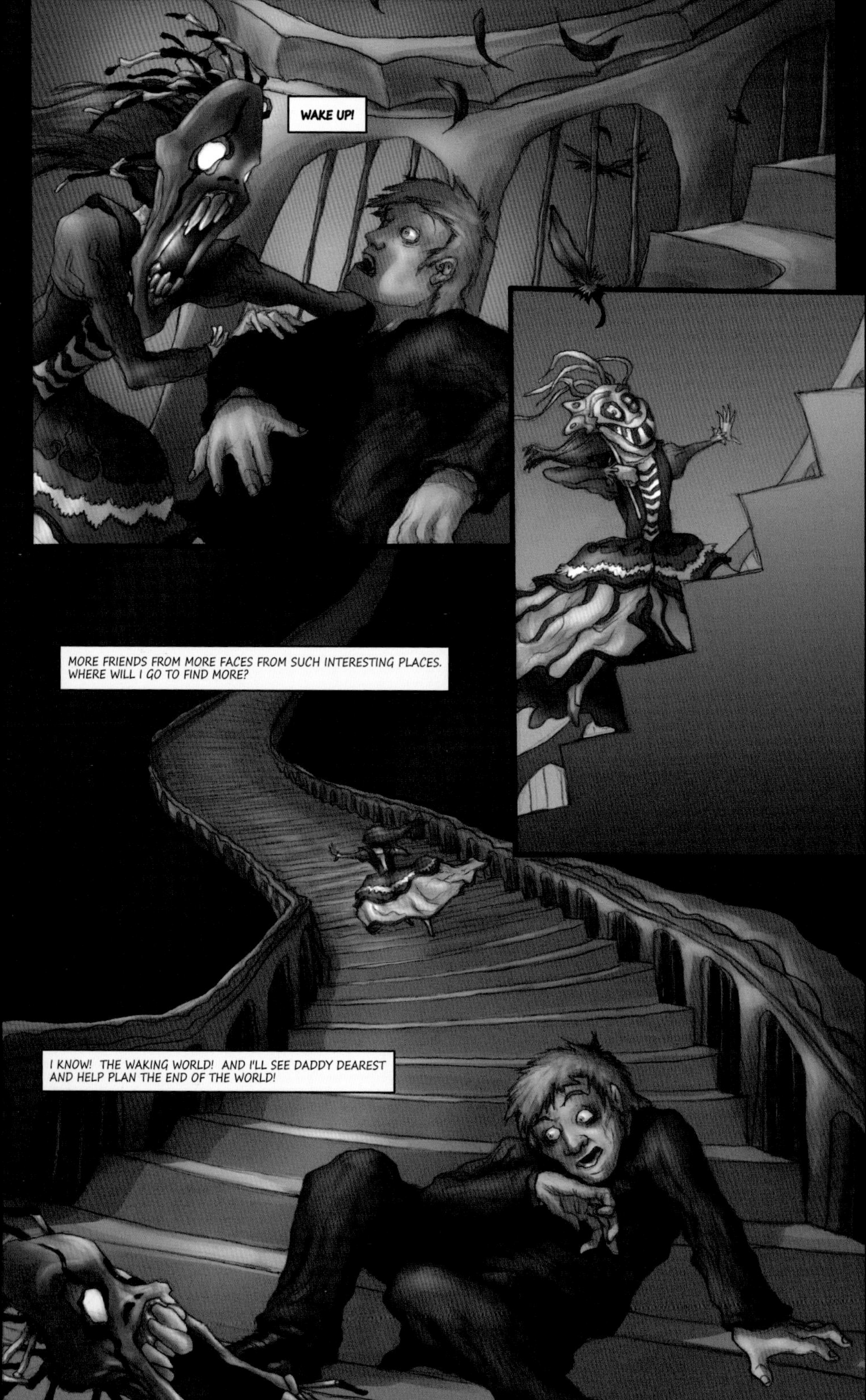
WAKE UP!
MORE FRIENDS FROM MORE FACES FROM SUCH INTERESTING PLACES. WHERE WILL I GO TO FIND MORE?
I KNOW! THE WAKING WORLD! AND I'LL SEE DADDY DEAREST AND HELP PLAN THE END OF THE WORLD!

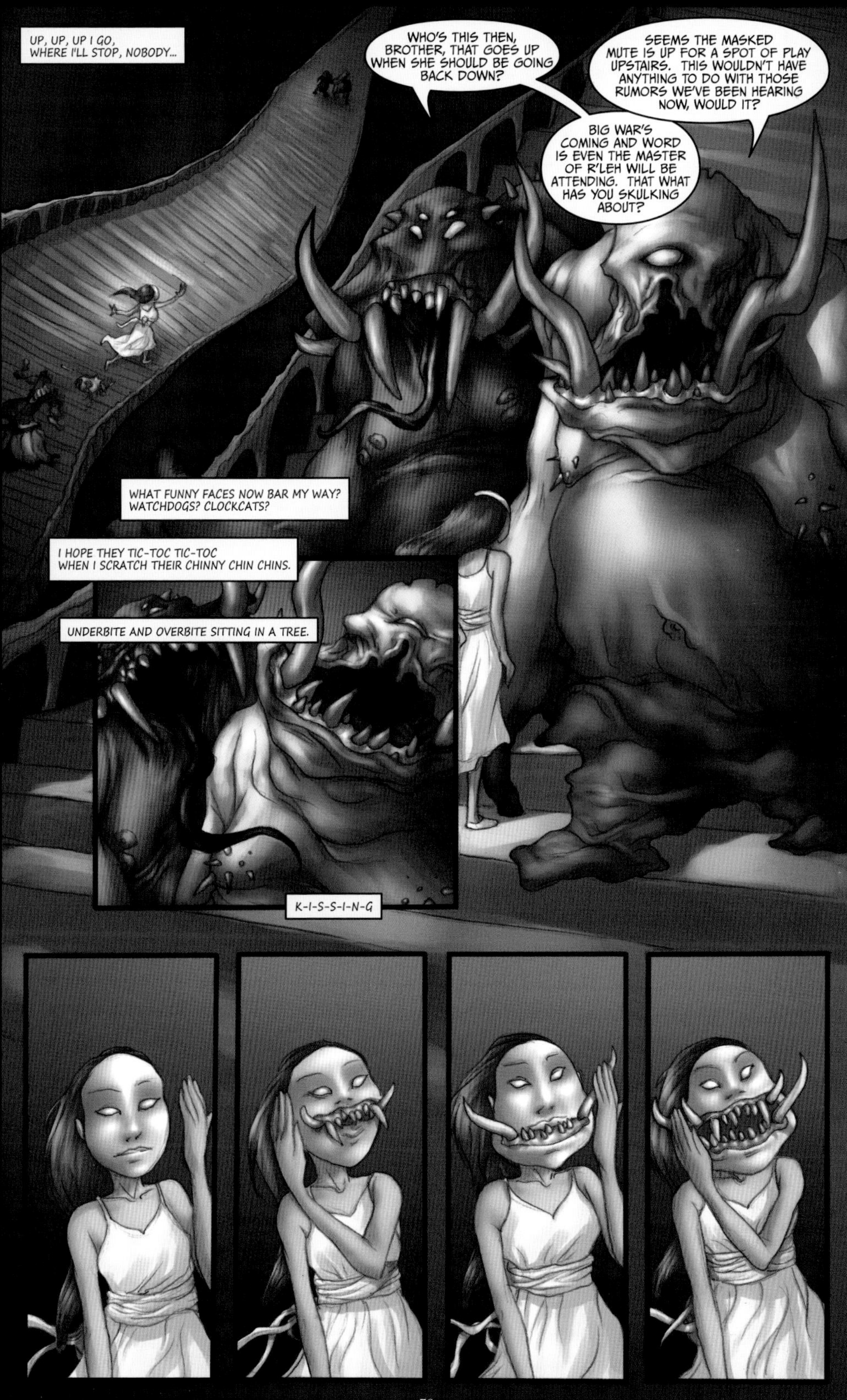
UP, UP, UP I GO,
WHERE I'LL STOP, NOBODY...
WHO'S THIS THEN, BROTHER, THAT GOES UP WHEN SHE SHOULD BE GOING BACK DOWN?
SEEMS THE MASKED MUTE IS UP FOR A SPOT OF PLAY UPSTAIRS. THIS WOULDN'T HAVE ANYTHING TO DO WITH THOSE RUMORS WE'VE BEEN HEARING NOW, WOULD IT?
BIG WAR'S COMING AND WORD IS EVEN THE MASTER OF R'LEH WILL BE ATTENDING. THAT WHAT HAS YOU SKULKING ABOUT?
WHAT FUNNY FACES NOW BAR MY WAY?
WATCHDOGS? CLOCKCATS?
I HOPE THEY TIC-TOC TIC-TOC
WHEN I SCRATCH THEIR CHINNY CHIN CHINS.
UNDERBITE AND OVERBITE SITTING IN A TREE.
K-I-S-S-I-N-G

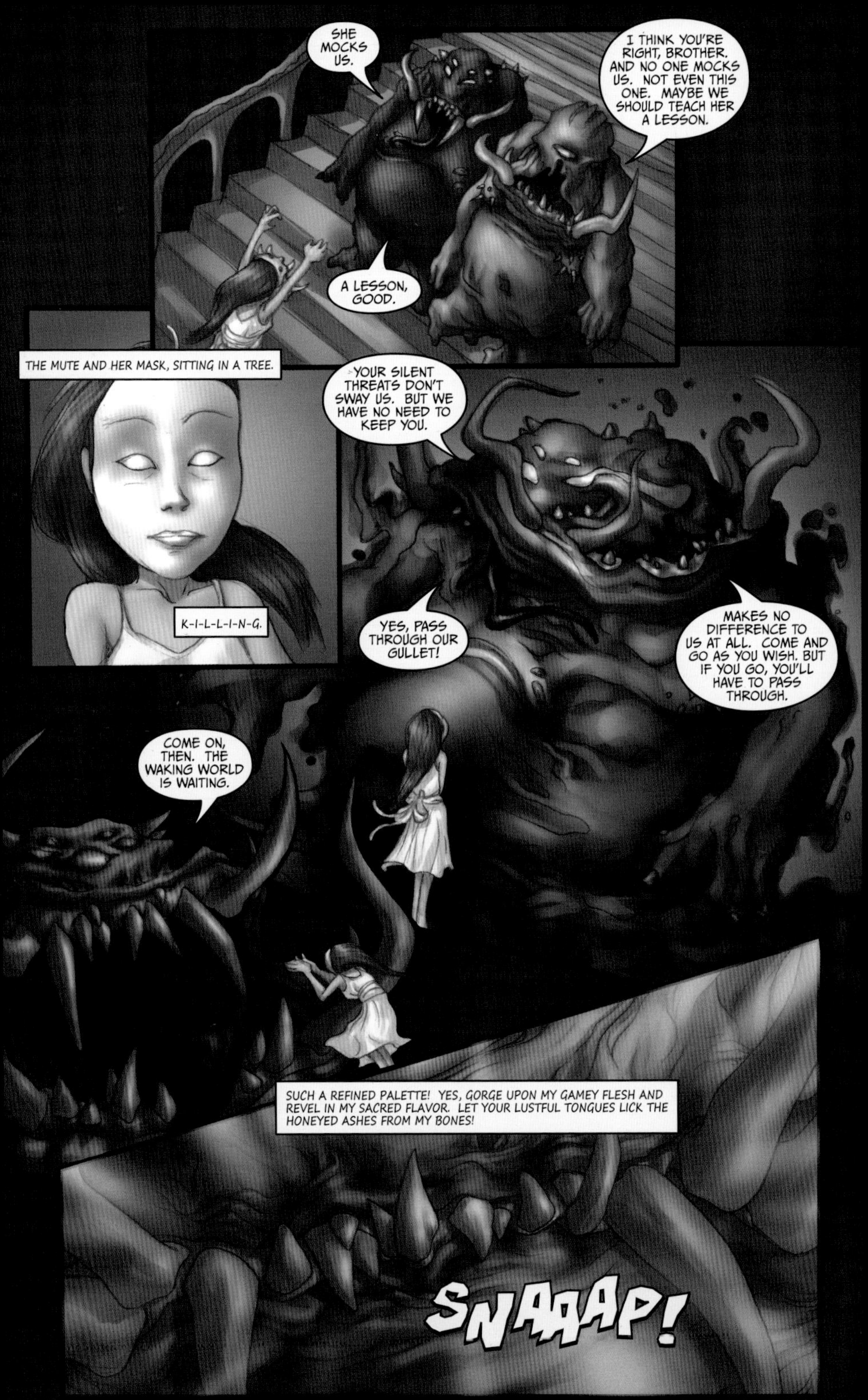
SHE MOCKS US.
I THINK YOU'RE RIGHT, BROTHER. AND NO ONE MOCKS US. NOT EVEN THIS ONE. MAYBE WE SHOULD TEACH HER A LESSON.
A LESSON, GOOD.
THE MUTE AND HER MASK, SITTING IN A TREE.
K-I-L-L-I-N-G.
YOUR SILENT THREATS DON'T SWAY US. BUT WE HAVE NO NEED TO KEEP YOU.
YES, PASS THROUGH OUR GULLET!
MAKES NO DIFFERENCE TO US AT ALL. COME AND GO AS YOU WISH. BUT IF YOU GO, YOU'LL HAVE TO PASS THROUGH.
COME ON, THEN. THE WAKING WORLD IS WAITING.
SUCH A REFINED PALETTE! YES, GORGE UPON MY GAMEY FLESH AND REVEL IN MY SACRED FLAVOR. LET YOUR LUSTFUL TONGUES LICK THE HONEYED ASHES FROM MY BONES!
SNAAAP!

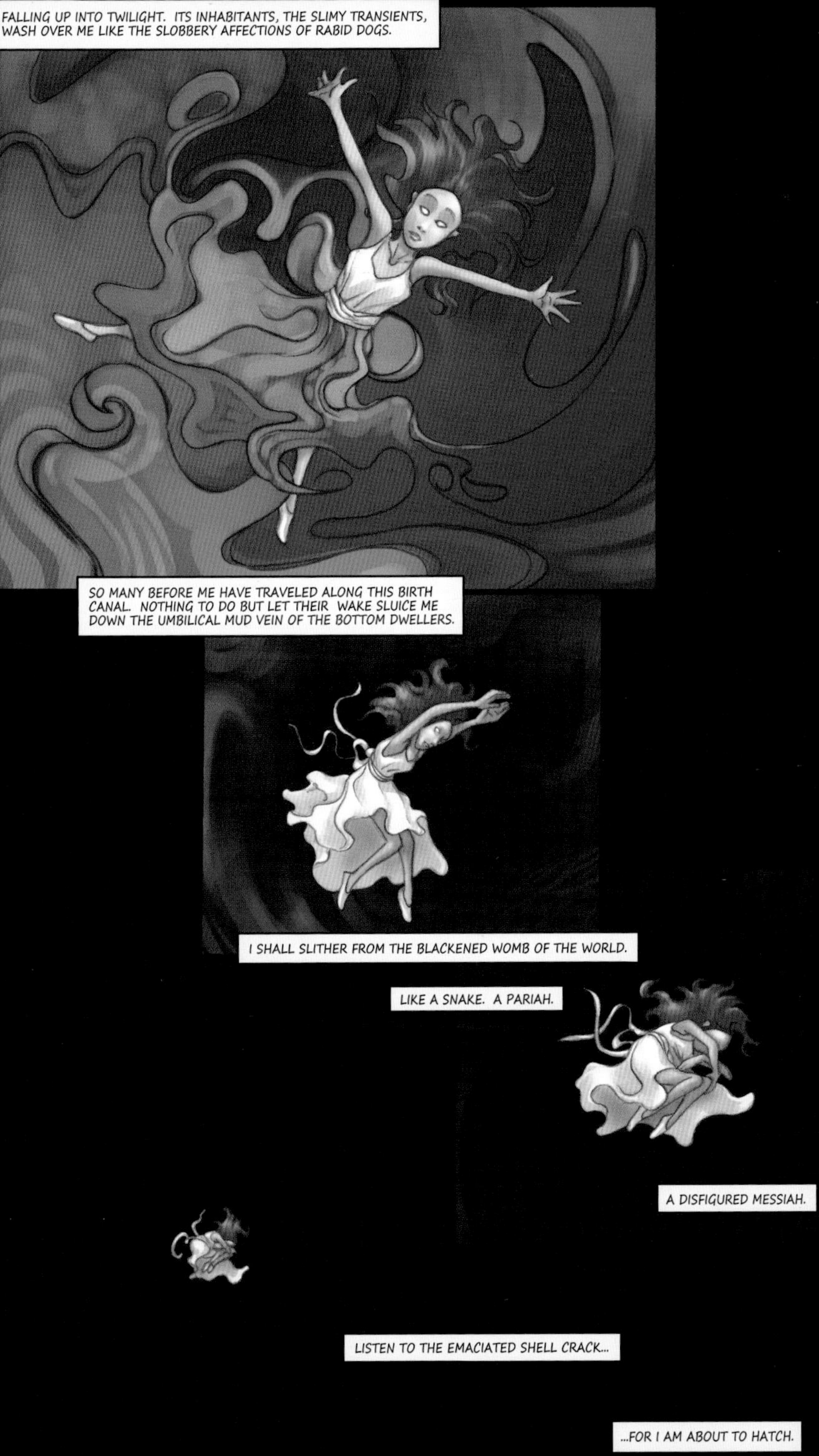
FALLING UP INTO TWILIGHT. ITS INHABITANTS, THE SLIMY TRANSIENTS, WASH OVER ME LIKE THE SLOBBERY AFFECTIONS OF RABID DOGS.
SO MANY BEFORE ME HAVE TRAVELED ALONG THIS BIRTH CANAL. NOTHING TO DO BUT LET THEIR WAKE SLUICE ME DOWN THE UMBILICAL MUD VEIN OF THE BOTTOM DWELLERS.
I SHALL SLITHER FROM THE BLACKENED WOMB OF THE WORLD.
LIKE A SNAKE. A PARIAH.
A DISFIGURED MESSIAH.
LISTEN TO THE EMACIATED SHELL CRACK...
...FOR I AM ABOUT TO HATCH.

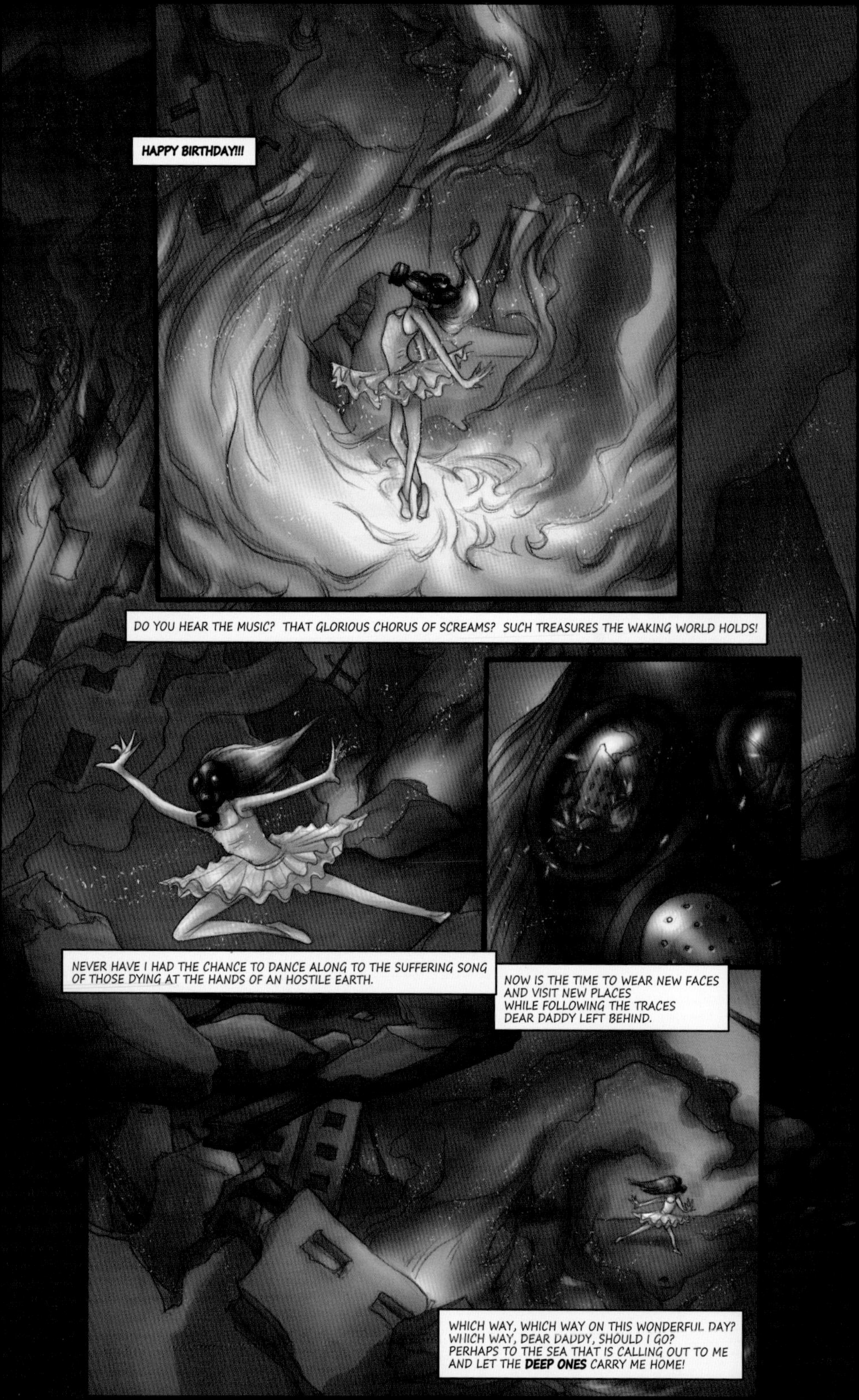
HAPPY BIRTHDAY!!!
DO YOU HEAR THE MUSIC? THAT GLORIOUS CHORUS OF SCREAMS? SUCH TREASURES THE WAKING WORLD HOLDS!
NEVER HAVE I HAD THE CHANCE TO DANCE ALONG TO THE SUFFERING SONG OF THOSE DYING AT THE HANDS OF AN HOSTILE EARTH.
NOW IS THE TIME TO WEAR NEW FACES AND VISIT NEW PLACES WHILE FOLLOWING THE TRACES DEAR DADDY LEFT BEHIND.
WHICH WAY, WHICH WAY ON THIS WONDERFUL DAY? WHICH WAY, DEAR DADDY, SHOULD I GO? PERHAPS TO THE SEA THAT IS CALLING OUT TO ME AND LET THE **DEEP ONES** CARRY ME HOME!

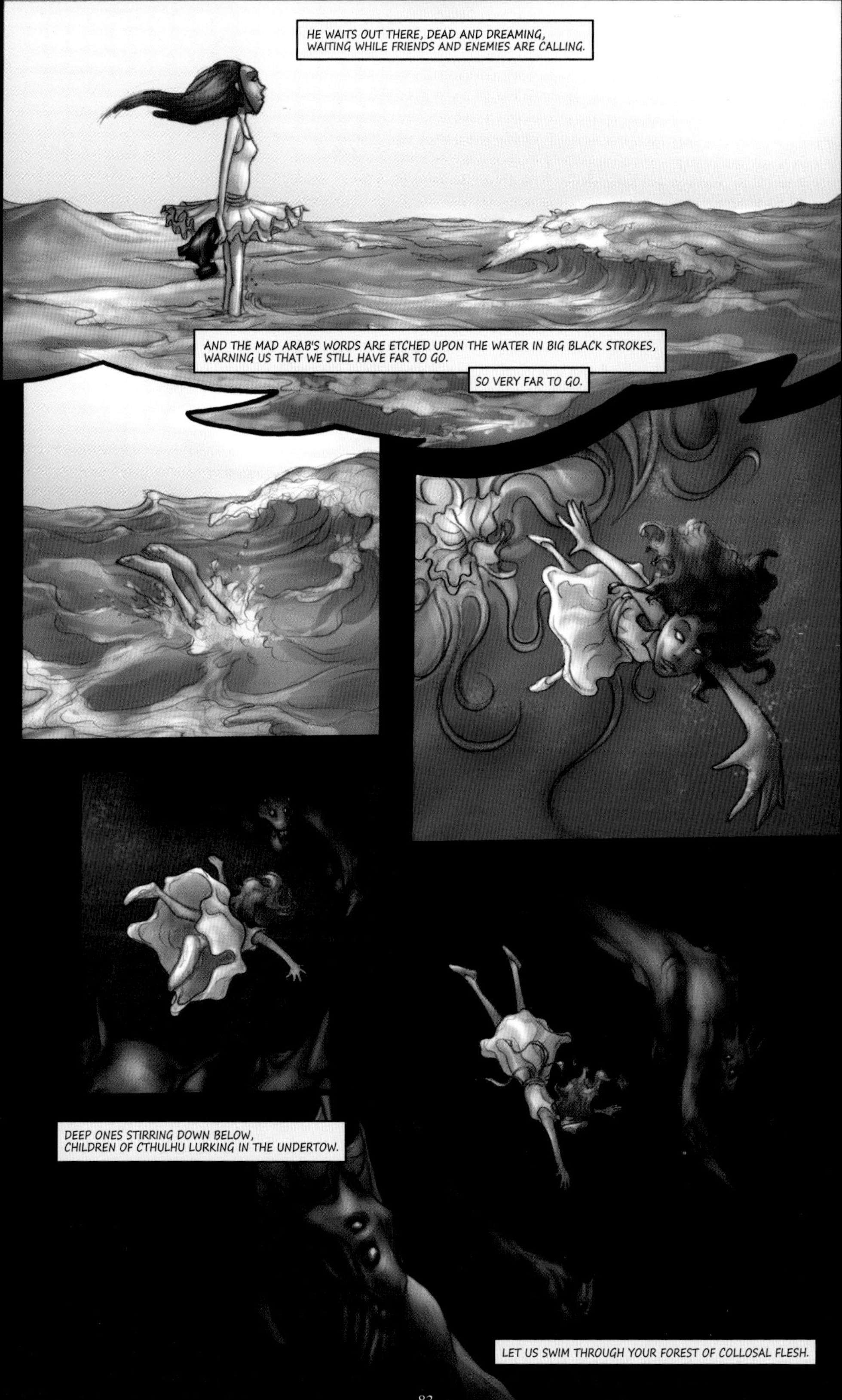
HE WAITS OUT THERE, DEAD AND DREAMING,
WAITING WHILE FRIENDS AND ENEMIES ARE CALLING.
AND THE MAD ARAB'S WORDS ARE ETCHED UPON THE WATER IN BIG BLACK STROKES,
WARNING US THAT WE STILL HAVE FAR TO GO.
SO VERY FAR TO GO.
DEEP ONES STIRRING DOWN BELOW,
CHILDREN OF CTHULHU LURKING IN THE UNDERTOW.
LET US SWIM THROUGH YOUR FOREST OF COLLOSAL FLESH.

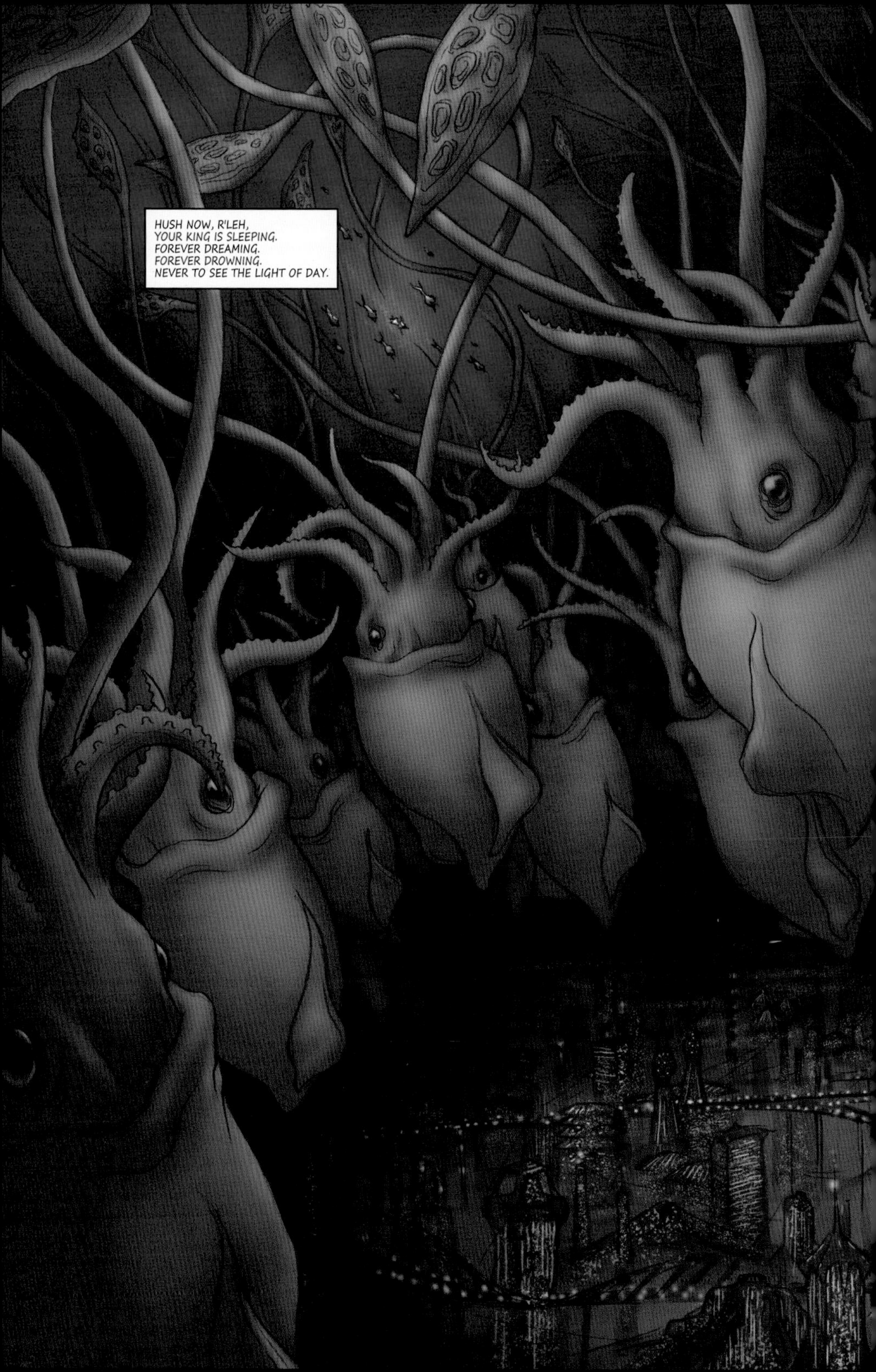
HUSH NOW, R'LEH,
YOUR KING IS SLEEPING.
FOREVER DREAMING.
FOREVER DROWNING.
NEVER TO SEE THE LIGHT OF DAY.

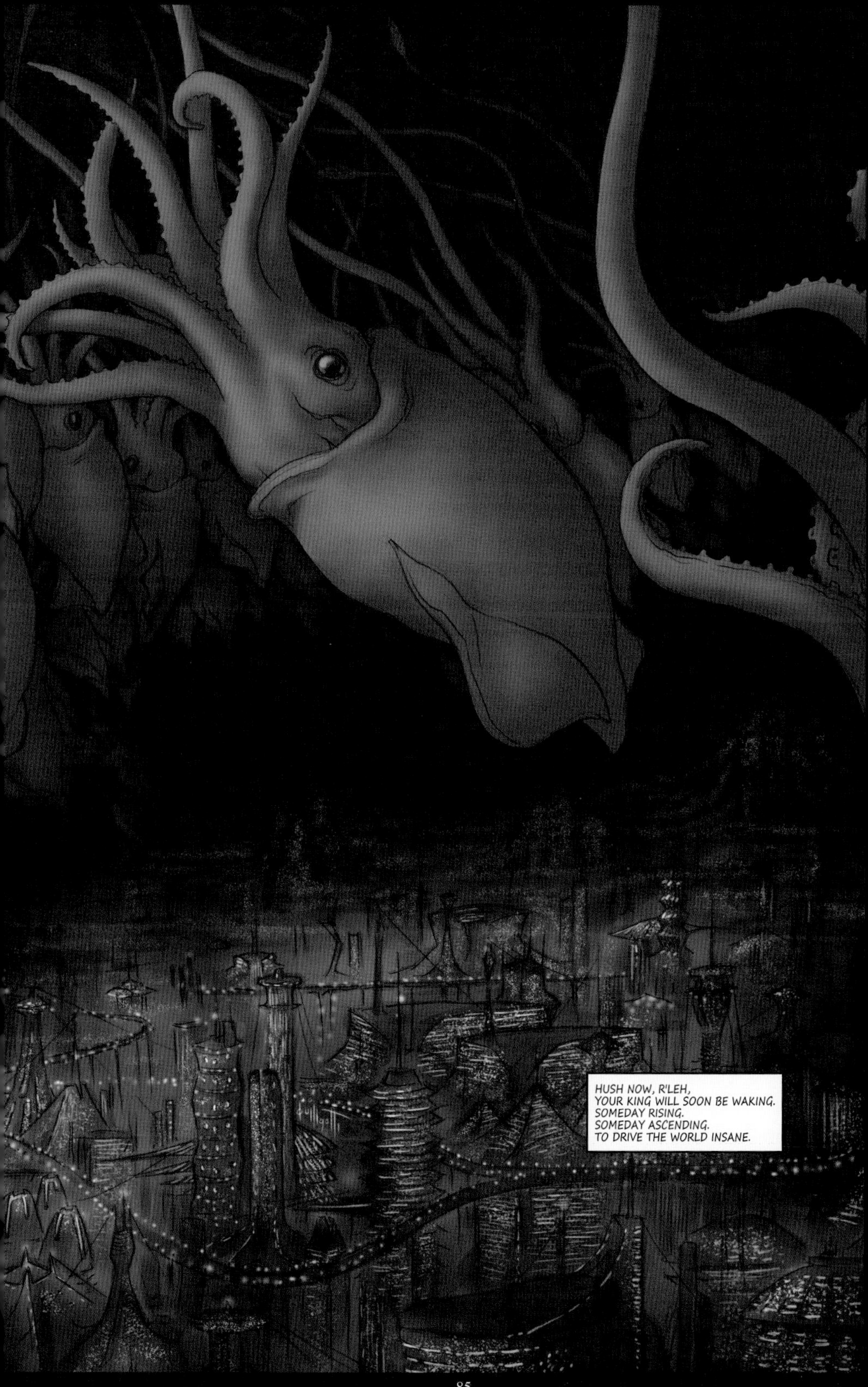
HUSH NOW, R'LEH,
YOUR KING WILL SOON BE WAKING.
SOMEDAY RISING.
SOMEDAY ASCENDING.
TO DRIVE THE WORLD INSANE.

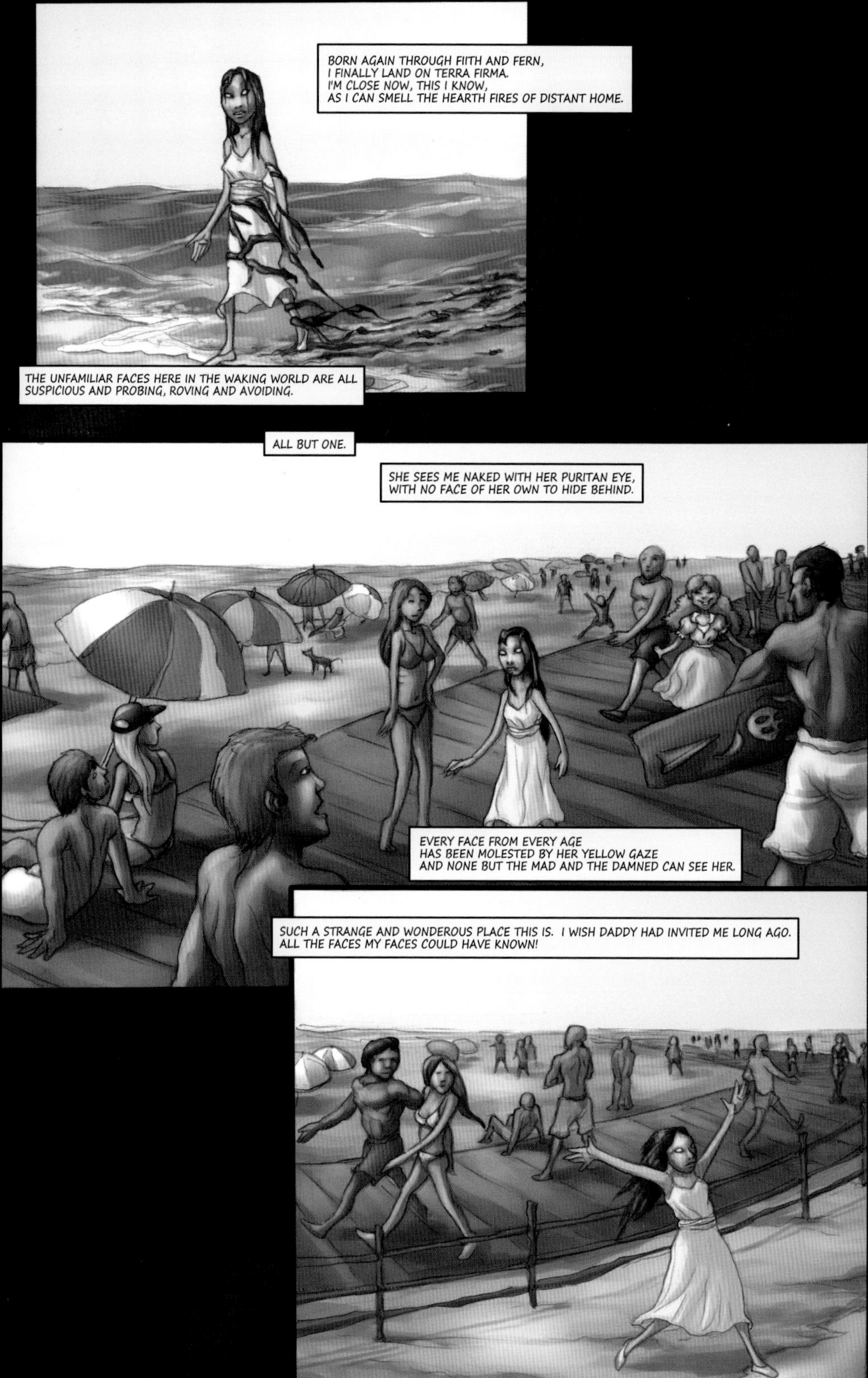
BORN AGAIN THROUGH FIITH AND FERN,
I FINALLY LAND ON TERRA FIRMA.
I'M CLOSE NOW, THIS I KNOW,
AS I CAN SMELL THE HEARTH FIRES OF DISTANT HOME.
THE UNFAMILIAR FACES HERE IN THE WAKING WORLD ARE ALL SUSPICIOUS AND PROBING, ROVING AND AVOIDING.
ALL BUT ONE.
SHE SEES ME NAKED WITH HER PURITAN EYE,
WITH NO FACE OF HER OWN TO HIDE BEHIND.
EVERY FACE FROM EVERY AGE
HAS BEEN MOLESTED BY HER YELLOW GAZE
AND NONE BUT THE MAD AND THE DAMNED CAN SEE HER.
SUCH A STRANGE AND WONDEROUS PLACE THIS IS. I WISH DADDY HAD INVITED ME LONG AGO.
ALL THE FACES MY FACES COULD HAVE KNOWN!

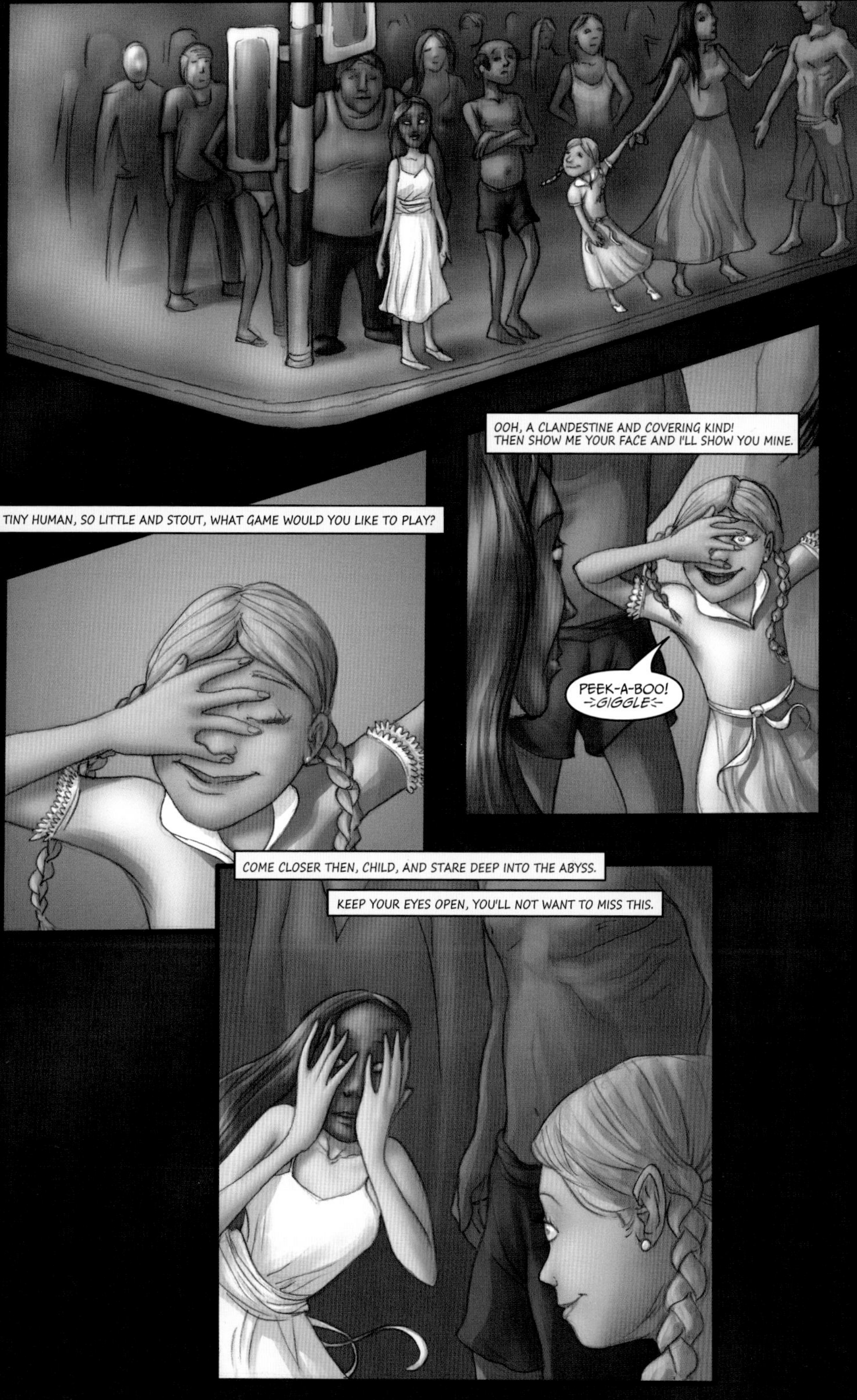

TINY HUMAN, SO LITTLE AND STOUT, WHAT GAME WOULD YOU LIKE TO PLAY?
OOH, A CLANDESTINE AND COVERING KIND! THEN SHOW ME YOUR FACE AND I'LL SHOW YOU MINE.
PEEK-A-BOO! ⇝GIGGLE⇜
COME CLOSER THEN, CHILD, AND STARE DEEP INTO THE ABYSS.
KEEP YOUR EYES OPEN, YOU'LL NOT WANT TO MISS THIS.

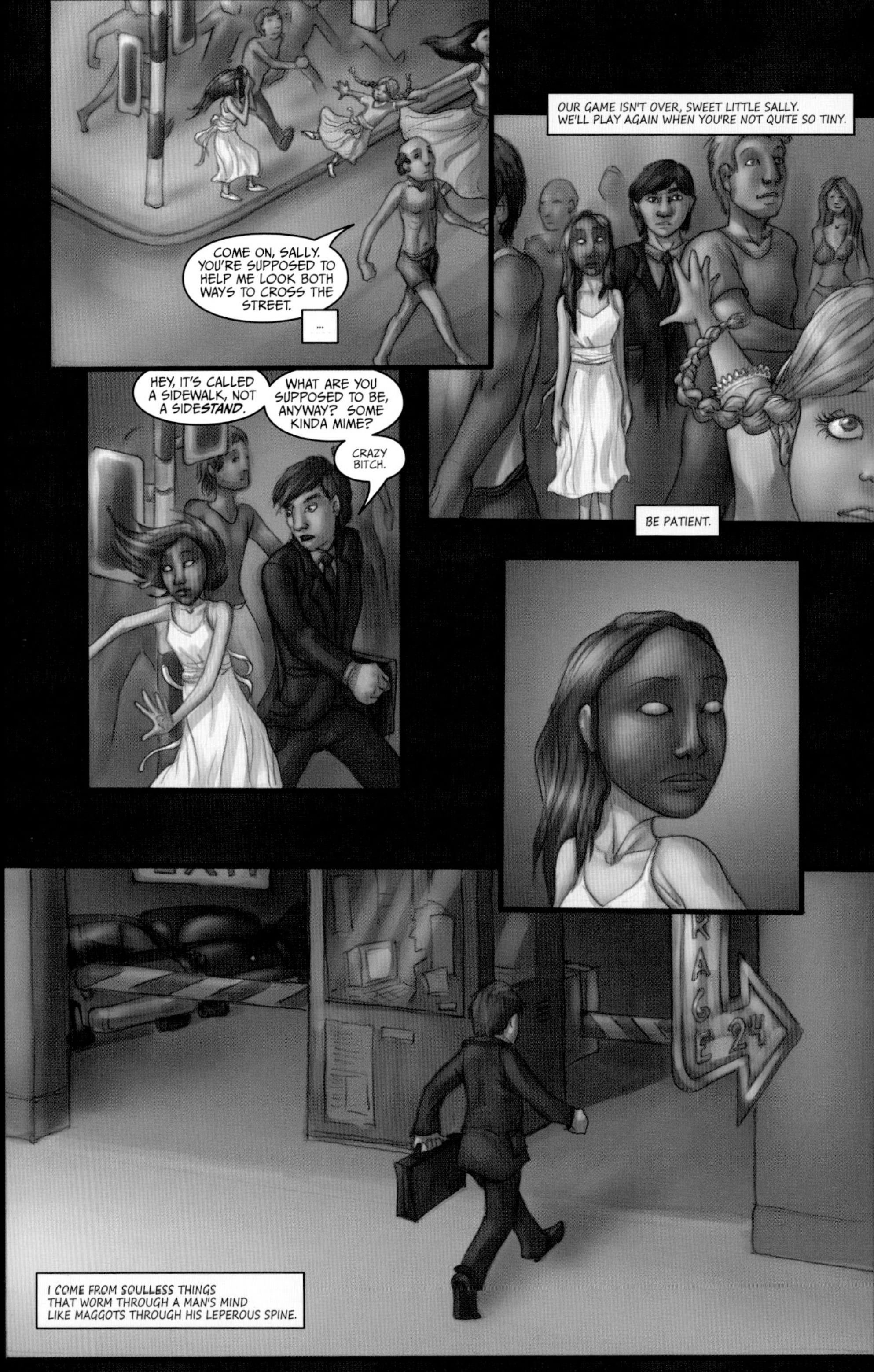
COME ON, SALLY. YOU'RE SUPPOSED TO HELP ME LOOK BOTH WAYS TO CROSS THE STREET.
...
OUR GAME ISN'T OVER, SWEET LITTLE SALLY. WE'LL PLAY AGAIN WHEN YOU'RE NOT QUITE SO TINY.
HEY, IT'S CALLED A SIDEWALK, NOT A SIDE*STAND*.
WHAT ARE YOU SUPPOSED TO BE, ANYWAY? SOME KINDA MIME?
CRAZY BITCH.
BE PATIENT.
I COME FROM SOULLESS THINGS THAT WORM THROUGH A MAN'S MIND LIKE MAGGOTS THROUGH HIS LEPEROUS SPINE.

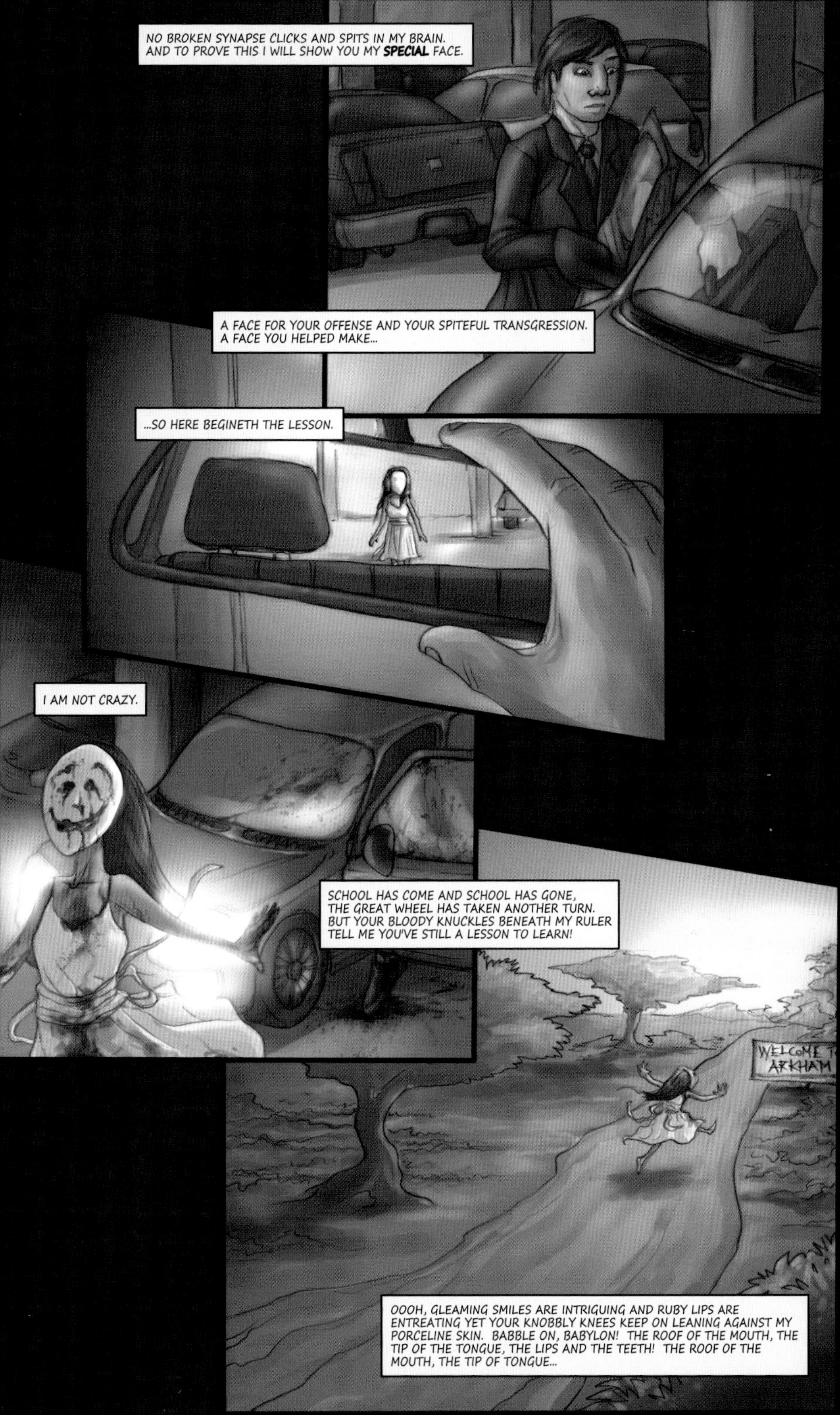
NO BROKEN SYNAPSE CLICKS AND SPITS IN MY BRAIN. AND TO PROVE THIS I WILL SHOW YOU MY **SPECIAL** FACE.
A FACE FOR YOUR OFFENSE AND YOUR SPITEFUL TRANSGRESSION. A FACE YOU HELPED MAKE...
...SO HERE BEGINETH THE LESSON.
I AM NOT CRAZY.
SCHOOL HAS COME AND SCHOOL HAS GONE, THE GREAT WHEEL HAS TAKEN ANOTHER TURN. BUT YOUR BLOODY KNUCKLES BENEATH MY RULER TELL ME YOU'VE STILL A LESSON TO LEARN!
OOOH, GLEAMING SMILES ARE INTRIGUING AND RUBY LIPS ARE ENTREATING YET YOUR KNOBBLY KNEES KEEP ON LEANING AGAINST MY PORCELINE SKIN. BABBLE ON, BABYLON! THE ROOF OF THE MOUTH, THE TIP OF THE TONGUE, THE LIPS AND THE TEETH! THE ROOF OF THE MOUTH, THE TIP OF TONGUE...

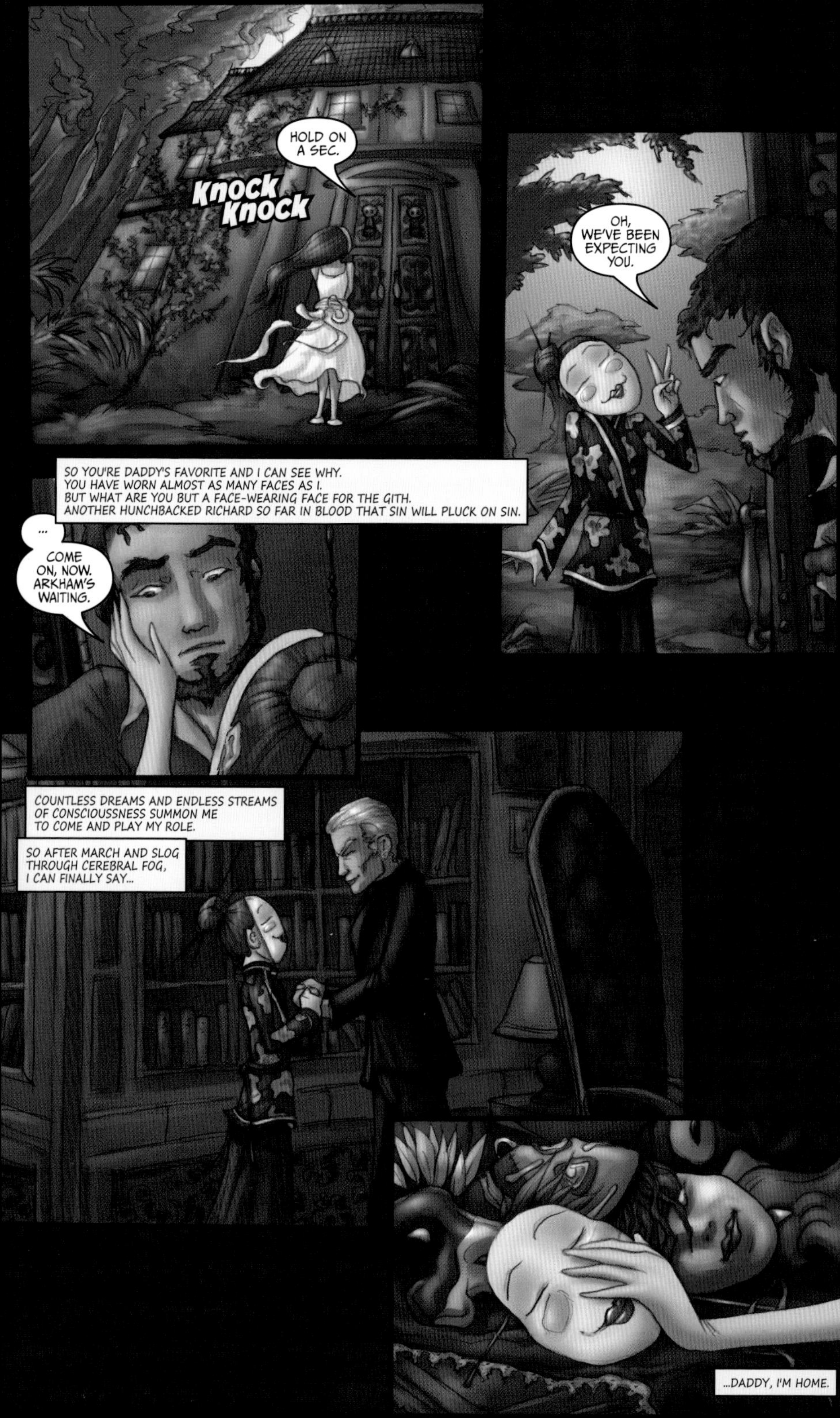
HOLD ON A SEC.
Knock Knock
OH, WE'VE BEEN EXPECTING YOU.
SO YOU'RE DADDY'S FAVORITE AND I CAN SEE WHY. YOU HAVE WORN ALMOST AS MANY FACES AS I. BUT WHAT ARE YOU BUT A FACE-WEARING FACE FOR THE GITH. ANOTHER HUNCHBACKED RICHARD SO FAR IN BLOOD THAT SIN WILL PLUCK ON SIN.
...
COME ON, NOW. ARKHAM'S WAITING.
COUNTLESS DREAMS AND ENDLESS STREAMS OF CONSCIOUSSNESS SUMMON ME TO COME AND PLAY MY ROLE.
SO AFTER MARCH AND SLOG THROUGH CEREBRAL FOG, I CAN FINALLY SAY...
...DADDY, I'M HOME.

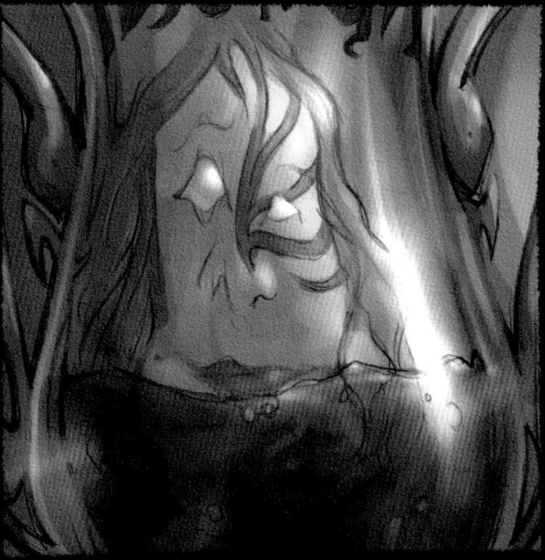

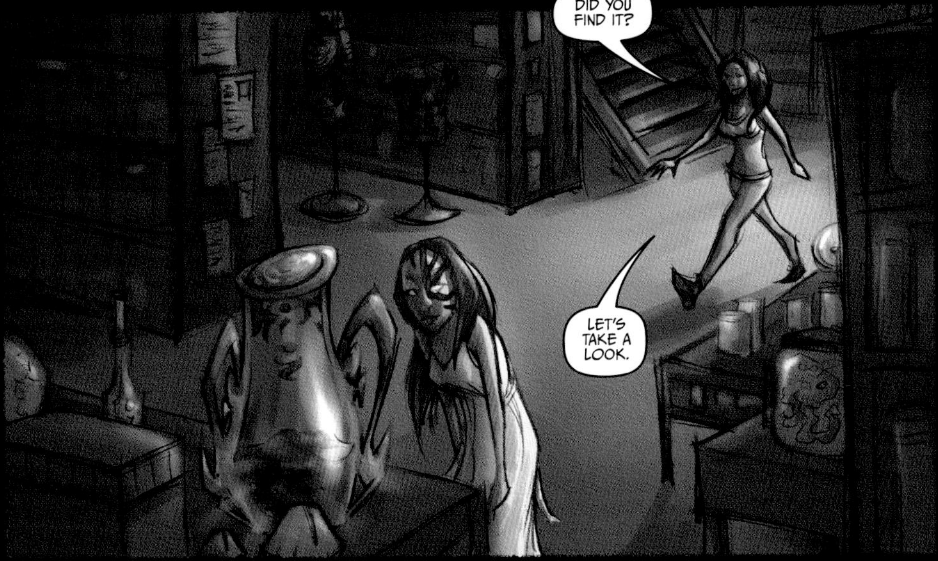
DID YOU FIND IT?
LET'S TAKE A LOOK.

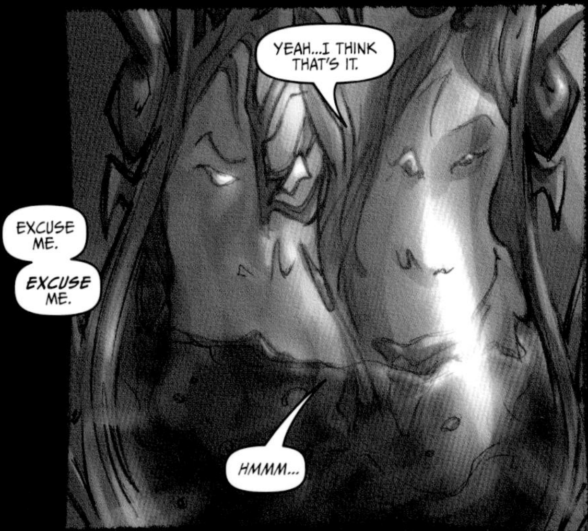
YEAH...I THINK THAT'S IT.
EXCUSE ME.
EXCUSE ME.
HMMM...

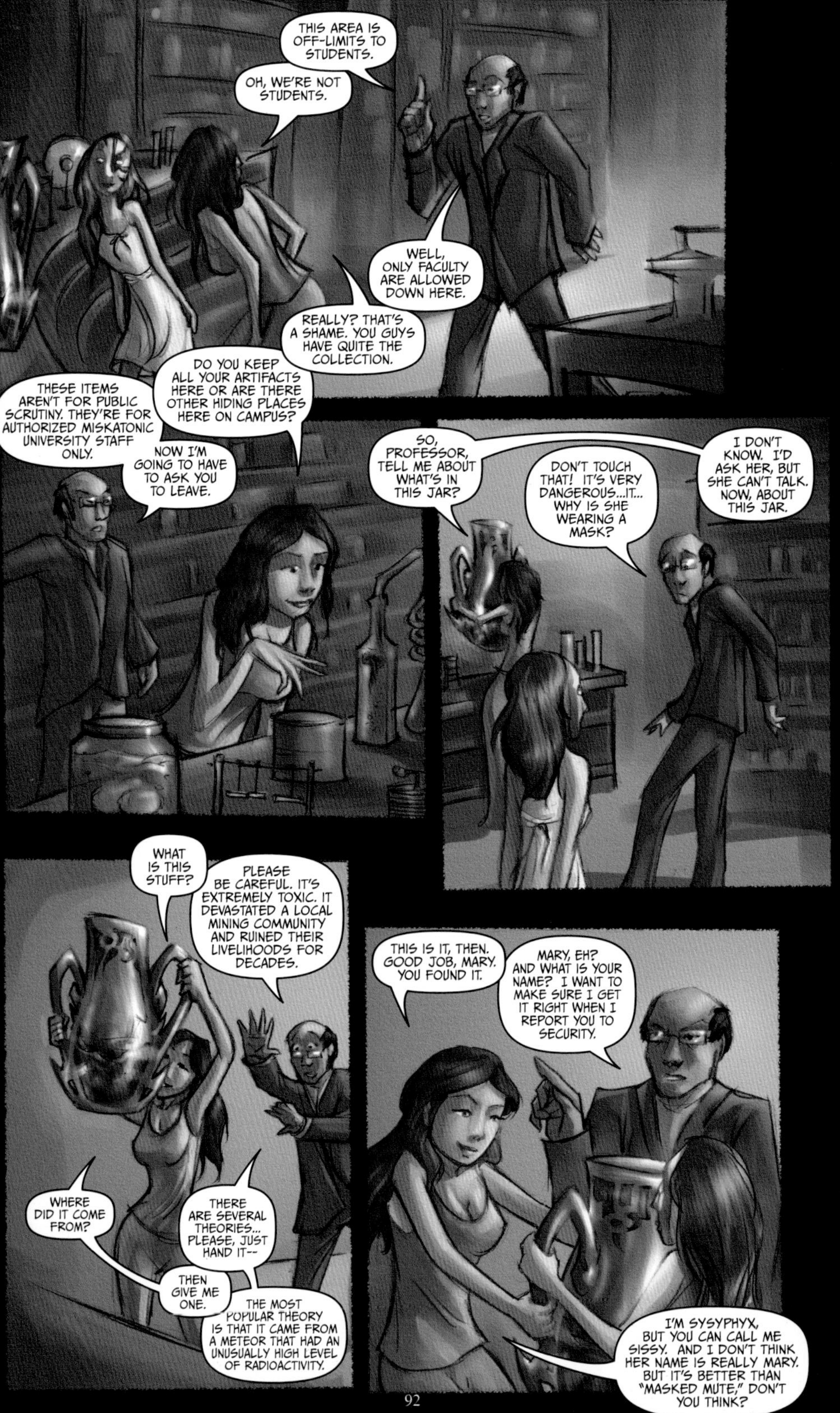
THIS AREA IS OFF-LIMITS TO STUDENTS.
OH, WE'RE NOT STUDENTS.
WELL, ONLY FACULTY ARE ALLOWED DOWN HERE.
REALLY? THAT'S A SHAME. YOU GUYS HAVE QUITE THE COLLECTION.
DO YOU KEEP ALL YOUR ARTIFACTS HERE OR ARE THERE OTHER HIDING PLACES HERE ON CAMPUS?
THESE ITEMS AREN'T FOR PUBLIC SCRUTINY. THEY'RE FOR AUTHORIZED MISKATONIC UNIVERSITY STAFF ONLY.
NOW I'M GOING TO HAVE TO ASK YOU TO LEAVE.
SO, PROFESSOR, TELL ME ABOUT WHAT'S IN THIS JAR?
DON'T TOUCH THAT! IT'S VERY DANGEROUS...IT... WHY IS SHE WEARING A MASK?
I DON'T KNOW. I'D ASK HER, BUT SHE CAN'T TALK. NOW, ABOUT THIS JAR.
WHAT IS THIS STUFF?
PLEASE BE CAREFUL. IT'S EXTREMELY TOXIC. IT DEVASTATED A LOCAL MINING COMMUNITY AND RUINED THEIR LIVELIHOODS FOR DECADES.
WHERE DID IT COME FROM?
THERE ARE SEVERAL THEORIES... PLEASE, JUST HAND IT--
THEN GIVE ME ONE.
THE MOST POPULAR THEORY IS THAT IT CAME FROM A METEOR THAT HAD AN UNUSUALLY HIGH LEVEL OF RADIOACTIVITY.
THIS IS IT, THEN. GOOD JOB, MARY. YOU FOUND IT.
MARY, EH? AND WHAT IS YOUR NAME? I WANT TO MAKE SURE I GET IT RIGHT WHEN I REPORT YOU TO SECURITY.
I'M SYSYPHYX, BUT YOU CAN CALL ME SISSY. AND I DON'T THINK HER NAME IS REALLY MARY. BUT IT'S BETTER THAN "MASKED MUTE," DON'T YOU THINK?

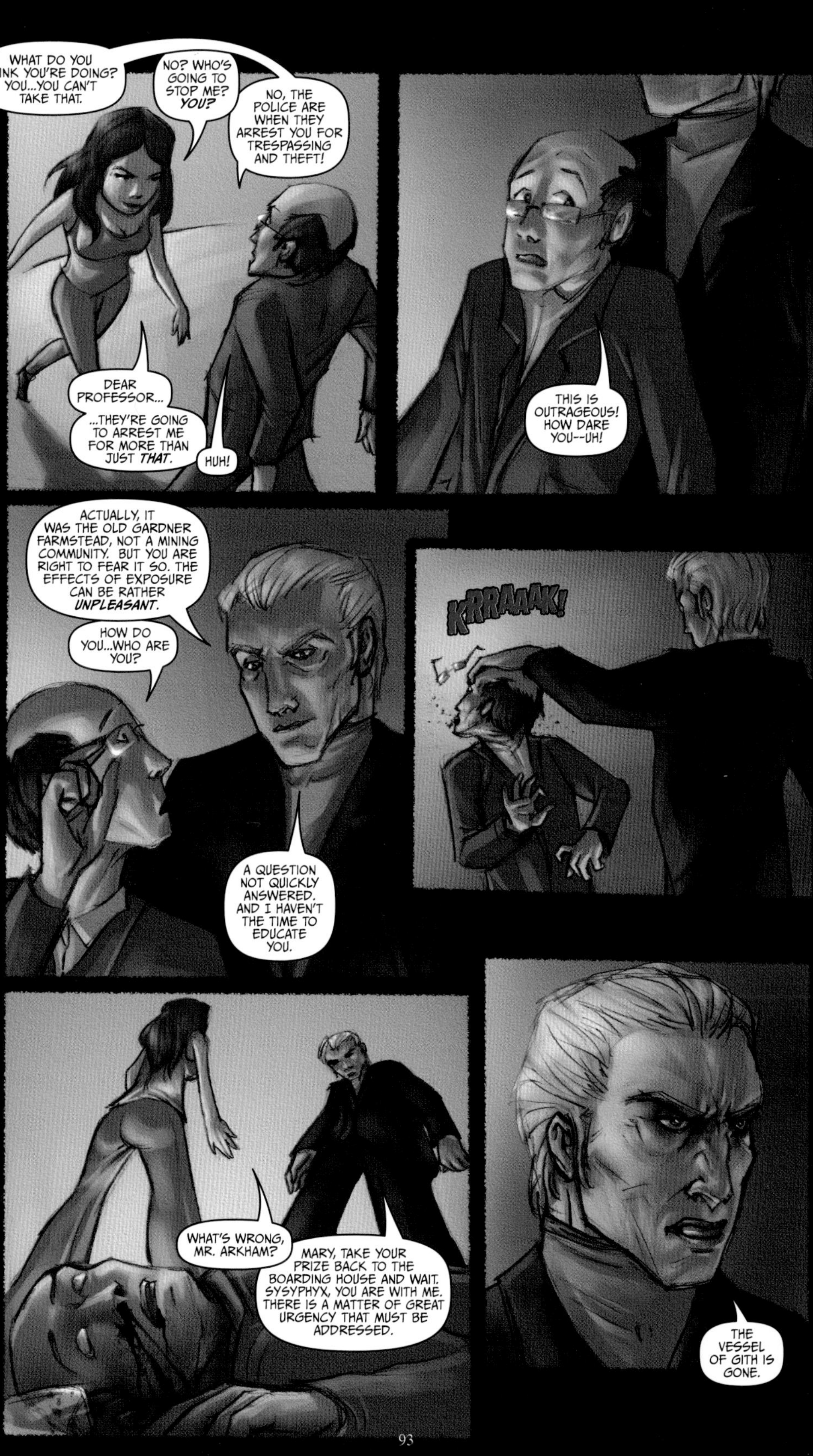
WHAT DO YOU THINK YOU'RE DOING? YOU...YOU CAN'T TAKE THAT.
NO? WHO'S GOING TO STOP ME? YOU?
NO, THE POLICE ARE WHEN THEY ARREST YOU FOR TRESPASSING AND THEFT!
DEAR PROFESSOR...
...THEY'RE GOING TO ARREST ME FOR MORE THAN JUST THAT.
HUH!
THIS IS OUTRAGEOUS! HOW DARE YOU--UH!
ACTUALLY, IT WAS THE OLD GARDNER FARMSTEAD, NOT A MINING COMMUNITY. BUT YOU ARE RIGHT TO FEAR IT SO. THE EFFECTS OF EXPOSURE CAN BE RATHER UNPLEASANT.
HOW DO YOU...WHO ARE YOU?
A QUESTION NOT QUICKLY ANSWERED. AND I HAVEN'T THE TIME TO EDUCATE YOU.
KRRAAAK!
WHAT'S WRONG, MR. ARKHAM?
MARY, TAKE YOUR PRIZE BACK TO THE BOARDING HOUSE AND WAIT. SYSYPHYX, YOU ARE WITH ME. THERE IS A MATTER OF GREAT URGENCY THAT MUST BE ADDRESSED.
THE VESSEL OF GITH IS GONE.

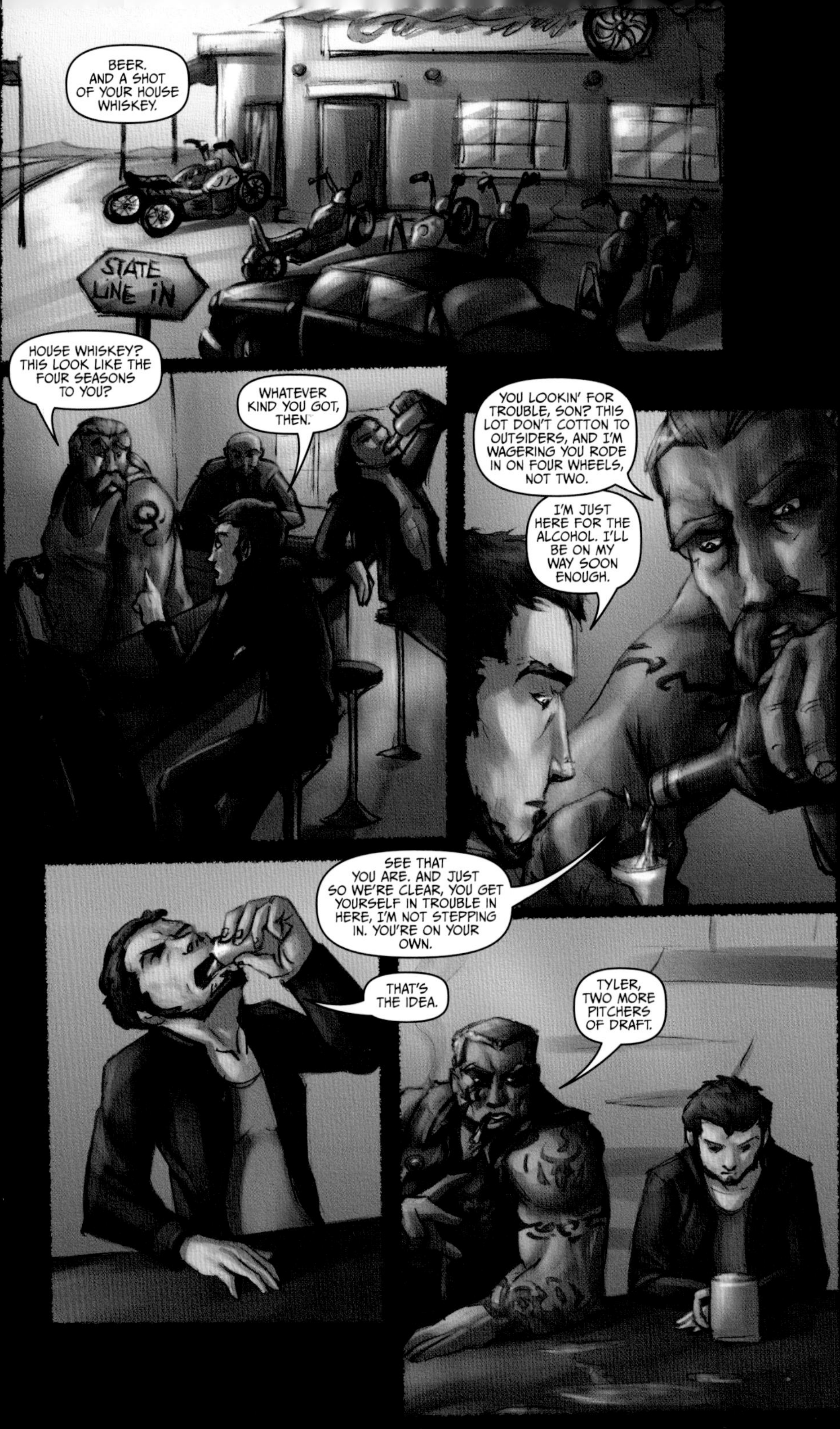
BEER. AND A SHOT OF YOUR HOUSE WHISKEY.
STATE LINE IN
HOUSE WHISKEY? THIS LOOK LIKE THE FOUR SEASONS TO YOU?
WHATEVER KIND YOU GOT, THEN.
YOU LOOKIN' FOR TROUBLE, SON? THIS LOT DON'T COTTON TO OUTSIDERS, AND I'M WAGERING YOU RODE IN ON FOUR WHEELS, NOT TWO.
I'M JUST HERE FOR THE ALCOHOL. I'LL BE ON MY WAY SOON ENOUGH.
SEE THAT YOU ARE. AND JUST SO WE'RE CLEAR, YOU GET YOURSELF IN TROUBLE IN HERE, I'M NOT STEPPING IN. YOU'RE ON YOUR OWN.
THAT'S THE IDEA.
TYLER, TWO MORE PITCHERS OF DRAFT.

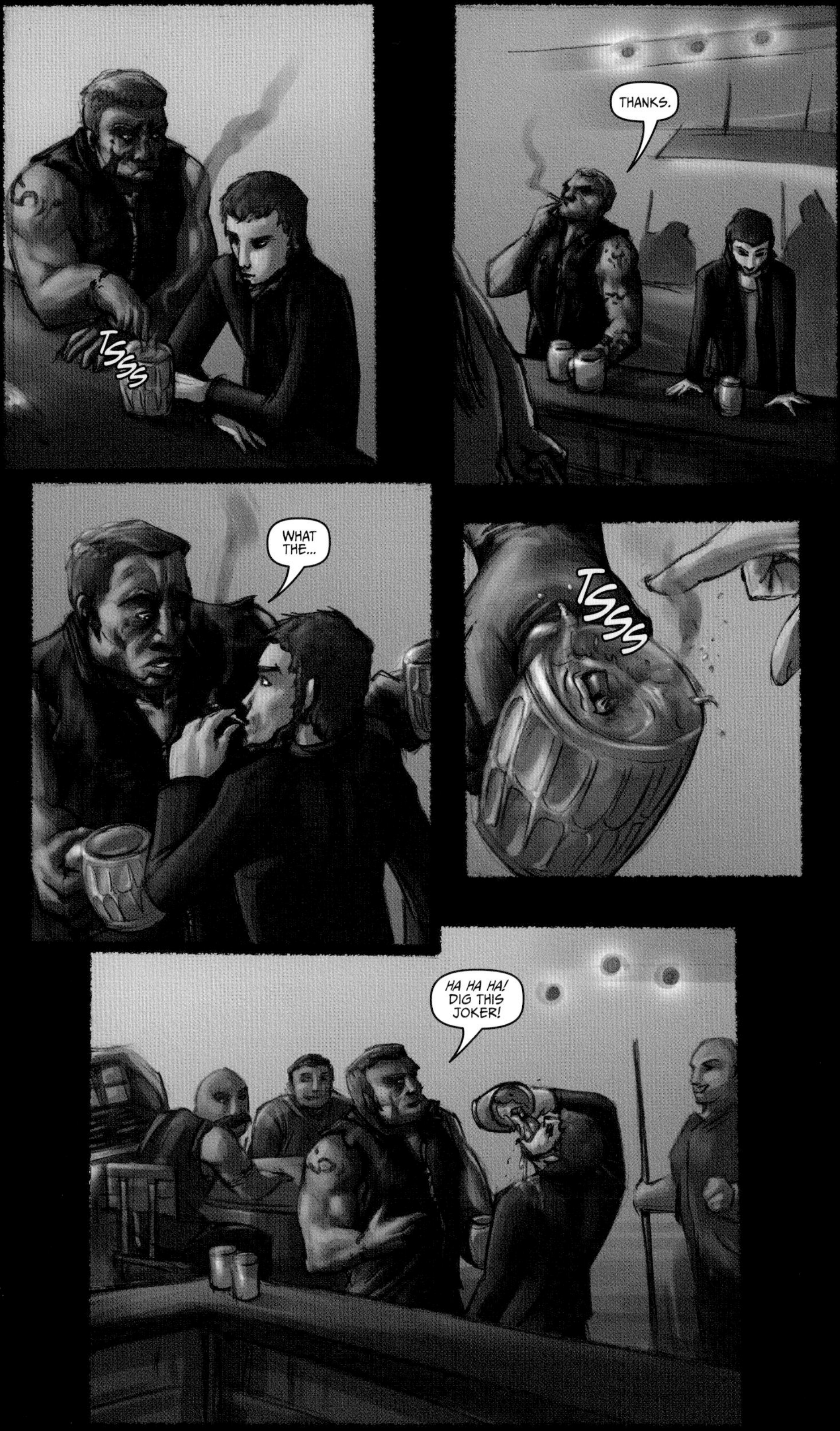
TSSS
THANKS.
WHAT THE...
TSSS
HA HA HA! DIG THIS JOKER!

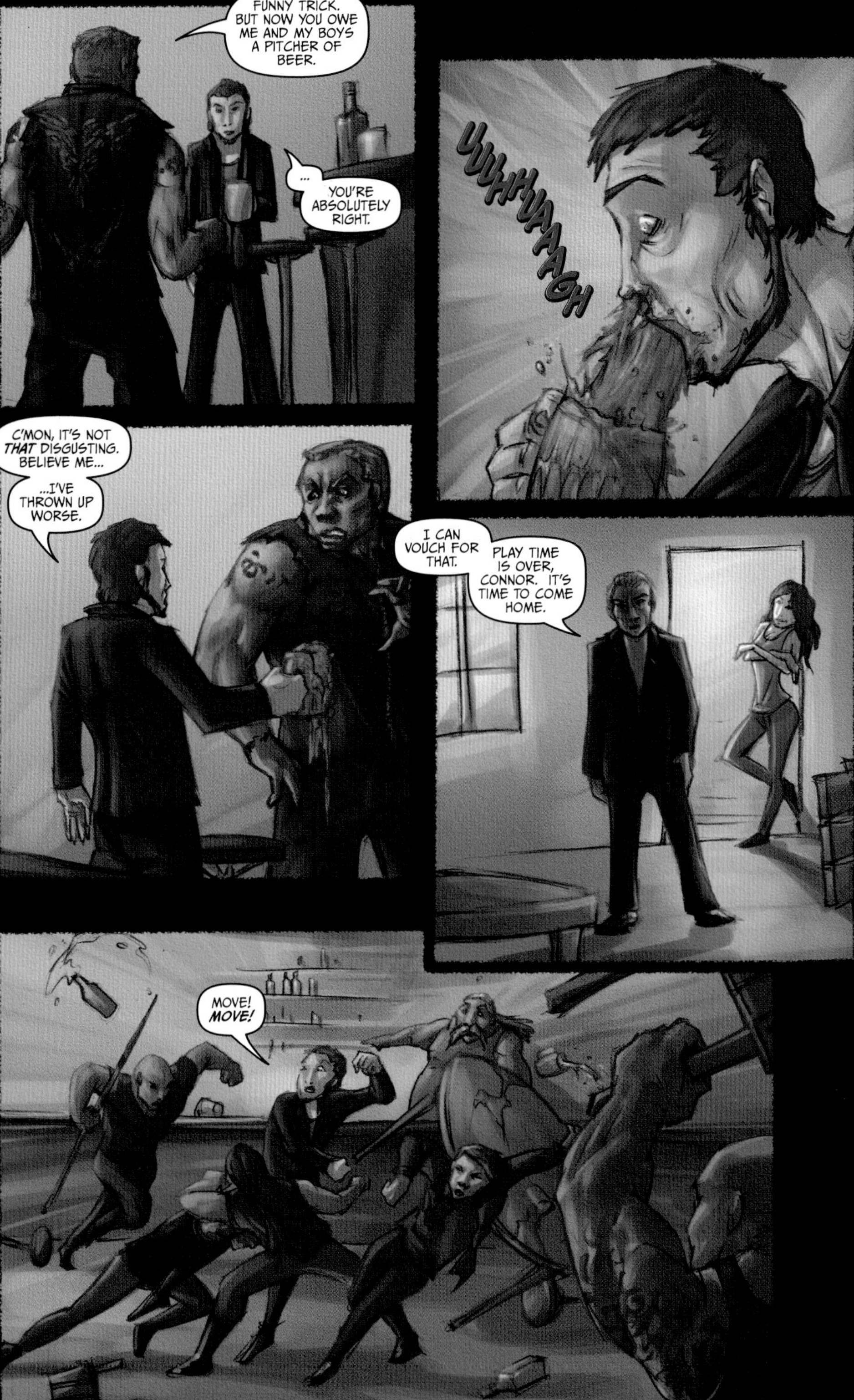
FUNNY TRICK. BUT NOW YOU OWE ME AND MY BOYS A PITCHER OF BEER.
... YOU'RE ABSOLUTELY RIGHT.
UUUHHUAAAGH
C'MON, IT'S NOT *THAT* DISGUSTING. BELIEVE ME...
...I'VE THROWN UP WORSE.
I CAN VOUCH FOR THAT.
PLAY TIME IS OVER, CONNOR. IT'S TIME TO COME HOME.
MOVE! *MOVE!*

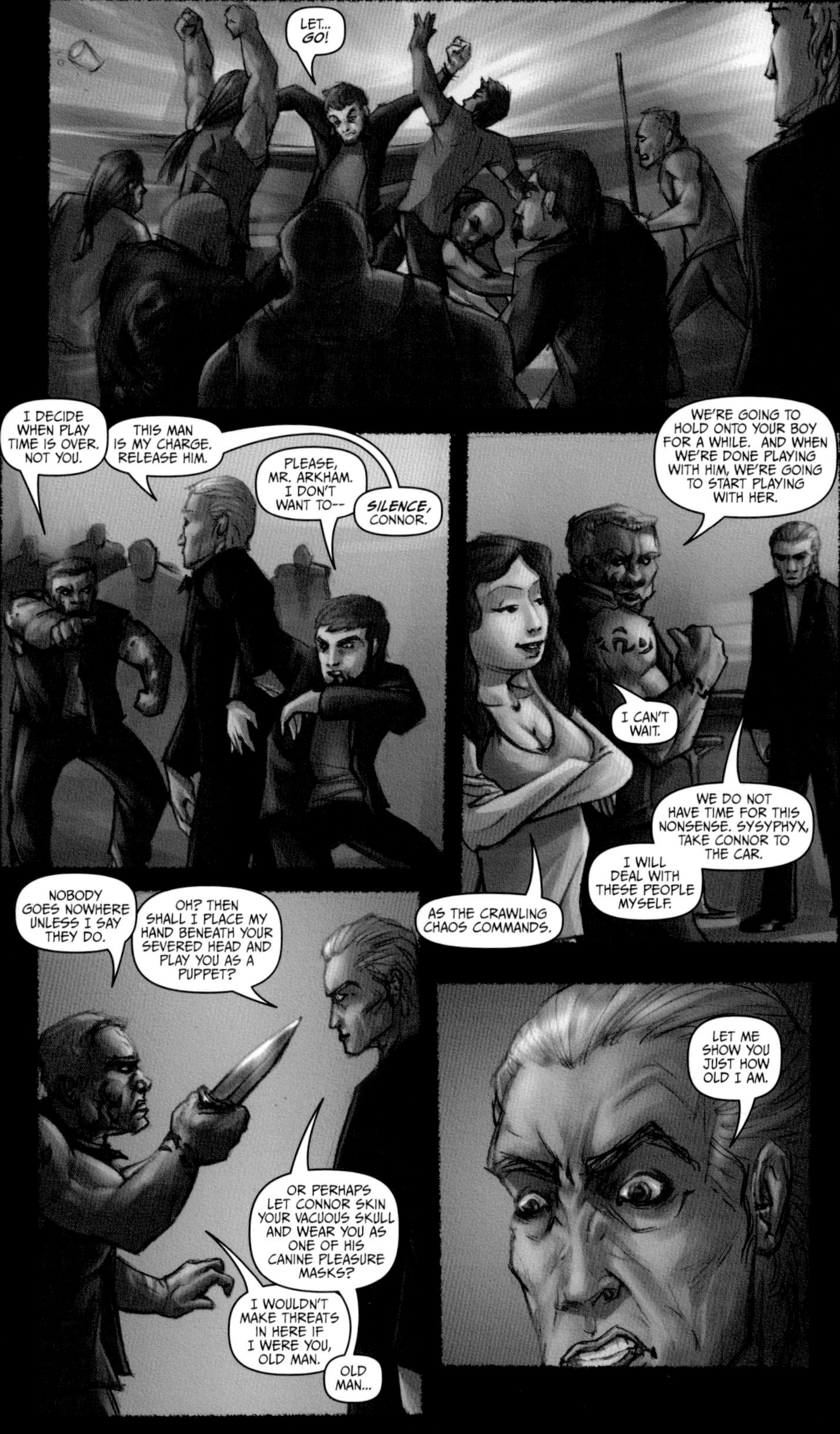
LET... GO!
I DECIDE WHEN PLAY TIME IS OVER. NOT YOU.
THIS MAN IS MY CHARGE. RELEASE HIM.
PLEASE, MR. ARKHAM. I DON'T WANT TO--
SILENCE, CONNOR.
WE'RE GOING TO HOLD ONTO YOUR BOY FOR A WHILE. AND WHEN WE'RE DONE PLAYING WITH HIM, WE'RE GOING TO START PLAYING WITH HER.
I CAN'T WAIT.
WE DO NOT HAVE TIME FOR THIS NONSENSE. SYSYPHYX, TAKE CONNOR TO THE CAR.
I WILL DEAL WITH THESE PEOPLE MYSELF.
AS THE CRAWLING CHAOS COMMANDS.
NOBODY GOES NOWHERE UNLESS I SAY THEY DO.
OH? THEN SHALL I PLACE MY HAND BENEATH YOUR SEVERED HEAD AND PLAY YOU AS A PUPPET?
OR PERHAPS LET CONNOR SKIN YOUR VACUOUS SKULL AND WEAR YOU AS ONE OF HIS CANINE PLEASURE MASKS?
I WOULDN'T MAKE THREATS IN HERE IF I WERE YOU, OLD MAN.
OLD MAN...
LET ME SHOW YOU JUST HOW OLD I AM.

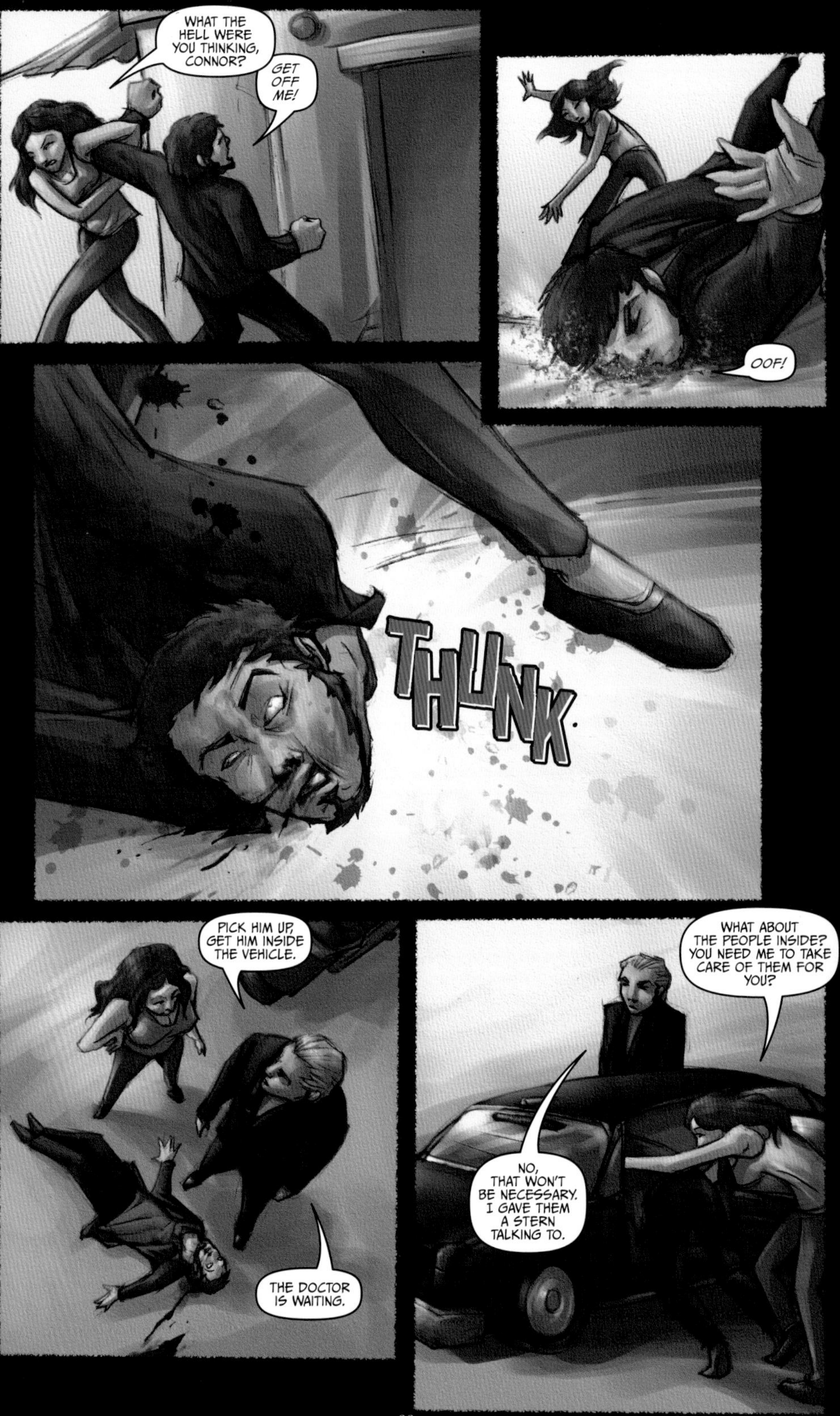
WHAT THE HELL WERE YOU THINKING, CONNOR?
GET OFF ME!
OOF!
THUNK.
PICK HIM UP, GET HIM INSIDE THE VEHICLE.
THE DOCTOR IS WAITING.
WHAT ABOUT THE PEOPLE INSIDE? YOU NEED ME TO TAKE CARE OF THEM FOR YOU?
NO, THAT WON'T BE NECESSARY. I GAVE THEM A STERN TALKING TO.

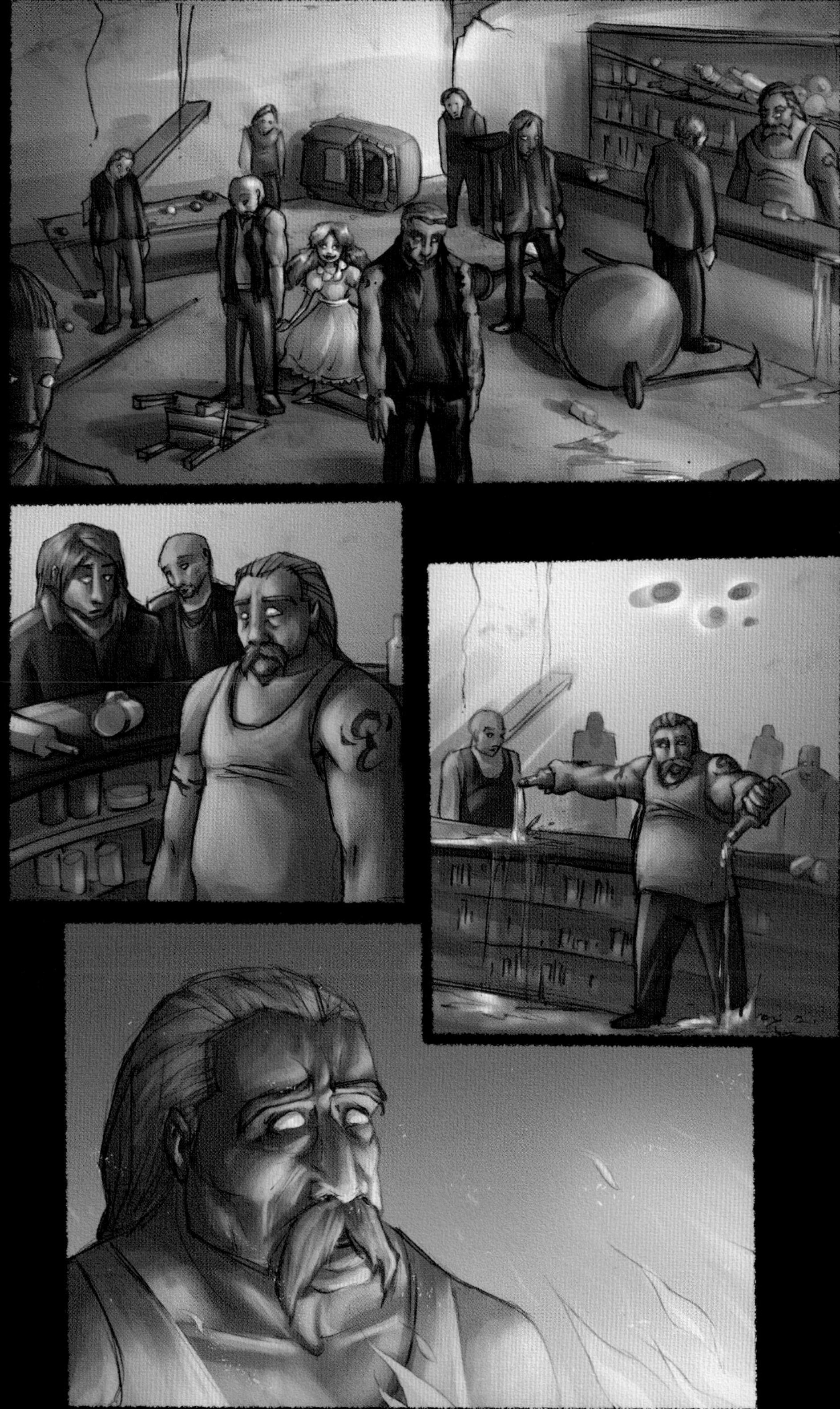

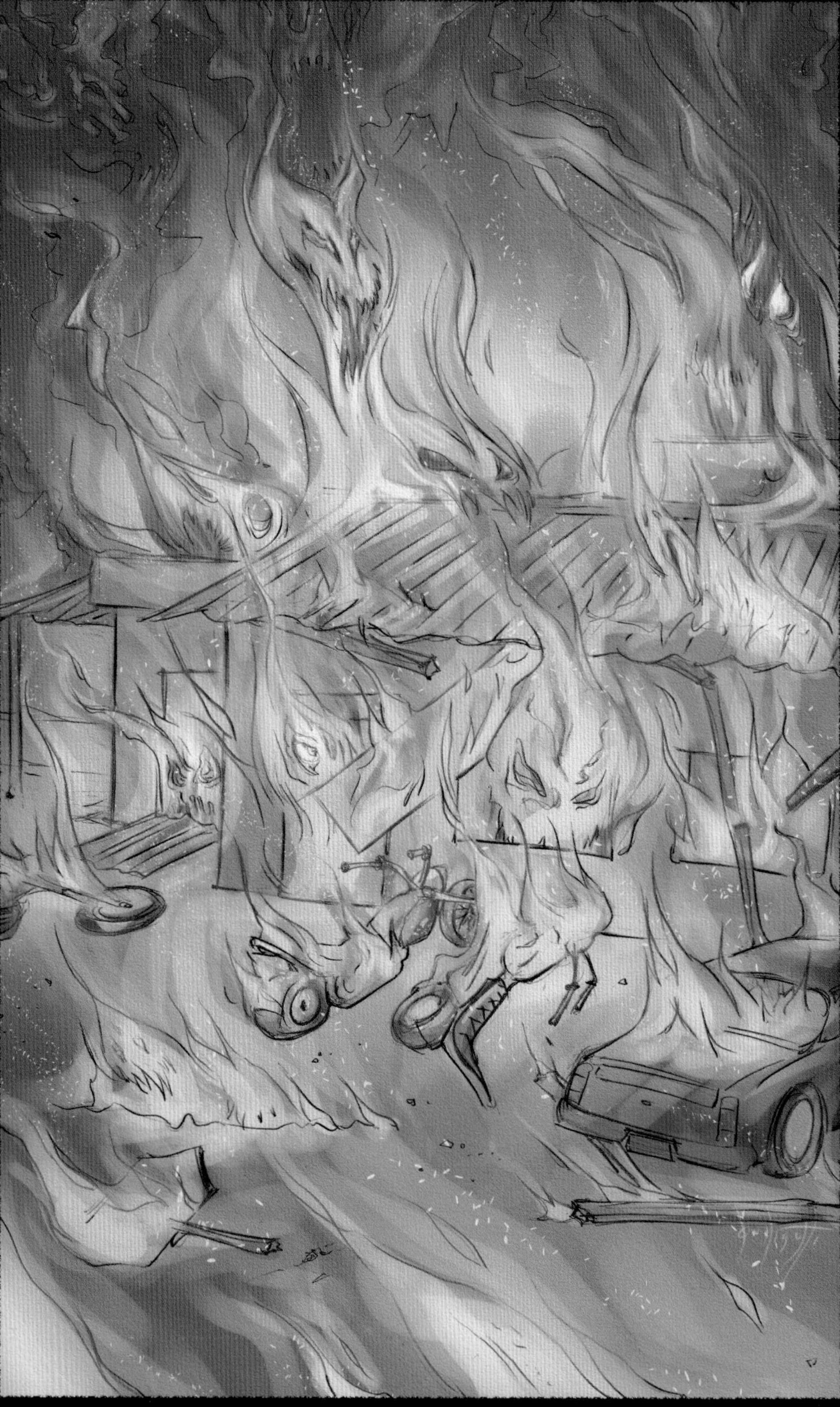

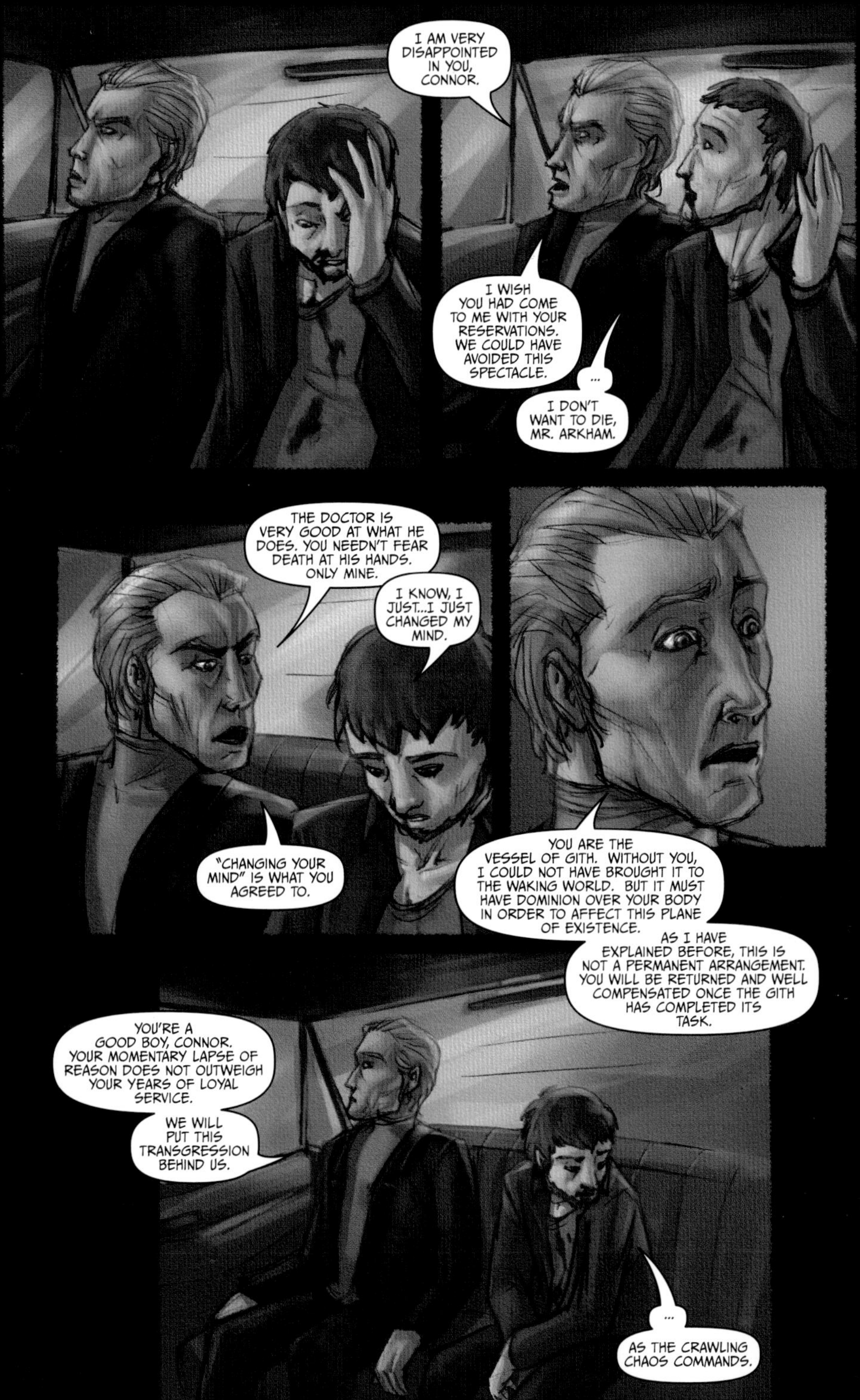
I AM VERY DISAPPOINTED IN YOU, CONNOR.
I WISH YOU HAD COME TO ME WITH YOUR RESERVATIONS. WE COULD HAVE AVOIDED THIS SPECTACLE.
...
I DON'T WANT TO DIE, MR. ARKHAM.
THE DOCTOR IS VERY GOOD AT WHAT HE DOES. YOU NEEDN'T FEAR DEATH AT HIS HANDS. ONLY MINE.
I KNOW, I JUST...I JUST CHANGED MY MIND.
"CHANGING YOUR MIND" IS WHAT YOU AGREED TO.
YOU ARE THE VESSEL OF GITH. WITHOUT YOU, I COULD NOT HAVE BROUGHT IT TO THE WAKING WORLD. BUT IT MUST HAVE DOMINION OVER YOUR BODY IN ORDER TO AFFECT THIS PLANE OF EXISTENCE.
AS I HAVE EXPLAINED BEFORE, THIS IS NOT A PERMANENT ARRANGEMENT. YOU WILL BE RETURNED AND WELL COMPENSATED ONCE THE GITH HAS COMPLETED ITS TASK.
YOU'RE A GOOD BOY, CONNOR. YOUR MOMENTARY LAPSE OF REASON DOES NOT OUTWEIGH YOUR YEARS OF LOYAL SERVICE.
WE WILL PUT THIS TRANSGRESSION BEHIND US.
...
AS THE CRAWLING CHAOS COMMANDS.

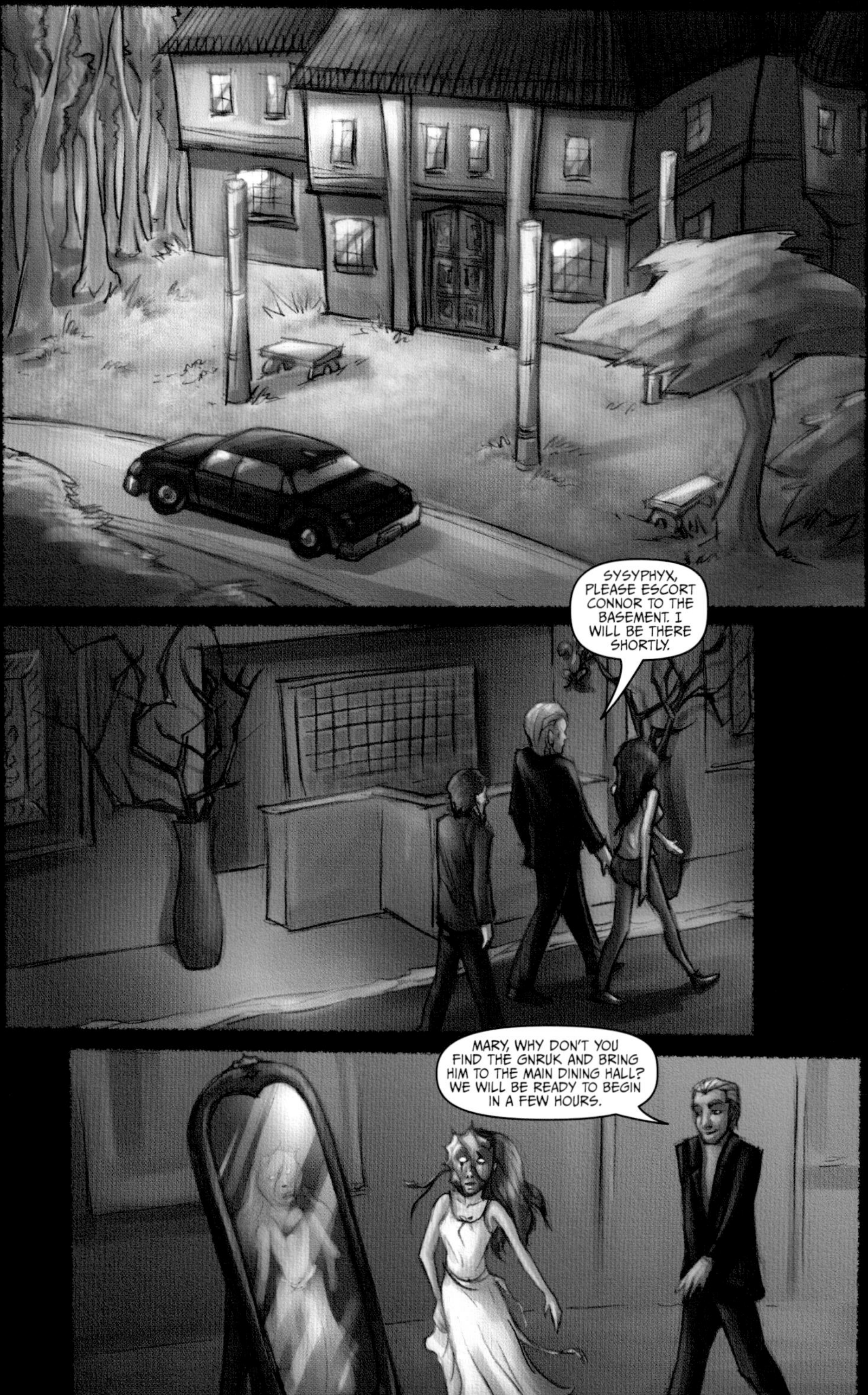
SYSYPHX, PLEASE ESCORT CONNOR TO THE BASEMENT. I WILL BE THERE SHORTLY.
MARY, WHY DON'T YOU FIND THE GNRUK AND BRING HIM TO THE MAIN DINING HALL? WE WILL BE READY TO BEGIN IN A FEW HOURS.

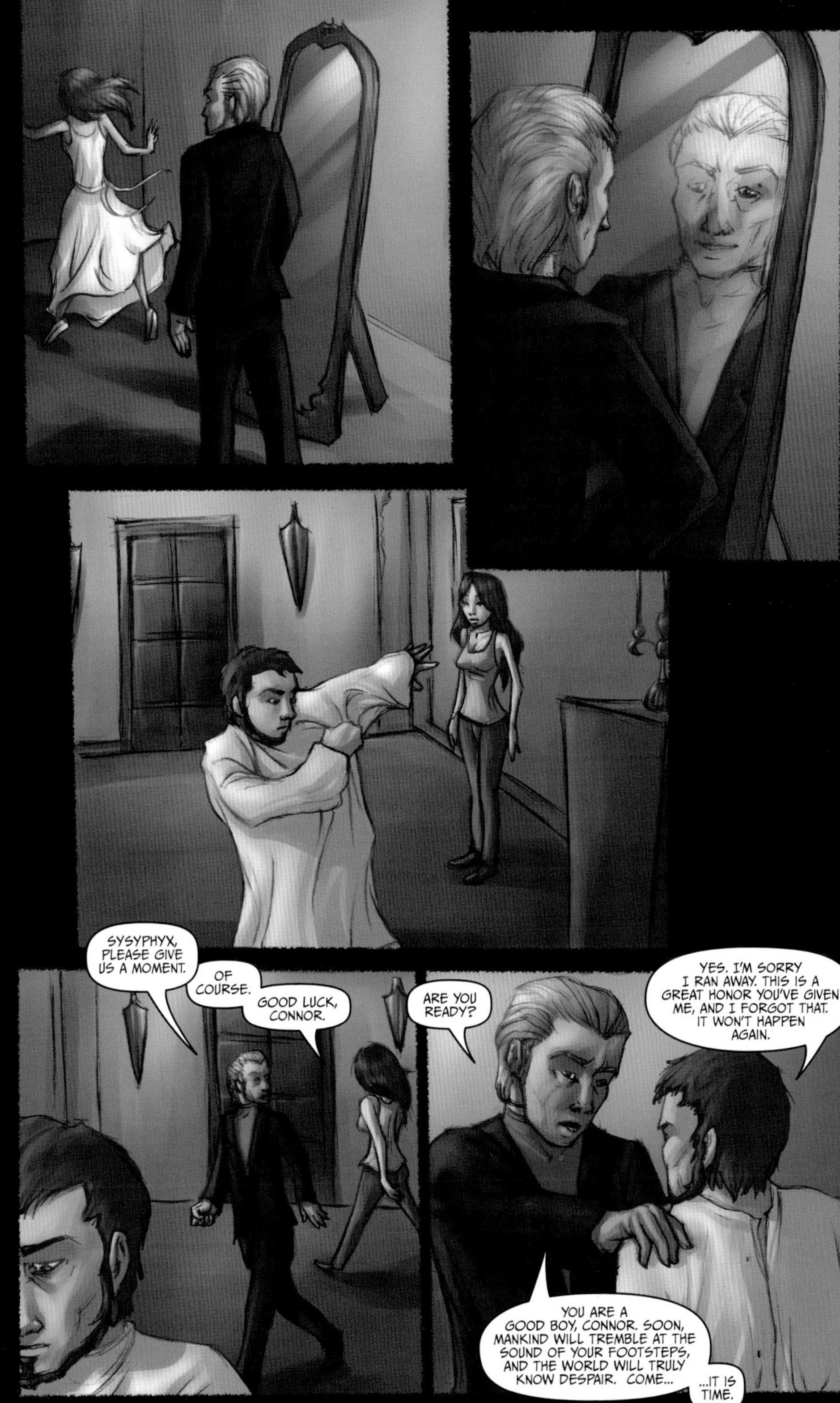
SYSYPHYX, PLEASE GIVE US A MOMENT.
OF COURSE.
GOOD LUCK, CONNOR.
ARE YOU READY?
YES. I'M SORRY I RAN AWAY. THIS IS A GREAT HONOR YOU'VE GIVEN ME, AND I FORGOT THAT. IT WON'T HAPPEN AGAIN.
YOU ARE A GOOD BOY, CONNOR. SOON, MANKIND WILL TREMBLE AT THE SOUND OF YOUR FOOTSTEPS, AND THE WORLD WILL TRULY KNOW DESPAIR. COME...
...IT IS TIME.

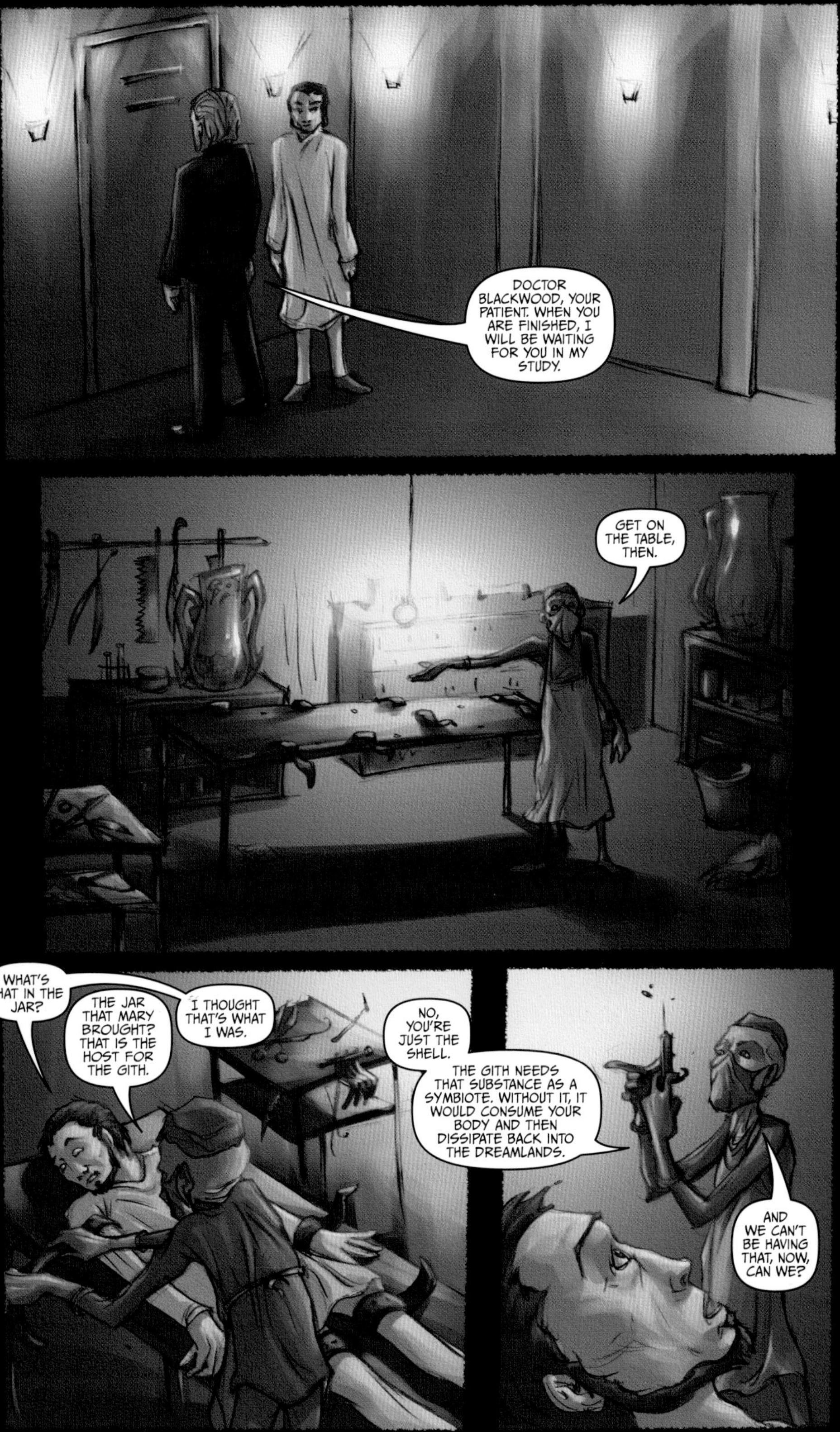
DOCTOR BLACKWOOD, YOUR PATIENT. WHEN YOU ARE FINISHED, I WILL BE WAITING FOR YOU IN MY STUDY.
GET ON THE TABLE, THEN.
WHAT'S THAT IN THE JAR?
THE JAR THAT MARY BROUGHT? THAT IS THE HOST FOR THE GITH.
I THOUGHT THAT'S WHAT I WAS.
NO, YOU'RE JUST THE SHELL.
THE GITH NEEDS THAT SUBSTANCE AS A SYMBIOTE. WITHOUT IT, IT WOULD CONSUME YOUR BODY AND THEN DISSIPATE BACK INTO THE DREAMLANDS.
AND WE CAN'T BE HAVING THAT, NOW, CAN WE?

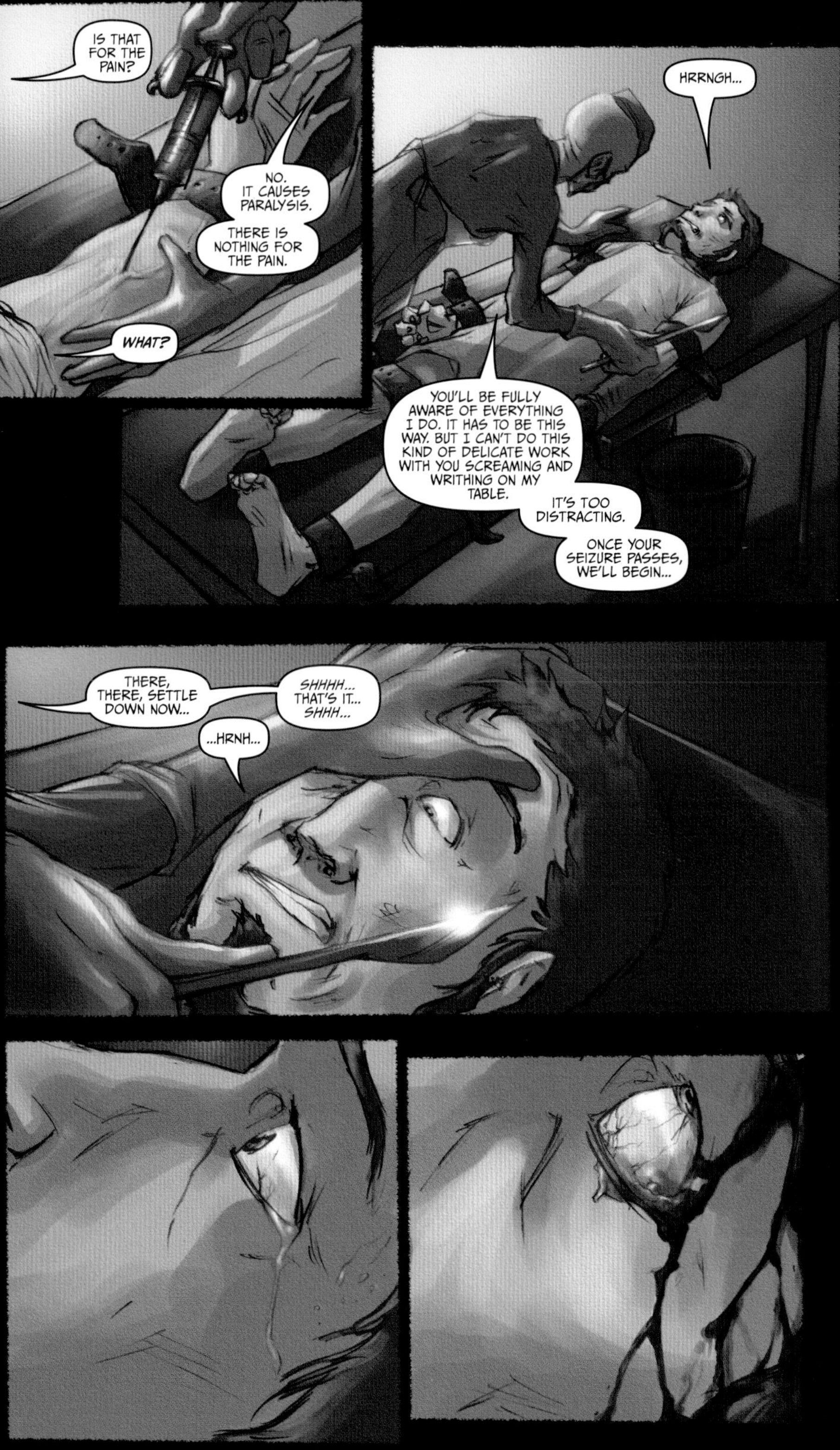
IS THAT FOR THE PAIN?
NO. IT CAUSES PARALYSIS.
THERE IS NOTHING FOR THE PAIN.
WHAT?
HRRNGH...
YOU'LL BE FULLY AWARE OF EVERYTHING I DO. IT HAS TO BE THIS WAY. BUT I CAN'T DO THIS KIND OF DELICATE WORK WITH YOU SCREAMING AND WRITHING ON MY TABLE.
IT'S TOO DISTRACTING.
ONCE YOUR SEIZURE PASSES, WE'LL BEGIN...
THERE, THERE, SETTLE DOWN NOW...
SHHHH... THAT'S IT... SHHH...
...HRNH...

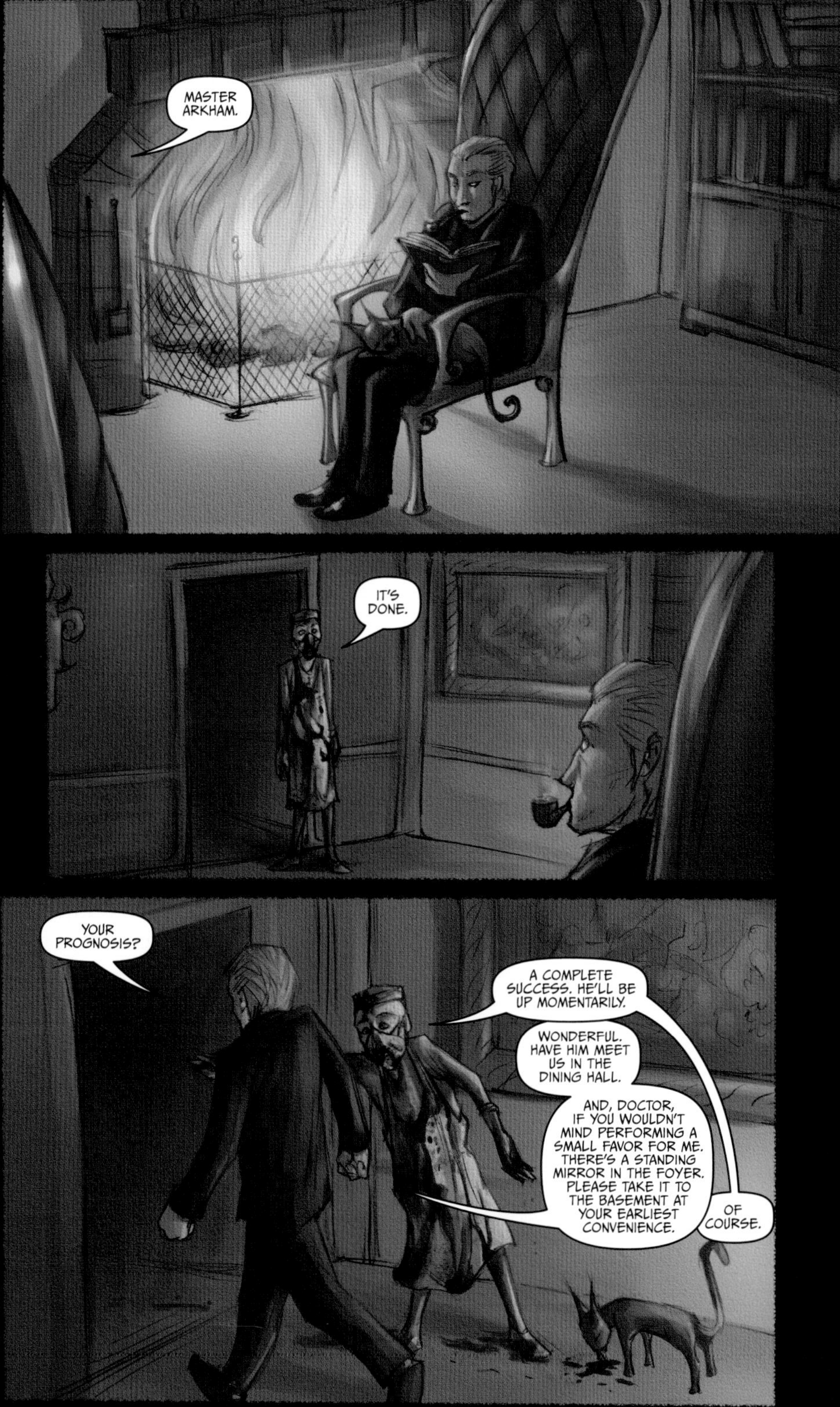
MASTER ARKHAM.
IT'S DONE.
YOUR PROGNOSIS?
A COMPLETE SUCCESS. HE'LL BE UP MOMENTARILY.
WONDERFUL. HAVE HIM MEET US IN THE DINING HALL.
AND, DOCTOR, IF YOU WOULDN'T MIND PERFORMING A SMALL FAVOR FOR ME. THERE'S A STANDING MIRROR IN THE FOYER. PLEASE TAKE IT TO THE BASEMENT AT YOUR EARLIEST CONVENIENCE.
OF COURSE.

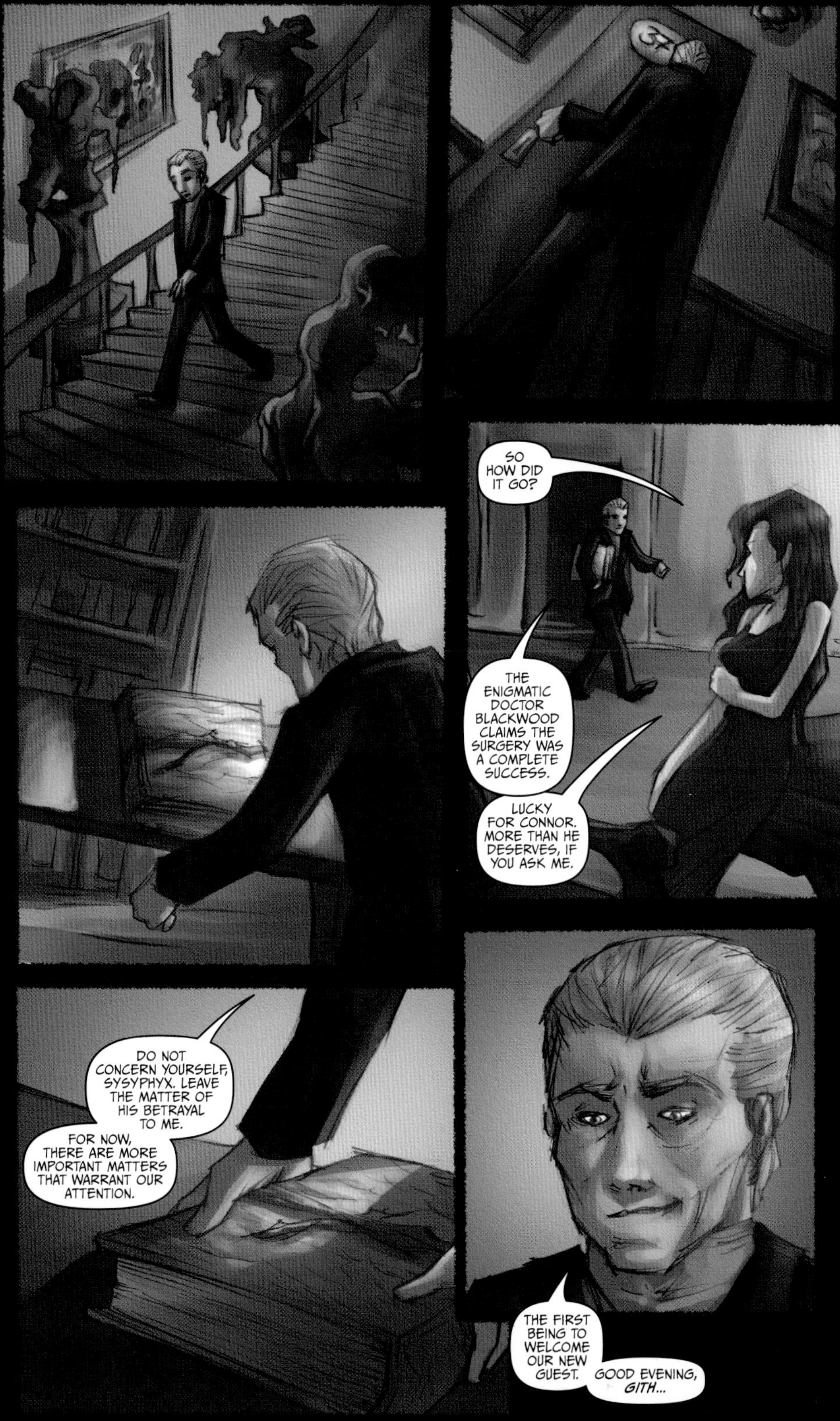
SO HOW DID IT GO?
THE ENIGMATIC DOCTOR BLACKWOOD CLAIMS THE SURGERY WAS A COMPLETE SUCCESS.
LUCKY FOR CONNOR. MORE THAN HE DESERVES, IF YOU ASK ME.
DO NOT CONCERN YOURSELF, SYSYPHYX. LEAVE THE MATTER OF HIS BETRAYAL TO ME.
FOR NOW, THERE ARE MORE IMPORTANT MATTERS THAT WARRANT OUR ATTENTION.
THE FIRST BEING TO WELCOME OUR NEW GUEST.
GOOD EVENING, GITH...